WARRIOR JUDGE

ONE MAN'S JOURNEY FROM GRIDIRON TO GAVEL

WARRIOR JUDGE

ONE MAN'S JOURNEY FROM GRIDIRON TO GAVEL

BY:

ED NEWMAN
AND
HOLLY NEWMAN GREENBERG

ISBN 978-1-63784-457-1 (paperback)
ISBN 978-1-63784-459-5 (hardcover)
ISBN 978-1-63784-458-8 (digital)

Hawes & Jenkins Publishing
16427 N Scottsdale Road Suite 410
Scottsdale, AZ 85254
www.hawesjenkins.com

Printed in the United States of America

For media, acquisition, and collaboration inquiries, contact the author at: info@warriorjudge.com

To Marvin, for leaving the world a better place.
—Ed Newman

To Dad, for making my dream to tell your story a reality. And to
Blair, Jordan, and Henry for giving me the time and space to do so.
—Holly Newman Greenberg

CONTENTS

Disclaimer ix

Chapter 1: Samson, a Warrior Judge 1
Chapter 2: Nothing but Gold 8
Chapter 3: Second Chance 15
Chapter 4: Konga 23
Chapter 5: The Pushback 33
Chapter 6: Frustrated Competitors 40
Chapter 7: Play Another Day 49
Chapter 8: Innovations 57
Chapter 9: The Brotherhood 63
Chapter 10: Make No Mistake 73
Chapter 11: Hungry for More 82
Chapter 12: Game of Chicken 89
Chapter 13: The Reality of Mortality 97
Chapter 14: The Man in the Mirror 104
Chapter 15: Matters That Matter 112
Chapter 16: Here, There, and Everywhere 118
Chapter 17: Two Thumbs Up 124
Chapter 18: Wheels Up, Wheels Down 134
Chapter 19: Relevance 141
Chapter 20: The Warrior's Way 147
Chapter 21: Got Man 153
Chapter 22: The Crazy 159
Chapter 23: Purple Patch 164
Chapter 24: Who's Who 172
Chapter 25: Perspiration and Perseverance 180

Chapter 26: Another Season, Another Opportunity..................188
Chapter 27: The Plan B Pact 197
Chapter 28: Oil and Water 203
Chapter 29: A Separation...211
Chapter 30: A Better Narrative 219
Chapter 31: Tough on the Field…Tough on the Bench! 225

Epilogue: On the Hop...233
Postscripts 243
Acknowledgments 247

DISCLAIMER

This is a work of nonfiction sprinkled with a dash of license. While the stories are based on my memories, some details have been changed to protect the privacy of those involved or fill in the gaps stolen by time. Even so, a great truth is preserved, and the bulk is pretty darn close to reality.

CHAPTER 1

SAMSON, A WARRIOR JUDGE

Nothing else existed. Not the pain in my shoulder, the metal brace shielding each knee, or the ruckus of 75,000 fans in Miami's Orange Bowl during the 1984 AFC Conference Championship. From the huddle, Dan Marino politely asked the linemen to give him another second. I amplified my concentration because I was the Miami Dolphins' starting right guard, and it was my job to protect my quarterback. This meant neutralizing the Steelers' 260-pound defensive tackle, who was glaring across the line of scrimmage, determined to disrupt Marino's pass. The stakes were high in this sudden-death playoff game. Victory meant Super Bowl. Loss meant—no, I can't even go there. Loss was not an option. We clapped our hands, broke the huddle, and pivoted to the line of scrimmage.

"Hut! Hut!" shouted Marino as he sequentially signaled the snap, secured the ball, and scanned the field for his target. Kinetic energy coursed through my legs. In unison with the other offensive linemen, I exploded backward and formed a protective pocket around Marino, shielding him from the marauding Steelers. Marino stepped deep into the pocket. The defensive tackle charged, and I surged straight into his onslaught. *WHACK!* Our bodies collided. But the impact did not faze me. Pain had been forgotten ten thousand hits ago. It was merely a consequence of contact sports that felt as natural as breathing.

Now engaged in a remarkably physical dance, I pounded my right hand onto the defensive tackle's chest and stared into his eyes. I could hear his grunts. They registered just a smidge louder than the hometown's rapturous roar. I could feel the guy's sweat and the warmth of his breath on my face. I could sense his urgency. Like a wild animal, he was mad to break up Marino's pass. He grasped my shoulder pads and yanked violently to throw me off balance, but I held my ground. In one last desperate attempt to free himself, the defensive tackle placed his left arm under my right triceps. But with my hand anchored on his chest, he couldn't get past me. My bone wouldn't snap. With a growl, I channeled the power gained from thousands of hours in the weight room—bench-pressing upward of five hundred pounds—and plowed the Steeler farther upfield. His body softened, and his resolve eased. I smiled ever so slightly because the crisis was over. Marino had the time and space he needed to complete his pass. Touchdown, Miami!

You'd think I'd join my teammates and revel in this win. The Miami Dolphins were Super Bowl–bound, after all. But no. That was a luxury I couldn't afford. As a first-year law school student, I had another epic challenge before me: law school finals. Heck, one exam needed to be rescheduled so I could travel to the big game in Palo Alto without conflict. Like football, success in the academic arena required total dedication and focus. No joke. This isn't fiction. I was living in the two extremes of professional football and a professional law degree. And if I wasn't careful, either would drown me. But I'm getting ahead of myself. Let me tell you how I got there in the first place.

***

Legend has it that shortly before I was born in the summer of 1951, my father gave my mother a peck on the cheek and whispered in her ear, "I hope it's a boy…a son to carry on the Newman name." My mom sighed in relief two hours later when the doctor placed me, a healthy and hungry eight-pound, eight-ounce baby boy into her arms. As the sun rose above the horizon on that June 4 day, she dreamed about my future. Maybe I'd become a dentist or a scientist. My dad, however, hoped that I'd become a partner in the family radiator business, just as he had done with his father. It was the "Newman way." Only moments in the world, and I already faced diverging expectations.

Something like a cross between the Tasmanian Devil and Bamm-Bamm Rubble, I ran around wild and broke things in my path the moment I found my legs. It was almost as if I was destined to crash into things. Realizing we needed more space, my parents traded our small tenement in Brooklyn for a larger, cookie-cutter home in the wholesome neighborhood of North Bellmore, Long Island.

The bigger home came with greater expenses. I watched as my dad stepped up to the challenge to cover them. He supplemented his bread-and-butter income from Newman's Auto Radiator with revenue from subsidiary garages, coin-operated laundromats, bingo halls, and trotter racehorses. I marveled at Dad's work ethic as he doubled his week and spent upwards of seventy hours managing his businesses.

All this meant less time at home and less time with me. Yearning for more, I'd crawl to the foot of his bed each morning and lie quietly, with my eyes patiently fixed on his television's black-and-white Indian-head test pattern, waiting for him to rouse. Like clockwork, Dad would wake at 5:15 a.m., turn off the tube, and greet me with a "Good morning, son." A bowl of Chex cereal and a few philosophical chestnuts later, he'd extend his arm for a manly handshake and leave, only to return late in the evening.

Sensing I needed more, Dad made time for me wherever he could. We'd go to synagogue on Saturday, out for a bagel run on Sunday, or to his radiator repair shop whenever possible. While Dad maintained his dream that I'd play a vital role in the family business,

3

I wasn't so sure. Even so, I became a regular at Newman's by the time I turned seven. With Mom's urging, I spent most of my days doing administrative work in the clean, quiet, and safe back office. That all changed on one sweltering day in the summer of 1958 when, with a knowing smile, Dad called me to the production floor and tasked me to remove several yards of inch-thick grease caked on the floor. "Hard work is honorable," he advised while handing over a hoe-like scraper.

What followed could have been a scene plucked from *Dante's Inferno*. Working strenuously to remove the scum in that sulfuric acid cloud, set in the stifling ninety-degree heat, with fire torches blowing everywhere and large fans loudly pushing the exhaust outside, I kept my head down and plugged away. Two hours later, I was covered head to toe in sweat and grime when Dad tapped me on my shoulder and praised, "You're doing a great job, son."

My chest puffed up at his approval.

Seeing the positive effect his words were having on me, Dad laid it on thick. "I'm so proud of you," he said. With a glance toward my soot-covered fingers, he added, "There's no shame in getting your hands dirty. Now get cleaned up."

To help pass the time on our long commute back to North Bellmore, Dad told me tales about great leaders and warriors—all with a focus on exceptionalism. "Life is too precious to squander," he preached. "Ordinary is not enough." With a shift of his blue eyes from the road to my face, Dad added, "You must make the most of the time you've got. If you do that, Eddy, the world will be your oyster. And never forget this"—Dad raised his voice and pointed to the sky—"you're a Newman!"

As we turned onto the Jericho Turnpike, Dad let out a little yawn. He reached into his center console, grabbed a short-bristled brush, and rhythmically stroked his curly black hair to stay awake. After a little while, he said, "Eddy, I want to tell you about Samson. I think you'll get a kick out of this guy because you're a little like him."

My ears perked as he told the tale of the long-haired biblical Hebrew hero who was said to dispatch a lion with his bare hands, defeat a thousand soldiers, and knock down a coliseum single-handedly. I loved learning about Samson because he was the antithesis of the stereotypical Jew. And there was more. The super-strong warrior had a good brain and served the Israelites as a judge! Even though I was young and insecure, I liked being compared to this warrior judge.

Little by little, I sought opportunities to develop my strength. In the fall of 1961, my Saw Mill Road Elementary School physical education teacher announced that President John F. Kennedy had launched a fitness initiative where students across the country would be assessed on timed push-ups, sit-ups, sprints, and other exercises. Instantly, I coveted the shiny gold medallion that would be awarded to the top performers from each grade. I studied my competition. There were five viable contenders. Two were bigger; three were stronger. No matter, I assured myself I'd be ready come test day.

Knowing that it would be easy to do 50 sit-ups, that I'd feel the burn at 100, and that it would be quite an effort to reach 150, I set a goal to complete 200 sit-ups without rest every night. I lay on my bedroom's blood-red carpet that first evening and hit a stone wall at 190 sit-ups. With veins popping and muscles spasming, I told myself, *Do more. Get to 200.* Grunting, I managed to achieve my goal. But it felt insufficient. With my internal monologue spurring me on, I lay back down and proceeded to do 220 sit-ups. That evening, 100 push-ups extended to 150, and 500 jumping jacks doubled to 1,000.

I became stronger with each passing day. Dad noticed my transformation. He started to show me off. One day he took me to Newman's and, in front of his buddies, instructed, "Tighten up, son." I constricted my abdominal muscles before—*POW*— he slammed a controlled fist into the center of my stomach. The calm and stoic face I maintained throughout the demonstration was not false bravado. The impact just didn't hurt.

Soon enough, it was the Presidential Fitness Test Day. I took my stance and gave the timed exercises every ounce I had. When I blasted past the average number of sit-ups for the ten-year-olds, my classmates gathered around me and cheered, "Go, Ed! Go!" Their attention made me push even harder.

"TIME!" shouted the gym teacher. She checked her clipboard and announced, "It looks like we've got a future star over here. Eddy's numbers match those of the top twelve-year-olds."

The joy of winning overtook me. I realized that even more than the medallion prize, I valued the respect of others. My classmates and teachers would now associate me with this accomplishment.

***

Even though I was attaining success in the athletic quarter of my life, my social skills struggled to keep pace. Many of the older neighborhood kids saw me as an easy target. They'd compare me to that goofy, freckle-faced character Alfred E. Neuman, who appeared on the cover of *Mad* magazine. Others would call me "Nudi." I found it frustrating that there was no training, exercise, or advanced preparation to get strong on the social playing field.

While I generally laughed along with their banter, all this changed on one crisp winter day when two North Bellmore kids hurled a dozen snowballs at me from across the street. Feeling extremely irritated, I roared at them, "STOP! Leave me alone, or else!" In the recesses of my brain, I was stunned that I raised my voice to those bullies. But I guess a little warrior within was begging to come out.

The antagonists ignored my plea and pelted me with another chunk of ice. I couldn't believe it. *ENOUGH!* My brain burned. I warned through gritted teeth, "The next person who throws a snowball at me is going to get a punch in the face."

Those boys must have assumed I was bluffing because one of them fearlessly launched yet another snowball. Ignoring that there were two of them, I turned around and furiously marched across the street. With my heart pounding, I flexed my fingers into my palms, held my breath, and felt an overload of energy charge through my body. From that close-up angle, my larger and heavier tormentor stared down his nose and into my face. I could feel the heat of his breath on my brow when he sniggered, "Whatcha gonna do about it, Nudi?"

Without hesitation, I landed a knuckle sandwich squarely onto his tinsel mouth. The blow mushed his lips into his wire braces and shredded his flesh from within. In shock, I looked from my young hands to the blood pouring from his mouth onto the white snow. Time stopped. My mind spun. This was something new. I wasn't a violent guy, but man…they goaded me! In the slow-motion moments that passed, I feared they'd pounce on me. But instead, the one not bleeding screamed, "Get out of here, you bully!"

Huh? I shook my head in confusion. Weren't they the ones hurling snowballs at me? But then it clicked. I was like a little Samson—a force to be reckoned with. When tested, I would defend myself. Instantly, my emotions shifted from fear to elation because I had tasted the respect given to warriors, and I liked it.

CHAPTER 2

NOTHING BUT GOLD

All my senses were alerted by the major production unfolding on Mepham High School's gridiron across the way. The air was redolent with freshly mowed grass, the field was chalked with bright-white five-yard lines, and the atmosphere was supercharged with energy from fans flooding into the bleachers. I turned to a buddy, whom I had joined for a game of two-hand touch on the adjacent baseball field, and naively asked, "Is there a football game tonight?"

"You kidding?" my friend looked at me as if I had a third eye. "It's Friday night! Of course, there's a game! The Mepham Pirates are playing the Sewanhaka Indians. It's gonna be a big game. Anyway"— he pointed toward the pitcher's mound and urged—"the others are waiting. Come on."

I walked to my crew, yet my focus remained on the high school teams. They entered the neighboring field from opposite end zones as a bevy of beautiful high school cheerleaders melodically shouted, "Let's go, MEPHAM!"

"—Ed! Let's play!" coaxed my friend. "You're with the Shirts. We're the—"

"—*TOOT! TAT! TAT! BOOM!*" a cacophony of sounds from Mepham's band drowned out his words, making it even harder for me to prioritize our game over the varsity spectacle.

After a few more nudges, I finally got into our action which was, quite frankly, just okay. There were arbitrary and rinky-dink rules, uncoordinated passes, sloppy ball control, clumsy efforts, and slackers who were there only for the exercise. About twenty minutes in, I exploded into a sprint and caught the ball 30 yards down the field just as a fleet-footed guy on the Skins' team planted two hands on my lower back and effected a stop. *Damn it!* I trotted to the huddle and prepared for the next play, but the loud crack of a helmet striking a shoulder pad 150 yards away lured my attention back to the varsity players.

My eyes blinked rapidly at the high-octane scene. A zebra threw a yellow flag and signaled a Sewanhaka infraction. A second umpire recovered the ball and placed it 5 yards back. The chain's men adjusted: second down, 15 yards to go. The visiting fans groaned. The Sewanhaka coach stomped out orders, and the home team band rhythmically banged their drums: "*BOOM! BOOM! BOOM!*" My heart raced.

The Mepham quarterback pointed toward the maroon eight-by-eight scoreboard. I imagined he was telling his teammates that now was the moment. I held my breath and watched closely as Mepham stepped to the line of scrimmage. At the ref's signal, the quarterback passed the ball, which a Mepham receiver acrobatically snagged out of the air for a 13-yard gain. Then, from out of nowhere, three Sewanhaka defenders appeared and crushed him. *Holy crap!* I inched closer and kept my eye on the receiver, who miraculously jumped up as if nothing had happened.

"Did you guys see that?" I bellowed back to my friends on the baseball diamond.

"Ed! Enough!" our team captain hollered. "Get in our game or get out of here!"

My head swiveled from my friends to the varsity players. I couldn't help but compare. They were the best athletes, handpicked from each high school and coached to perform. We were a mixed bag of awkward sixth graders. Their accommodations were supreme. Ours…well, we were playing on a makeshift field with no coaches, no officials, no fans, and no protective gear whatsoever. Half the crew didn't even have shirts on! Instantly, I saw that this level of play was no longer sufficient. I wanted to be where those varsity guys were. I craved that sort of challenge.

The thought stayed with me all the way through the end of our match and into the weekend. When I couldn't shake it, I pulled out a calendar and counted the days until junior high school because there I'd get a crack at junior varsity football. I could wait—six months until sign-ups. But the best-laid plans…

***

Mom, who was pregnant with her fourth, shouted from the kitchen that dinner was ready one evening in the spring of '64. My sisters, Terri and Gayle, bounded down the stairs to eat. I took my usual seat next to Dad. After some small talk, Dad winked at Mom and announced, "We've outgrown this house. We're going to move this summer." My eyes widened as he shared the details, "…Long Island…in the Gates of Woodbury."

Moving? A new home. Good? Maybe? While I liked the idea of new friends and experiences, I felt sad because my earliest memories were from North Bellmore.

The days that followed were busy. We packed, moved, and prepared to start at our new schools. Naturally, some things slipped through the cracks—most notably, South Wood's JV football registration deadline. I repeat, I missed the football registration deadline. I didn't even realize the oversight until school had started and the team was practicing without me.

I shared my disappointment with Mom. She arranged for a meeting with the school's athletic director to see if an exception could be made. But the guy refused to yield. He instead suggested I join the JV cross-country team. With Mom's encouragement, I decided to give it a go.

10

"Line up," instructed the cross-country coach as he pulled a stopwatch from his pocket and cued the start on my first day of practice. I got into position and, on his command, foolishly burst out ahead of the rest.

For the first few minutes, I maintained my lead, but I started to sweat heavily and heave for air. *Thump!* My ambition to win quickly wilted to simply finishing. *Thump!* My heart painfully pounded against my ribcage. *Thump!* Everyone passed me, and I rationalized that my broad shoulders and heavy bones were a disadvantage to long-distance running.

Despite my subpar performance, I trusted things would improve. But the pattern persisted for several weeks, and the lack of progress weighed on me. Mom noticed I was getting mopey and asked what was going on. With my forehead leaning in and the blues of my eyes peering up, I told her about the cross-country running debacle. "I think I should leave the team," I admitted. "But I don't want to be considered a quitter."

"That's right, son. Newmans don't quit," Dad dismissed the idea.

But Mom delved a little deeper. She asked, "Do you even like cross-country?"

"No," I grumbled with a frown. "Not at all."

Mom and Dad exchanged looks.

I bit my upper lip and explained, "I want a shot at being the best, but I don't have the build needed to succeed in this sport."

"I see," said Mom empathetically. "Then I think you're right, Eddy. You probably should quit."

Dad gave her a quizzical look. Mom shared her philosophy that continual failure would hurt my self-confidence. She didn't want that for me. Upon reflection, Dad didn't either. He yielded with instructions for me to seek out some other sport that I'd enjoy and have a better chance of excelling at. Luckily, that wasn't hard to do because South Wood was posting flyers for wrestling tryouts.

***

"Show me what you've got, kid," encouraged South Wood's JV wrestling coach, Mr. Ohjweiler, after pairing me with an older yet similarly sized 106-pounder and challenging me to escape from the bottom position during wrestling tryouts. I set up on all fours and tensed as my counterpart hunched his body over mine.

"Go!" shouted Coach Ohjweiler as he slashed his hand toward the ground, and I...I froze.

Do something! My mental chatter commanded action, but I didn't know what to do. *Do anything!* I desperately latched onto my competitor's left arm, and with brute strength, I attempted to pull him underneath me. The upperclassman easily countered that by using his feet, back, and shoulder muscles to pull away. I thrashed about like a crazed cat in a cage, but he maintained control! My blood pressure spiked. My heart thudded. I recklessly rotated and found myself in an extremely vulnerable position, with my back six inches off the mat. *Avoid the pin!* My internal coach cheered me on. I frantically sucked in air, gathered my feet, and gained a base before— SNAP!—I erupted off the floor, threw my arms into my opponent's chest, and to everyone's surprise, including my own, I managed to escape.

A stunned Coach Ohjweiler let out a good-natured chuckle and called me a "tiger." I debated whether he meant "tiger" as a compliment. No matter, I resolved that I liked it either way.

"Ed, you've got potential," said Coach Ohjweiler. He elaborated, "But there's a lot of technique to work on before you'll be any good."

I beamed because here was a sport where I had what it took. I joined the team and poured my heart and soul into the wrestling program. Each day I worked to perfect the reversals, takedowns, breakaways, hand plays, and feints. I must have practiced them thousands of times. In doing so, I developed great strength, stamina, and speed. I even won a few matches.

Unexpectedly, the more enamored I became with the sport, the more my grandparents griped. With their old-world values, traditional Jewish viewpoints, and focus on fostering a sustainable, longterm career, they'd say things like, "Wrestling? For a Jewish kid? I've never heard of such a thing." It frustrated me that they didn't understand how I was finding a place for myself through wrestling.

By eighth grade, I was logging two wins out of every three matches, but Coach Ohjweiler wouldn't let it go to my head. "Aim higher," he'd say. "Sixty-six percent is nothing to write home about." One day he added, "I'll show you what a true champion looks like when we watch the big boys compete in the upcoming Nassau County Tournament."

I was speechless the moment I stepped into that huge gymnasium for the competition. Suffused with ethyl alcohol and perspiration, the arena was packed with family, friends, and fans watching multiple concurrent matches taking place under bright ceiling lamps. My eyes darted from the wrestlers in their competitive togs, to the coaches pumping up their athletes, to the nests of teams and fans clustered throughout. Just like my reaction to the Mepham football game, I was hooked.

"Look, Ed," my teammate smacked my shoulder and pointed toward Syosset's scarlet mat, where our hometown wrestling hero, Eddy Fisher, was waiting to compete in the finals. I drummed my knuckles in anticipation because I knew of Fisher. He was one of the "true champions" Coach Ohjweiler had mentioned. The wiry, blond-haired, 136-pound competitor with an oversized jaw and cauliflower ears was a legend. And word was he'd been preparing for this match for months.

I studied Fisher as he got mentally ready. He tilted his head from left to right, paced the mat, and flared his nostrils. With thin lips and piercing eyes, Fisher approached the point of combat. When the ref blew his whistle, Fisher cuffed his right hand around the back of his opponent's neck. In jerky motions, he pushed and pulled to gain an opening. But Fisher's lightning-fast counterpart warded off each takedown attempt, and the two gladiators rotated around the mat with only thwarted lunges and retreats, completing a scoreless first period.

In the second period, Fisher worked a half nelson from the top position and tried to lever his adversary onto his back. But the tough nut wouldn't yield. The stalemate continued until Fisher loosened his grip, and his opponent took advantage by making a reversal.

"Two points!" the ref shouted.

Fisher's face flushed in fury.

In the third period, Fisher marshaled all his reserves to make up the difference, but his opponent wouldn't allow it. He pushed Fisher off the mat—three times. It looked as if Fisher's chest billowed 20 percent in those last few moments. He was so determined to rebound. But Fisher couldn't close it. The clock ran out, and the devastated competitor fled the gymnasium in shame.

Twenty minutes later, when the officials called for the place-holders to collect their medals, Fisher was nowhere to be found. His varsity coach, William Blossfield, who ordinarily looked so professional and ordered with a jacket, pressed shirt, and tie, now appeared disheveled. He deputized us South Wood kids for help. "Go find Fisher," he desperately pleaded. "Hurry! Please."

We scoured the stadium and found Fisher taking refuge in a dark corner of the boys' locker room. When the anguished competitor returned to the gymnasium, he slogged past the fans, coaches, and photographers over to the trilevel podium and compliantly stood a step beneath gold. But the moment the ref draped the silver medallion over Fisher's neck, he forcefully removed it as if it were an intolerable irritant and slung it thirty yards into the stands. *Whoa!* I gasped along with the others. I understood him. Fisher gave it his all, and it was for naught. Second place doesn't count when you accept nothing but gold. Immediately the standard was set, and I wanted to follow it.

CHAPTER 3

SECOND CHANCE

Tuesday, chicken day. *Mmm*, I was hungry. I devoured my dinner in seconds and asked for another serving. Mom was astonished, Dad was impressed, and my siblings were amused. With freshman wrestling over at Syosset High School, I could eat as I pleased. Wednesday, hungry again. Thursday, same thing. I wolfed down my meal and all my family's scraps.

Dad chafed about our ballooning grocery bill. Mom explained, "It's Eddy. He's hungry all the time. I can't keep up when he eats a family-sized box of cereal for a small snack."

Dad waffled. With a concealed smile, he concluded that I was healthy, muscular, and going through a growth spurt. "Fine," he backpedaled, "feed Eddy all he wants."

The next day, Mom entered the kitchen with two extra bags of groceries and happily told me, "Tonight I'm going to roast a chicken for the family and another just for you." The prospect of a bigger portion pleased me, but my satisfaction was short-lived because after consuming nearly half the bounty for our family of six, my stomach grumbled for more. When I asked for another plate, Mom looked to Dad because there was no more food to give.

Skeptical that any person my size could consume that much food, Dad opened his wallet, pulled out two crisp dollar bills, and instructed me to bike to the local Burger King to get whatever I wanted. Five miles later, I scarfed down a double Whopper, a large side of fries, and a thick chocolate milkshake. I followed that up with a bowl of cereal when I got home.

The more I ate, the more I grew. Syosset's varsity football coach, John Miller, noticed my bigger build as he was planning out the position roster for the 1966 season. He decided to move me from my prior JV fullback position to the varsity team's offensive line as a tackle for my sophomore year.

When I learned of the change, I felt disappointed— like I had been robbed of an opportunity to gain the attention of fans because I found fullback far more glamorous than tackle. I mean, fullbacks carried the ball and scored touchdowns; offensive linemen did not. I went to Coach Miller's office to discuss my concerns and tentatively tapped on his door.

"It's open," Coach Miller shouted from within.

When I entered his office, I noticed an impressive collection of sports memorabilia and college All-American trophies, conveying that this guy was the real deal. One prominent picture hanging on the wall featured a much younger Coach Miller in military garb, standing next to a few soldiers on the beach.

Seeing that it caught my attention, Coach Miller stated, "You know, that photo was taken on June 6, 1944, in France. It was the day the Americans invaded."

I lifted my brows. D-Day!

"You'll get a kick out of this, Ed," he continued. "The Germans had us pinned down on the beach with machine-gun fire when army command ordered us to dig in for a while. I was so exhausted after that sleepless night that I used my shirt as a pillow and slept on a sand dune all morning, completely unaware that my armpits were exposed to the rising sun." Coach Miller demonstrated the T-shape in which he lay, and with a touch to his underarms, he chuckled. "My pits got so damn burnt that I was walking around like the Frankenstein monster for days!"

Coach Miller's story put me at ease. I relaxed a little and explained the purpose of my visit. "Coach, I thought I was doing well at fullback. Why did you switch me?"

Coach Miller gave me a sensitive smile that barely concealed four missing teeth on the lower part of his mouth. "Ah," he said as he stood up from his desk and approached me with open hands. "I've been keeping an eye on you. And I think you've got what it takes to go far if you're willing to work with me."

I tensed. This wasn't what I wanted to hear.

Coach Miller recognized my resistance and encouraged, "Give it time. You'll see. Being on the O-line is good for you, and it's good for the team."

"But," I protested, "I really want fullback!"

Coach Miller passed one hand over the bald spot on his head and raised the other to cut me off. "You've grown a bit recently, haven't you?" There was no denying it. He scanned my large frame and continued, "I'd say you've gained an inch in height and, what… twenty pounds of muscle since the JV football season?"

I nodded.

"Here's the thing, Ed. If you were the starting fullback, every team we faced would key in and intercept you before you even took the handoff." Coach Miller inched backward and reasoned, "But if you were a lineman, you'd make our running backs look great and still be the superstar responsible for it."

Superstar? That magic word appeased me, so I resolved to go with it.

***

There was much to learn in the fall of '66 when the football season began. Credit goes to Coach Miller and his staff, who taught me rudimentary assignments and techniques. Immediately, I could see that my wrestling skills crossed over nicely to offensive lineman play. My proficiency increased, and results and recognition followed.

The team also performed better with me on the O-line. Syosset's game attendance increased, and the student body rallied behind us. They invited us to parties and other events as VIPs. Their friendly embrace helped me emerge from my cocoon and become—hmm, how can I describe it? I guess, popular? Yes, that's right. As a sophomore, I was becoming popular. Everyone on the team was. And with our shared experiences, we were becoming brothers bonded in the crusade. Inevitably, the fun extended off the field.

***

After a good football season, my compadres and I met at Howard Johnson's for their Wednesday night dinner special: all-you-can-eat fried chicken for $5.99. Twenty-five voracious high school football players filed in and took up nearly half the restaurant's seats while one worried manager watched the horde advance. The guy visibly frowned when he heard offensive lineman Roy Kaplan invite a few of us to compete in a chicken-eating contest.

"Winner eats for free?" I confirmed and cleared my first serving before the plate even hit the table. In rapid succession, I asked for another round and another after that. My teammates followed suit. But some, with eyes bigger than stomachs, fell off before their third plate arrived. By my fourth helping, the meat tasted like it had been supersaturated in old frying fat. No matter. I kept going.

Despite the manager's antagonistic glares, Roy and I pounded twenty-five pieces. *Got to win.* Then thirty pieces. *I have a legacy to maintain.* My teammates got up, formed a circle around us, and fervently chanted, "Go! Go! Go!" just as I downed my thirty-fifth piece and flagged the waiter for another plate to catch up to Roy's thirty-sixth piece.

"Stop!" the manager screeched and hurried over to our table. "The two of you"—he angrily peered down at us—"you're putting this restaurant out of business. Please, you have to leave right away."

I gazed down at our plates. This was no way to end a contest. In my most nonconfrontational tone, I pointed to the promotional signage hanging over the kitchen and implored, "That over there says 'All you can eat.'"

The manager tensely tapped his foot.

Not missing a beat, two stocky Hells Angels—dangerous-looking men with unruly salt-and-pepper beards, oversized denim jackets, and miles of road behind them—drew the stage light to their corner stall. One raised a large mug of beer and hollered, "Settle down, buckaroo. Give da kids da chicken!"

The manager's face started to twitch.

I considered the scene. Only two pieces of chicken stood between me and the win. But it wasn't worth a fight. Not over this. I met the troubled eyes of the manager and tried to reason with him, "We're almost done," I explained. "It's just the two of us now, and we've got a bet going. Just give us one more serving each, and I promise you, we'll pay our bill and leave."

As our final plates came out, the Hells Angels settled down, and our teammates resumed their cheering even louder than before. "Eat the meat!" they screamed. I swallowed my thirty-ninth and final piece just as Roy scarfed down his fortieth. Contest over. Second place. The worst! Not only did I lose, but to the jeers of my buddies, I had to pay for my meal and a share of Roy's. My biggest regret was that I could no longer boast that I was "the greatest eater on the team."

My teammates mocked me as I sought consolation in a medium-sized strawberry Slurpee from the 7-Eleven next door. But the torrent of their taunting turned to Roy when he upchucked pounds of *pollo*. May the recordkeeper place an asterisk in the book: "Roy Kaplan ate the most chicken in a single sitting, but he kept none of it down. Ed Newman did."

***

In the following wrestling season, the Syosset student body continued to appreciate me for my athletic achievements. However, it seemed that the better I performed, the more my grandparents complained. They harangued that sports were "hurting my education." This all came to a head in late August 1967, days before the start of my junior year, when my dad's parents were over for dinner, and my Grandpa Harry asked about school. While he anticipated I'd talk about something academic, like algebra or world history, I expounded on my great expectations for football and wrestling.

"You're still wrestling?" Grandpa Harry cut me off. "And playing football too? All these athletics," he objected, "I want better for you, Eddy. Tell me, what about your schoolwork?"

I stared blankly across the dining room. While Grandpa Harry was big on education, I had little passion for it.

"It's okay, Harry," Mom piped in and explained. "We're working with Ed to take his schoolwork more seriously. He knows he'll be applying to college next year."

"Exactly!" Grandpa Harry interjected. "If Eddy wants to get into a good school, he must devote more time to his studies."

I tried to pacify my grandfather by telling him I had everything under control. But Grandpa Harry pressed, "Eddy, your strong mind will take you far only if you train it. This fixation with sports will sidetrack you."

Seeing the pained look on my face, my Nana Anna tapped Grandpa Harry's hand and said, "Enough." Then, just as quickly as the subject flared, it shifted to the playoff-bound St. Louis Cardinals baseball team. But like a bad penny, it resurfaced later that evening.

With a handful of freshly roasted chestnuts, Nana Anna approached. "Here. Have a little snack, *Tatala*." She gingerly placed the treat in my palm and sat next to me while I peeled the warm black skin off the treat. She explained, "Papa wants to protect you. We all do."

I glanced down at the floor because all this harping was getting old. Nana Anna placed a thumb and finger under my chin and gently lifted my face upward to meet hers. "I'm worried," she continued. "This football…it's so dangerous. Is it really worth the risk of serious injury?"

Injury? That was the furthest thing from my seventeen-year-old mind. I smiled at Nana Anna and assured her that I was more than capable of defending myself, but Nana Anna wouldn't buy it.

Without saying the words, she suggested I quit football. This left me feeling very unsettled.

I awoke early the following morning to talk it over with Dad. To my surprise, he told me that he had no problem with me playing football as long as my academics came first. "If your grades slip," he warned, "even a little, we will pull you out of sports. But there's more, Eddy," Dad added, "and this is important."

I pushed my meal aside and paid attention as he explained how, rather than derailing me, sports could open doors for me. I perked up, and Dad elaborated, "But you have to be the best, for only the best can parlay their reputation off the field."

I liked what Dad was saying. I also wanted to be the best, so I promised to focus on my studies and athletics. Yet I was young and immature. My academic world yielded whenever there was a conflict. Girls, like my first steady, Alyse, stole my attention. Parties were way too much fun to miss. My best buddy, Eugene, had no problem convincing me to play hooky. And sports occupied so much of my time that little was left to hit the books. By the end of an excellent junior year football season and the start of a promising wrestling season, my devil-may-care attitude caught up with me, and my grades slipped.

"No, Eddy!" Mom gasped at the sight of that dreadful C on my report card. "This will not do." With a frown, she echoed Dad's ultimatum. "No sports until your grades improve." I thought Mom was kidding, but Dad made it clear that this was not a joke.

With a broken heart, I appeared at Coach Blossfield's office the following morning and blurted, "My folks insist I quit sports immediately."

"What?" Coach Blossfield's face drained of blood, and his head swayed from left to right as I explained the situation.

"You're our heavyweight! The wrestling season just started!" he sputtered while anxiously fidgeting with his tie.

I looked away. I already felt so bad.

Coach Blossfield collected his thoughts and stated, "There's a lot more going on here than you realize. I'm going to loop in Coach Miller because, after all, you were with him during the football season when your grades dropped." Coach Blossfield immediately picked up his office phone and arranged for the meeting.

Coach Miller had preloaded his film projector with footage from a recent football game when Mom, Dad, and I arrived. He invited everyone to take a seat, darkened the lights, and began rolling the film. "I want to show you something, Mr. and Mrs. Newman. — LOOK!" Coach Miller raised his voice and pointed toward the screen. "Here's your son flattening the linebacker and creating a lane for our running back." He expanded, "And there…see? Ed doesn't stop!" The energy in his voice surged as he explained, "Your son easily catches up to the ball carrier and throws another block. Don't you realize?" Coach Miller looked from the screen to their faces and exclaimed, "Nobody does that!"

Dad's eyes glimmered with pride. Mom remained apprehensive.

Addressing her skepticism, Coach Miller stated, "Ed is an extraordinarily talented athlete. If he stays the course, he'll have colleges fighting over him. They'll offer him full scholarships."

Scholarships? This was another magic word. Dad did a little happy dance. Mom eased up. And noting he was gaining some ground, Coach Miller pressed for a decision. "Mr. and Mrs. Newman, if you can give Ed a second chance, Coach Blossfield and I will ensure he focuses on his studies and improves his grades. What do you think?"

I took in a deep breath and considered a life without sports. It was unfathomable when I had so much potential and could achieve so much through athletics. I looked at my parents, who were silently deliberating. With interlocked fingers, I begged, "Please?"

We sat there for a while. Finally, Dad looked at Mom. She nodded slightly. And with that, he answered, "Okay. We'll give you a second chance. But only this one time, Eddy. If your grades drop again, that's it."

"Okay," I promised. "I won't let you down."

CHAPTER 4

KONGA

"Hey, Ed! Got a sec?" Coach Miller intercepted me on my way to wrestling practice and asked if I was ready for my AP American History test.

"I am," I answered a little too quickly because I had totally forgotten about it. But now alerted, I knew to get ready.

"Great," said Coach Miller. With a twinkle in his eye, he explained how I needed to keep my grades up because scouts from Annapolis and West Point were looking to make me a junior-year scholarship offer. He boasted, "Other schools will come like locusts next year, so you ought to give me your college criteria, and I'll act as your gatekeeper."

The days that followed were hectic. With classes, wrestling, social obligations, and several meetings with recruiters, there was little time for anything else. Still, I studied, and my grades improved. I also earned All-Division wrestling honors and received full scholarship packages from the academies. I felt optimistic about my future, trusting that other universities would see me reaching new levels on the gridiron in the fall of '68.

***

"Remove your helmet and shoulder pads to cool off," instructed Syosset's special teams coach, Mr. Cerullo, while reviewing assignments on a brutally hot September day at the beginning of my senior year. After doling out a few coaching points, Mr. Cerullo suggested we try it with him set up as the punter.

As Syosset's center spiraled the ball into Mr. Cerullo's grasp, I raced past the front linemen with my hands held high to stop the ball. But in moving so fast, I didn't realize that my head crossed the ball's trajectory, and, like a wet slap, it crashed straight into my unprotected right eye. *Shit*. I fell to the ground in pain. *Chaos*. This was a terrible run-in with Chaos, the destroyer of dreams.

"You okay?" Mr. Cerullo yelped.

I squinted and tried to make sense of the surreal panorama of colors flooding in. Greens were purple, and yellows were pink. Mr. Cerullo's face was a bluish blur. "Something's not right," I answered.

Mr. Cerullo immediately alerted Coach Miller, who had me showered, dressed, and waiting with an ice pack on my eye for my mom to take me to the doctor.

As the ophthalmologist examined my eye, I considered my late Nana Anna's cautions. "Football is dangerous," she used to say. "Is it really worth the risk?" I held my breath, realizing she might be right. My stomach dropped as I waited for the doctor's diagnosis. Without emotion, he pronounced that it was retinal hemorrhaging.

"You need to rest that eye," the doctor cautioned, "because if you're not careful, your retina could detach, and that could lead to blindness."

The doctor must have noticed my vacant stare because, after a few seconds, he confirmed, "You understand?"

In slow, measured words, I asked, "When can I return to ball?"

"Son," he clarified, "you're done with ball."

"No!" I protested. "Please! Football is my ticket to college scholarships. You don't know what you're taking from me."

Mom reached for my hand and implored, "You're hurt, Eddy. You can't risk your vision."

"No!" With a quiver in my voice, I entreated, "I understand the value of erring on the side of caution but," I begged, "there must be another way."

The doctor looked from my bloodshot eye to my mother's worried face. After what seemed like an eternity, he said, "Well…maybe. I can't promise you anything, but I'll at least reassess things in a few weeks after all the swelling has gone down. In the meantime," he soberly added, "I insist that you refrain from any physical activity."

"That sounds like a good idea," Mom whispered.

The days that followed were awful. I suffered sympathetic glances from almost everyone I passed in Syosset's hallways. I hated being the object of their pity. I clenched my jaw and got caught up in negative thinking: No football, no wrestling, no good. I feared that my physical conditioning would fall off. Man, that follow-up appointment couldn't come soon enough.

And then, finally, it was time for my follow-up appointment. I sat in the examination chair with clammy hands and waited while the doctor placed dilating drops into my eye. Thirty long minutes later, he looked through his ophthalmoscope and evaluated my progression. My good eye circled the room. I focused on my mom's angst-ridden face. I found myself considering a life without sports all over again. *Chaos. Fucking Chaos.* But I hoped that, like any opponent, Chaos could be barred or sidestepped—at least some of the time.

The doctor scooted his chair back. With a serious face, he said, "You're cleared to play football. But be careful, son. You got very lucky this time."

Exhilarated is an understatement—I was nearly jumping out of my skin.

Ed Newman, #71, Syosset tackle (1968)

What followed were glorious days on the gridiron. Displayed before the college scouts' discerning eyes were win after win delivered by the best football team Syosset High School had ever produced. We finished the year with a stellar record and a first-time win over our perennial spoiler, Hicksville. Moments after the victory, Coach Miller gathered the team and praised, "You guys accomplished something no Syosset football team ever has. Today you made history."

The fool's grin monopolizing my face straightened when I noticed a few seniors were crying. When I asked what was going on, one shared that they were mourning their separation from football. While it hadn't occurred to me, this was their football finale. Meanwhile—with Princeton, Columbia, Virginia Tech, and William and Mary lining up to sign with me—this was just my beginning. Now understanding their pain, I also shed a tear.

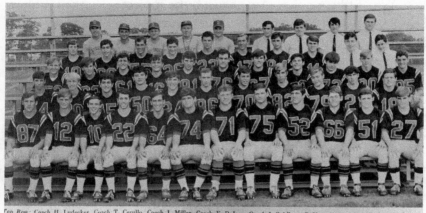

Top Row: Coach H. Ludecker, Coach T. Cerullo, Coach J. Miller, Coach F. DeJong, Coach J. Goldberg, P. Katz, D. Petzel, J. Woulfin, R. Spence. *Row 2:* R. Silvestri, H. Giragosian, J. Drew, J. Murnane, R. Naranjo, S. Hanson, B. DelSavio, J. Villizon, J. Kay, E. Alwais. *Row 3:* R. Rohr, M. Tesseraro, D. Carro, D. Krasanic, T. Zahar, J. Lusardi, T. Brust, M. Mark, G. Welikson, C. Kupec, D. Mattina. *Row 4:* G. Rossetti, T. Scherer, B. Jalli, L. Thomas, M. Saladino, F. Puchalski, R. Rudnick, A. Abrams, A. Charlton, D. Ney, D. Brady. *Bottom Row:* G. Olt, B. Schondelmier, J. Burke, S. Parker, R. Rosenfeld, P. McQuade, E. Newman, T. Wieler, Captain L. Mueller, E. Kanowitz, J. Greene, R. Hoda.

Syosset's varsity football team (1968)
Photo credit: Syosset High School Yearbook

***

"The Baltimore Colts are favored to win Super Bowl III against our very own New York Jets this Sunday, January 12, at 3:05 p.m. Eastern in Miami's Orange Bowl," announced the radio broadcaster in early 1969.

Dad handed me a glass of Bosco chocolate milk and asked, "Who do you think will win?"

I downed the drink and admitted that I wasn't up on the Super Bowl.

"More of a participant than a fan, huh?" Dad laughed. He turned the radio down and tried to pique my interest by explaining how the Colts were expected to win but that the Jets' quarterback, Joe Namath, had brazenly guaranteed that his team would win.

Dad refilled my glass and declared, "In my day, no athlete would make such a bold statement. I'm sure Namath's prediction is riling up the Colts and their coach, Don Shula." He concluded, "I think the Colts will win, but it would be cool if we had a Super Bowl champ in our backyard."

When I kept quiet, Dad changed the subject. He asked if I had heard from the recruiter from his alma mater, Duke University. I hadn't, but explained how things were looking good with Columbia and Princeton.

"You've got to wait for Duke," Dad insisted. "You can't beat that education." With a nostalgic sigh, he elaborated, "If my GI benefits hadn't expired and Newman's hadn't taken me away from Durham, I would have been very proud to graduate with a Duke degree."

I liked the idea of following in Dad's footsteps, so when Blue Devil football called, I explained that I would only play ball with Duke if their head football coach, Tom Harp, also allowed me to compete on the school's wrestling team. Coach Harp agreed, and I signed the papers to join Duke University's class of 1973 on a full football scholarship.

***

"Now that your future is all set with Duke," Coach Blossfield kidded at the start of my senior wrestling season, "you'll probably go lazy on me."

"Nah, you must be thinking of somebody else," I declared, "because I want to go undefeated this year."

Coach Blossfield tightened the already perfect knot on his tie and chided, "Wanting is not enough. If you plan to win all your matches, you've got a lot of hard work ahead of you."

"I'll be ready," I assured him.

Coach Blossfield immediately put me to the test. He doubled my wrestling time, tripled my strength routines, and told me to "cut the bullshit" when I resisted roadwork. My body responded to the extra effort, and I maintained an early winning streak.

By the season's sixth match, I was oozing confidence. I met the laser eyes of Coach Blossfield. His penetrating stare triggered an adrenaline rush that could not be contained. I started to pace like a lion in a cage. Back. I worked myself into a lather. Forth. I glowered at my opponent. Back. I sucked down oxygen. Forth. I approached the center of the mat.

Three seconds and a handshake later, the whistle blew. All 218 pounds of me charged at my 233-pound opponent. I hooked his neck with my right arm and jerked him downward. The guy countered with a backward jolt. I helped him along by dipping my head under his arm and pushing him upward, exposing his midsection. I then lunged in and lifted my opponent up from behind before sensationally bringing him down to the mat. To the enthrallment of the crowd, I followed that by mechanically slipping in a half nelson, levering him onto his back, and pushing his shoulder blades toward the ground for the pin.

I don't know why, but in that moment, I looked toward my girl, Alyse, and motioned a thumbs-up, followed by a thumbs-down, to theatrically solicit her input. Alyse played her part and pointed toward the ground. I obliged and cranked my adversary over like the lid on a can of tuna fish.

"—PIN!" the ref yelled. "Five points to Syosset!"

The small crowd roared.

Week after week, the intensity of my pre-match rituals built. The fans lapped it up, and attendance at Syosset's wrestling matches increased. Coach Blossfield noticed and arranged for the final matches of the 1969 wrestling season to take place on the court before Syosset's basketball team competed.

Nearly a thousand people came out to see "Newman's opening act" before our final regular season match against Hicksville. I paced back and forth as friends and family clustered on the wooden bleachers. Feeling high from the growing tension, I moved faster and faster. Some of the more vocal students started to bellow in sync with my strides, "KONGA! KONGA!" Their chants were lifted from that scene in the classic *King Kong* movie, when the indigenous people extolled the giant ape as he approached his sacrificial offering.

Their contagious cheers echoed off the gym's elevated ceiling. "KONGA! KONGA!" Hundreds joined the refrain. I puffed my chest and stoked their energy. With my overzealous movements, I must have looked like a professional wrestler, but there was no acting going on here. I was just young, immature, and swept up in the moment.

When the ref called for the heavyweights, I went to the center of the mat and waited for my opponent. Twenty seconds later, I noticed that the Hicksville coach was engaged in an animated discussion with his heavyweight. The coach shook his head in irritation and walked over to the ref, who, after a short exchange, boomed, "Hicksville disqualified!"

The Syosset fans went insane. I was astonished that a varsity wrestler was too afraid to compete against me. And while I probably should have been satisfied with remaining undefeated, I wasn't because I needed this competition to prepare for the postseason tournaments.

Luckily, Coach Blossfield had a plan to help me out. I was overcome with gratitude the moment I arrived at Syosset's gym and found fifteen of the largest guys from our football team waiting to grapple with me. Coach Blossfield cleared his throat and explained that each would face me in a series of forty-five-second speed matches.

I took my stance and listened as Coach Blossfield told my first counterpart to take control. A few seconds later, I effortlessly bulled him down—three times—before the clock ran out. I did the same with the following two opponents. Coach Blossfield screamed at each guy thereafter, "Take him down! Put Newman on his back!"

Not a fucking chance! One by one, I pinned each of those guys within seconds. While they fully recovered, I gasped for air, grunted, and fought fatigue.

"Enough of that," Coach Blossfield said about twenty minutes in. "Newman," he instructed, "get on top. The rest of you"—he pointed to the ballplayers—"escape from Ed's grasp."

When none of the guys could get out of my hold in this new, more challenging format, an agitated Coach Blossfield screamed, "Next period. Newman to the bottom. Make him eat the mat!" He egged the ballplayers on, "Can't you see that Ed is totally exhausted? Pin him already!"

By this point, I had been wrestling without rest for an hour. While I had handled the first twelve ballplayers quite well, my tank went dry when Joe Piscatelli, the largest guy on the team, plastered his

225 pounds onto my back. Coach Blossfield screamed at Piscatelli, "Flip Newman! Pin him!"

No! NEVER! I would never let anyone dominate me.

Piscatelli went batshit trying to be the guy who pinned Newman. I did all I could to prevent that while lying belly flat on the mat for several seconds. When our stalemate didn't break, Coach Blossfield called the match.

Piscatelli easily hopped up. I remained prone on the ground, heaving for air. Coach Blossfield inched forward. With his black leather shoes just a smidge from my nose, he sneered, "You loser. Go shower."

In some twisted way, his insult motivated me to do more.

Ed Newman, All-County wrestler (1969)
Photo credit: Syosset High School Yearbook

After earning gold in the Division 1A Championship and the Nassau County Wrestling Tournament, I set out to win States—the final competition of the postseason. But my adversary had an eighty-pound weight advantage over me, and I couldn't muscle him around.

With bile in my gut, the slow-motion exercise in futility ended with a score of 2–1, and my otherwise perfect season concluded with defeat.

I left States feeling ordinary because, best case, I'd get credit for coming in second. Worst case, I'd be forgotten along with the bulk of meaningless trivia. Disinterested in either, I renewed my vow to be the best of the best at Duke. To me, that was the only acceptable path forward.

CHAPTER 5

THE PUSHBACK

I rubbed my eyes in disbelief as Dad and I passed a disconcerting billboard on our journey south to Durham, North Carolina. It featured a white-cloaked man on horseback, holding an enflamed cross, with big and bold letters stating: "THIS IS KLAN COUNTRY, 'LOVE IT OR LEAVE IT.'"

I pointed toward the billboard and asked, "Did you see that?"

Dad slowly lifted his chin. After a bit of silence, he explained how some in the white community resisted an integrated society. With a look in his rear-view mirror, he expanded, "There's a lot of hate out there, son. It's no good." He proceeded to quote the late Martin Luther King Jr. and reminded me to judge others by their character, not by the color of their skin. Dad suggested that some might even judge me for being different—specifically, for being Jewish. He concluded, "Just be aware of the biases around you."

I didn't know what to say, so I kept quiet.

A little while later, we pulled onto Chapel Hill Road and took in the majesty of Duke's Gothic wonderland. Dad pointed across the well-manicured quad toward a series of beautiful, interconnected

Gothic buildings, each with cathedral-style doorways and a thick white stone bordering a tan, gray, and brown brick foundation, and declared, "That's where I stayed my freshman year." He inhaled Durham's crisp autumn air and recalled with a look of deep satisfaction, "College was the best time of my life. I hope you make the most of it."

Dad helped me unload my things. Once I was settled in, he gazed down at his polished black shoes and lingered before looking at me with his arm outstretched. "I wish I could stay a little longer, but I've got to get back to Newman's."

Feeling a mixture of anticipation and sadness, I pushed Dad's hand aside and lunged in for a full hug. Our typical handshake felt inadequate.

"I love you, and I believe in you," Dad softly encouraged from our embrace.

My stomach twisted at his words. I didn't want to let Dad down. Duke had some of the nation's brightest students. I secretly worried it'd be hard for me to keep up with a full athletic schedule. Those fears must have been written all over my face because, as Dad turned to leave, he added, "Remember, if you ever need me, I'm just a phone call away."

***

There's little to say about freshman-year ball except that the team, like the rest of Duke, was newly integrated. While most of my teammates were open-minded, the players seemed to self-segregate. I made it a point to treat everyone equally. However, when one player called offensive lineman Willie Clayton the "n-word," I scolded the offender, remonstrating that such behavior wouldn't fly.

Regarding my football/wrestling arrangement, Coach Harp followed through and allowed me to wrestle, even when it overlapped with football's spring training. Yet Duke's head wrestling coach, Bill Harvey, wasn't interested in making any accommodations on my behalf. He insisted that I beat his scholarship heavyweight, John Van Norman, in regular wrestle-offs to earn and maintain the start. No matter. I was up for the challenge.

What followed was epic. Possessing the build of a bear and the pride of a lion, the eighteen-year-old Virginia high school wrestling champ tested me every minute of every wrestling practice at championship levels. I countered his larger size with incredible speed and strength. John responded by doubling his efforts, and our daily war propelled me to levels of power I had never known before. Every night, my body protested from the extreme exertion. Every morning, I woke up muscle-bound and in great pain. But the stiffness and aches magically melted away at the start of our next grapple.

Within a week, I was as fit as I had ever been. Within two, I felt like Superman. After three, I had transformed into a fearless warrior who could handle any assault thrown his way. All the while, John remained a pure competitive athlete. He cheered me on when I took the start, went undefeated, became the ACC Heavyweight Champion, and made it to the ultimate competition of the postseason: Nationals—where, anticlimactically, I lost to another 325-pound beast.

Ed Newman, Duke wrestler (1970)
Photo credit: Duke University Archives

***

Duke football underperformed my sophomore year, and the university responded by firing Coach Harp and replacing him with Duke alum Mike McGee. From the rear of the room in a get-to-know-you meeting, I assessed the former offensive lineman from the St. Louis Cardinals as he projected a take-no-shit attitude and used his big, muscular build to take command of the room.

"Even though the season is over," Coach McGee outlined his expectations, "the work is not yet done. You need to stay in top shape by lifting weights and attending spring training."

Spring training? I naively assumed that Coach McGee's requirements didn't apply to me because I had that "Harp exception." I conducted my business as if nothing had changed. I dominated on the wrestling mat, won my second ACC heavyweight championship title, and thanks again to John Van Norman, secured an encore shot at Nationals.

All too familiar with the pain of losing, I upped the ante and put in an unbelievable amount of effort to win the final wrestling tournament just as football's spring training was kicking off.

"Newman, got a sec?" Coach McGee flagged me down on my way to wrestling practice. With his thick forehead leaning in, he drilled his dark eyes into mine and demanded, "You need to quit wrestling right away."

"What?" I stumbled backward.

He clarified, "You need to quit wrestling so you can learn our football scheme."

I didn't understand. Wasn't my wrestling good for Duke and good for the football program? I described to Coach McGee how it improved my athletic abilities far more than spring ball ever could, but Coach McGee wasn't interested. He maintained, "You've got to suit up now. Don't forget, Ed," he warned, "you're on a full football scholarship."

My brain flared white-hot as I considered the detour Coach McGee was demanding. I sputtered, "Wh…what about Nationals? I have a special deal with Duke and Coach Harp. Please!" I implored, "You don't know how much I've been preparing."

Coach McGee cut me off and cajoled in a disarming manner, "I've been watching the films. I think you're probably our best varsity player. In fact," he expanded, "I believe you can fill in the gaps where needed, and we need you as a middle linebacker."

What? He wants me to quit wrestling and switch positions? I exhaled loudly. Coach McGee tried to temper my concerns. "Don't get all worked up here," he assured. "You're a quick learner. You won't have any problem adapting to linebacker."

"This is a terrible idea," I protested. "I don't know jack shit about linebacker."

But Coach McGee wouldn't yield. It was his prerogative. All I could do was go with it. What a shame, all my effort for naught. My shot at winning Nationals, gone.

I felt so uncomfortable on my first day as a middle linebacker. Our team captain was barking unfamiliar words, and Duke's linebacker coach, Bill Thompson, was shouting play-by-play guidance at me from the backfield. "It's a second down, four yards to go, run-pass situation," Coach Thompson enlightened as we got into position. "You gotta read their lean real fast before the snap to determine your next move." I nodded blankly before completely botching the play.

I moped over to the sideline, feeling embarrassed, where Coach Thompson met me and said, "Don't worry, Ed. You'll get there after two thousand hours of practice." I shook my head in frustration. I didn't have two thousand hours in the remaining three weeks of spring ball.

The days that followed were more of the same—a lot of confusion, little progress, and ordinary play. When spring training ended, I was only as good as a backup player. I felt sorry for myself that I had little to show for missing Nationals.

I dedicated my summer to turning things around. I got leaner, gained some quickness, and felt optimistic when I returned to Duke at the beginning of my junior season, ready to master the linebacker position. As things started to gel on my first day of practice, Coach McGee yelled from the sideline, "Newman! Go over to Bossons. I want you to do a few snaps with the offensive linemen."

"What?" I ran toward him to better understand.

"It's...it's just for a little while. You know, in case there's an injury," Coach McGee stammered. "You're still our linebacker. But if the team needs you, you're already our best lineman."

Best lineman? I stood there dumbfounded because the football program was touting fellow junior Willie Clayton as the team's top offensive lineman in the school paper.

Coach McGee pointed toward Duke's O-line coach and ordered, "Get going. Bossons is waiting."

I did as I was told but assumed I'd be back with the linebacker corps by the next drill. Lord knows I needed the practice. Yet within fifteen minutes, Bossons made it clear that this was no backup in case of an injury situation. Coach McGee was returning me to the O-line—full-time.

A torrent of emotions cascaded as I realized I had learned linebacker at the expense of wrestling honors, only to be moved back to the offensive line. I slammed my helmet to the ground and screamed at Coach McGee, "You're messing with the wrong guy!"

Needing to unload, I stormed off the field and rushed to the first payphone I could find. I called Dad, who listened quietly as I explained the situation.

"Son," he calmly interrupted, "I believe you've been wronged. I fully support you to do whatever you need to."

Dad's words gave me a gigantic boost. I knew I had to push back on Coach McGee because I couldn't accept being treated like a sacrificial pawn on a chessboard, regardless of the consequences.

Over the four long days that followed, I walked around Duke's campus like a zombie with no soul, preparing to leave the football program and lose my scholarship. I wondered what my future would hold. Before this pushback, I had dreamed of making it to the pros. But now, all that was at risk. Perhaps I'd leave Duke and play football for another university? I wallowed in the unknown.

Meanwhile, in a universe of his own, Coach McGee expected I'd come crawling back and ask for his forgiveness. When he realized he had no hold on me, he asked a teammate to find me for a sit-down. I reluctantly complied.

Coach McGee was straddling a shellacked wooden bench in the empty locker room. He respectfully removed his Duke football hat, encouraged me to take a seat, and got right to it. "What are your grievances, Ed?" he asked.

With a tug at a loose nail cuticle, I said, "What were you thinking? You should have known that no college athlete could ever learn an entirely new position in just three weeks of spring ball."

Coach McGee shrank in his seat.

I continued, "I was fixated on being a linebacker. And then, without even talking to me about it, you switched me to the offensive line. What's worse is that you made me quit wrestling's Nationals on an experiment. You essentially stole from me something I can never get back." With nostrils flaring, I concluded, "You set me up for failure, and I don't do well with failure."

Coach McGee put his hands over his eyes and slowly swayed his head back and forth. "You're right," he quietly responded. "I messed up. I'm so sorry."

I was stunned. I never expected Coach McGee to admit fault—especially to one of his athletes. But he did, and almost instantly, my body relaxed, and my mind opened to hear what he had to say.

After explaining the team's needs, particularly how it would greatly benefit Blue Devil ball to have me back on the O-line, Coach McGee stated, "I'd like you in camp. What can I do to make that happen?"

I briefly considered his question and laid out my conditions. They included a pass from spring training if I made it to Nationals again and, most importantly, "ink." I insisted, "If I perform as the team's top offensive lineman, Duke Media should promote me as such." I said this because I needed the publicity to catch the attention of the NFL scouts.

Coach McGee listened closely. When I finished, he nodded and promised, "I'll do it. I'll do all of it if you perform."

I felt overcome with relief. I loved Duke and didn't want to leave the university. I saw Coach McGee's contrition as a hit on the reset button. It was an opportunity to start anew, and that was exactly what I needed. By instinct, I went to a pay phone and called Dad.

CHAPTER 6

FRUSTRATED COMPETITORS

Duke's 1971 football season was shaping up nicely as we charged out of the gate with three consecutive wins and earned the number 19 college football ranking. Even with that success, the pundits predicted that Stanford would whup our Blue Devil asses in the fourth game of the season.

"Newman! Clayton!" Coach McGee poked his fleshy face into the locker room and barked, "Come with me now. I want to run something by you guys."

Willie Clayton and I followed Coach McGee into his office, where an unflattering newspaper article about the game lay on his desk. Coach McGee crumpled the paper, and with his large fist pumping wildly in the air, he chafed, "These idiot reporters seem to think that Stanford is going to dominate us. Sure, Jones being out will hamper our offense. And…yeah, we're dreadfully thin on defense, but"—Coach McGee put down the rag, pointed at the two of us, and with a broad smile, revealed—"I have a secret weapon."

Willie and I looked at each other. Coach McGee elaborated, "Nobody does this, but I want the two of you to play both offense and defense during the Stanford game."

Whoa. My jaw dropped. *Double playtime.*

Coach McGee elucidated, "With you guys playing defensive tackle and your regular O-line assignments, we'll gain the advantage over Stanford. They won't know what hit them!" He boasted, "You'll be my 'Iron Dukes.'"

Come game day, I suited up in Stanford Stadium. After some back-and-forth pacing, I took the field as an offensive guard, where I easily manhandled Stanford's defensive counterparts. After a pass on a critical third-and-long situation was disrupted, I jogged to the sideline and met an animated Coach McGee, who commanded, "Get your wind quickly. You're back in on defense at the next snap."

A whistle and a huddle later, my counterpart shifted to a Stanford offensive guard. I popped that guy two yards into the backfield and forced a fumble, which Stanford's center recovered.

"Stanford brings out the punt team!" boomed the announcer.

With lungs working like a pair of fireplace bellows, I jogged to the sideline so the special teams could establish the line of scrimmage. Then, with just enough wind, I returned to the field—this time in service of the O-line.

And so a pattern of play was established. I transitioned between the offensive and defensive lines with only moments to rest in between. Willie did the same. All the while, Coach McGee watched for signs of fatigue – which I never showed. By the third quarter, Coach McGee offered me a few minutes to rest. I assured him I was okay. I wouldn't allow anything to stop me now.

As the seconds ticked away in the fourth quarter, Stanford's accomplished quarterback, Don Bunce, took his stance. The guy was desperate to erase Duke's six-point lead. A single message burned in my brain: *Don't let Bunce score.* Personally positioned as a defensive tackle and wound as tight as could be, I exploded when the ball snapped and darted to the inside, where I danced around the offensive guard like he wasn't there. Once free of that interference, I screamed like a crazy man at the top of my lungs, "YEAHHHHHAAAAAA!" and ran so close to Bunce that he took his eyes off his intended receiver and fearfully stared into mine. So determined to clinch the win, I flailed my arms, swatted, and roared anew, "YEAHHHHHAAAAAA!" Bunce ran for his life, straight to Stanford's sideline. *Success!*

Talk about an on-top-of-the-world moment. Coach McGee made a special trip through the locker room after the game to give Willie and me a pat on the back. The good got even better when Coach McGee placed a sealed envelope in my locker with the following words scribbled on the face:

> You asked for ink...you got it.
> —McGee
> P.S. NFL scouts are calling.

Enclosed within was a *Stanford Daily* article titled "Offense Dies Against Duke." The following segment was highlighted in yellow: "Coach Mike McGee of Duke made the best use of what talent he had by placing talented offensive linemen Ed Newman and Willie Clayton on the defensive line as well."[1]

Instantly, my addiction for praise was ignited. I was like a racehorse with blinders on. All I could see was the path immediately in front of me. There was the next step, the next play, the next game and hopefully, the next win. With that persistent discipline, I maintained a stellar junior year football season, where I played on both offense and defense.

Unfortunately, Blue Devil football didn't perform as well. We ended the season with a 6–5 win-loss record, and I found being a superior player on an average team frustrating because I couldn't really crow.

***

---

[1] https://archives.stanforddaily.com/1971/10/04?page=7&section=MODSMD_ARTICLE21

Around that time, in a league far, far away was another frustrated competitor. After suffering a humiliating defeat against the New York Jets in Super Bowl III, then-Colts head Coach Don Shula resolved that appearing in a championship game was not enough. He needed to win one—or two. By happenstance and a little sleight of hand, the young coach left Baltimore for Miami in the winter of 1970, where he cleared out the dead weight, whipped the committed into top-notch professionals, and transformed the Miami Dolphins into a Super Bowl–contending team. Yet victory was elusive. Shula suffered another humiliating loss, this time in Super Bowl VI when the Dallas Cowboys crushed Miami 24–3.

"Is Shula good enough to win a Super Bowl?" sports gossipers prattled. Their words poured fuel on his fire. Maybe Shula prayed? Maybe he meditated? Whatever it was, the man became obsessed with finding "the winning edge."

It was that intensity that motivated Shula to take the 1972 Miami Dolphins on a trip that no team had ever traveled before—or after. They sailed through a string of wins and a Super Bowl victory, ending the season with a perfect 17–0 record. I repeat, 17–0! This gold earned Don Shula and his '72 season talents a lifetime admittance into the pantheon of legends. Other coaches and teams could only aspire.

***

Despite their glory, I knew little of the Miami Dolphins. As a senior at Duke, I was preoccupied with finals, fraternity parties, a pair of postseason All-American bowl games, and a return to wrestling. It was a lot, especially when NFL scouts were knocking at my door, sports agents were vying to represent me, and professional football teams were inviting me to all sorts of physical and intellectual evaluations.

Trudy, Ed, and Marvin Newman at the East-West Shrine game (1972)

The question of my prospective player position also weighed heavily on my mind. While I had played exclusively on the D-line throughout the 1972 football season, I believed that my body and skill set were best suited for offensive lineman play. I told the scouts to draft me accordingly, but they insisted that that would hurt my chances for an early pick. Even so, I stuck to my guns.

Ed Newman, Duke defensive tackle (1972)
Photo credit: Duke University Athletics

"The draft is heating up," a friend intercepted me in Duke's mess hall on January 30, 1973, the first day of the two-day draft, and asked, "Do you think today is the day?"

I shrugged; it was unknowable. All I could do was wait. And wait I did, for several hours, and nothing happened. Nothing! My feelings were a jumble. I felt insecure when one day turned into the next, and Duke's Steve Jones got drafted in the fifth round.

I sat near my Phi Delta Theta fraternity house phone and listened to the slow-moving draft on the radio: 11:00 a.m., nothing; noon, still nothing; 1:00 p.m.—*ugh!* I wondered if my decision to be drafted as an offensive lineman was a fatal blow.

The endless inquiries from my fraternity brothers made me feel uncomfortable. I sought solitude on the bench at the front of the frat house and tried to escape in the pages of Robert Heinlein's novel *Stranger in a Strange Land*. I meditated on the story about the Martian-raised human who refused to accept limits when—

"Eddy! Steady Eddy!" a brother screamed from the common room window. "Hurry up and get to the phone. The Dolphins are on the line!"

I grok. I put down the book and trotted inside, where I met the impish smile of a Phi Delt brother, who whispered, "Good luck."

For a second, I feared this was a perfectly executed prank because brothers will do that, you know? Even so, I took in a calming breath and nearly sang the word, "Hello?"

"Congratulations, Ed," the faceless voice on the other end commended. "You're our sixth-round draft pick. I'd like to be the first to welcome you to the Miami Dolphins organization."

My heart sped up, and my pulse increased by twenty beats. I couldn't believe this was happening. It was like an out-of-body experience. My fraternity brothers bobbed around looking for answers, and I shared the happy news.

One Phi Delt volunteered, "The Miami Dolphins are the best! The very best!" When I cluelessly nodded, he explained, "Don't you see? They just won the Super Bowl. They had an undefeated season!" He clarified, "You're going to an undefeated team."

"That's cool," I replied tentatively, because it was a lot to process.

My brother cautioned, "You'll have some stiff competition in Miami. They've got exceptional guards with Larry Little and Bob Kuechenberg." With a tilt of his head, he expanded, "I hate to say it, Ed, but there's a chance you'll go to Miami and not make the team. I mean, not every draftee does."

Nah. I brushed the negativity away because I believed in myself. As far as I could tell, I was as ready as any rookie could be. But my heart thumped furiously at the big challenges ahead. It's said that one in thirty kids go on to play high school football, one in thirty high schoolers advance to college ball, and only one in thirty college football players make it to the pros. I ran the math. Was I really the one in twenty-seven thousand? *Ya damn right!*

***

A few weeks later, the Dolphins flew their draftees to Miami for the team's annual awards banquet. The pomp and ceremony nearly took my breath away. There was champagne, delicious food, a great band, Dolphins-branded swag, well-heeled fans, and a squadron of hot cheerleaders. Add to that the opportunity to meet fans, engage with my fellow draft class, and interact with the '72 season veterans—THE PERFECT 17–0 MIAMI DOLPHINS! Holy shit. The greatness of this team was starting to sink in.

With a dry smile, a drunken slur, and a little attitude, Miami Dolphins owner Joe Robbie took the mic and adjusted his oversized, silver-rimmed aviator glasses. He urged in an amplified voice, "Come on up, Coach. The show must go on."

I scanned the hall and found Don Shula in the far corner, savoring each well-deserved moment as he slowly advanced toward the stage. There were hands to shake and players to greet. The man would not be rushed. In all his glory, the greatest coach to ever grace the gridiron radiated like a bright bulb. His smile was so contagious that it overshadowed his otherwise piercing eyes and dominant jaw.

Once Shula made it to the podium, he stood proud and appeared at least three inches taller than he actually measured. He looked around the room. The din quieted, and all eyes snapped to his attention. Shula gave his State of the Union and handed out trophies to the season's MVPs, including Nick Buoniconti, Larry Csonka, Jake Scott, and Bob Griese. He then directed his attention to the draftees, some of whom he explained would help the team achieve victory once again. He invited us to the stage in draft pick order. There was Chuck Bradley, Leon Gray, Don Strock, and then he said it: "Offensive guard, Ed Newman."

I would have floated up had it not been for a beautiful Miami Dolphins cheerleader who met me at my table and offered me her arm. Standing in a row alongside the others, I took in the scene, particularly the flock of fans ogling up at us. My heart raced. It was awesome—like nothing I had ever experienced before. *Click!* Several bright lights flashed, and the cameras captured the incredible moment.

Once back in my seat, the noise settled, and Shula proposed, "There's no reason we can't do it again. There's no reason we can't win another Super Bowl." Insatiable hunger prompted the Don to raise his voice even louder, and midthought, he pinched the tip of his nose.

"That's one," the stalwart, big-boned, dark-haired center Jim Langer whispered to the thin-haired, Danish-looking blond guy sitting next to him, otherwise known as offensive guard Bob Kuechenberg.

That's one? I didn't know what they were talking about. I turned from Langer and Kuechenberg back to Shula as the energy in the room built. Shula launched into the Super Bowl ring presentation ceremony. He bellowed, "Let's hold onto perfect!" and flicked his nose again.

"That's two," Kuechenberg stated with a laugh.

I arched an eyebrow.

The festivities concluded a few hours later, and I left the banquet eager to launch into the next phase of my journey. I returned to Duke, finished out my senior year, and drove with Dad to New York's LaGuardia Airport with a one-way ticket to Miami in my hand. I was ready to dominate as a Dolphin. My dad, however, feared that the NFL would be my Waterloo. He pulled me in for a rare hug and urged, "Don't feel bad if you don't make the cut. You've done great, son. Besides," he reminded, "Newman's is always here waiting for you."

My body tensed in revulsion at the idea of failure. I gently pushed back, looked Dad square in the eyes, and promised, "I'm going to Miami, and I'm going to kick ass." I then grabbed my bags, turned, and stepped over the plane's threshold, leading with my right foot first.

CHAPTER 7

PLAY ANOTHER DAY

Sweat stains spattered my shirt as I walked from Miami International Airport's exit to the air-conditioned car waiting to take me to the Dolphins' facilities for rookie orientation camp. Even though I was used to hot northeastern summers with temperatures nearing triple digits, this stifling heat, paired with South Florida's extraordinarily high humidity, was excruciating. I wiped my brow and guzzled an ice-cold bottle of water. But it all proved insufficient. The driver picked up on my discomfort and offered me some chilled Gatorade and a Dolphins-branded hand towel.

Over the next twenty-five minutes, we drove past patches of newly developed land with all sorts of tropical, spiny greenery. There were vibrant robellinis with fronds fanning out in every direction, tall queen palms scraping the sky, and coconut trees dropping ripe husks onto the Bermuda grass below. I couldn't help but notice how different Miami's flora and flat terrain was from the lush vegetation that smattered the hilly and more populated roads of Long Island and Durham.

"We're here," the driver announced as he turned right onto an unfinished asphalt road and parked in front of two adjoining football fields with bleachers encircled by a chain-link fence. The driver explained that the Dolphins' camp was rented from Biscayne College. Pointing in various directions, he said, "You'll practice here, eat over there, and stay in the dorms across the way. Now grab your bags. I'll take you to your room."

I followed the driver to the university's dull yellow concrete dormitories. When we arrived at my drab, minimalist motel-style room, we were greeted by the scurry of startled cockroaches and a wave of stale heat. Damn, it was brutal. I went straight to the window AC unit and twisted the dial to the *max* before setting off on a self-guided tour through Dolphins Land.

Surprisingly, almost everything around the World Champions' facilities was underwhelming. The lockers were constructed of raw two-by-four lumber and chicken wire. The carpet was old, heavily stained, and dank, reeking of body odor, sweat, cigarette fumes, liniment, mildew, and a splash of mold. There was also a shit-brown couch near the small rundown equipment area that must have been someone's throwaway. None of this was what I expected of the Super Bowl champs, but I trusted there was some secret sauce at play. Perhaps Shula? Or his extraordinary veteran talent? Time would tell, and I realized that time was now because Shula's 7:00 p.m. rookie introduction meeting was about to begin. I sprinted to the meeting room.

Once seated alongside several large draftees and free agents sitting in XXXL elementary school-style chairs, I watched as an impatient Shula walked to the front of the room, checked his watch, and shot a death stare at some almost-late dude attempting to take his seat without being noticed. The moment the clock hit the top of the hour, Shula began, "Every team is gunning to knock us from our perch, and we're not going to let them."

Coach's words had me instantly. I leaned forward and watched as he tightly folded his arms across his chest, almost like a little Mussolini, and demanded we study our playbooks to keep up with the vets when they arrived in a week. Coach subtly adjusted his groin and jutted his chin toward offensive line coach Monte Clark and running back coach Carl Taseff, who began distributing the team's large three-ring binders.

Coach Clark appeared happy to be there as he donned a warm smile and alert eyes. With ten years of professional offensive tackle experience, I anticipated the recently retired thirty-something would have much battle-worn wisdom to impart.

Coach Taseff emitted a less pleasant vibe. He limped around in obvious pain from a ruined right knee. I suspected it was that knee that forced his early retirement from the NFL, where he had once played as a cornerback alongside Don Shula. Now somewhat sour, the bowlegged scamp scowled, "Five-hundred-dollar fine if you lose your playbook."

"Taseff's right." Shula raised his playbook and tapped the hardcover. "Consider this your bible. I expect you to study your assignments religiously because mistakes will not be tolerated." Shula flicked his nose and elucidated, "I have no patience for anyone who messes up. We're going to watch you like hawks." He paused for effect and expanded, "This is a numbers game. Some of you will be traded. Most of you will be cut. But I promise you this, each of you will have a chance. Do not waste your opportunity because you will not get another one."

I looked around and sized everyone up. Undoubtedly, any of these men would have been a superstar at Duke. But here, we were all just amateurs trying to step it up to the pros.

Coach next filled out the details of our daily jam-packed agenda. It included three practices interspersed by meetings, meals, and a mandatory evening curfew—with bed check. Once the clock struck 7:30 p.m., Shula directed us to get with our position coaches. The O-line players gathered around Coach Clark, who pulled an accordion-style divider across the ceiling track and presented his material on an overhead projector. I asked a lot of questions. Coach Clark doled out a lot of answers.

***

51

"Any relation to Paul Newman of *Cool Hand Luke*?" equipment man Dan Dowe joked as he handed over my Dolphins shirts, shorts, shoes, socks, and supporters and looked for an unassigned jersey number for me to sport.

"Nah," I answered with a pat on my belly. "Though I'm pretty sure I could eat fifty eggs without a problem."

Dan laughed as he placed a piece of white tape onto the front of my helmet and labeled it with "Newman #64."

Whoa, 64? My eyes widened with awareness: *64—June 4—that's my birthday!* I shared the happy coincidence.

"Well, look at that," Dan encouraged. "It must be a lucky number then. Now," he suggested, "go and find the locker also labeled #64 and get set up because practice will start soon. You don't want to be late." He cautioned, "Shula is ruthless with the tardy. I've seen guys get cut for much less."

Dan's ominous words sobered me to the fact that NFL could also stand for "not for long." Sure enough, fifteen rookies vanished a few days later. Gone. Just like that. And while I took a moment of silence for those guys, I couldn't pay it too much mind because the vets were already trickling into the locker room and coldly passing us rookies as if we were ghosts.

"Get your shit out of here," tight end Jim Mandich abruptly stomped up to my locker and began to peel the #64 label off the front frame.

"HEY?" I objected with a flinch. "This is my space."

With his black mop hairdo and glowering grimace, Mandich disregarded my plea and proceeded to reveal a more permanent nameplate that read "Mad Dog." He bared his canines and barked one word, "GET!"

As I grudgingly gathered my things, I overheard placekicker Garo Yepremian giggle in a heavy Armenian accent to safety Dick Anderson, "I got a joke that'll knock the hair off your head." Garo pointed at Anderson's prematurely balding crown, dropped his smile, and delivered, "Oh. I see you've already heard it." Proud of himself, Garo danced around like a little imp and mimicked Elvis Presley with a dropped voice, "Thank you very much."

Anderson chuckled, and with a finger now directed at Garo's also balding head, he responded, "Look who's talking, Garo."

"Hey, Dick," Mandich interrupted, "where's Jake?"

With a smirk, Anderson answered that his partner in crime, defensive safety Jake Scott, was up for contract renewal and holding out for more dough.

"Ah, he deserves it," said Mandich. "After all, he was our Super Bowl MVP."

"Yeah," red-assed starting offensive lineman Bob Kuechenberg from his metal folding chair. "Manny Fernandez should have gotten those honors." He scrunched his small nose and expanded, "Manny had a career game with seventeen tackles and a sack."

Anderson waved his hand as if to dismiss any debate and said, "Whatever it is, Kuech, Robbie brags that his 'World Champion Miami Dolphins' have the lowest gross salary expense in the league. Jake is going to force him to pony up."

"Damn right," interjected backup offensive guard Al Jenkins from his locker, situated a few from the one I was now claiming as my own. Noting that this was my man to beat, I gave Jenkins a once-over. He appeared carefree and confident. He stood tall—at least an inch higher than me and solid—with fifteen pounds on me. My adrenaline started to pump, and I reminded myself that I got this.

***

Coach Shula looked down his nose before our first hitting practice and reviewed his list of "winning edge" philosophies. "I expect no mistakes," he insisted, wagging a finger. "You understand? I want crystal-clear communication." He met our eyes and elaborated, "I expect each of you to take full responsibility for your assignments." Coach raised his voice, got more into it, and swiped at his nose before instructing, "Get your shoulder pads from Dowe."

"That's one," Kuechenberg whispered to Jim Langer behind a cupped hand, almost simultaneously with Shula's flick. Kuech wagered a bet with his buddy that Shula, whom he referred to as "Shoes," would "dig for gold" at least ten times that week. This conversation seemed to perk the center up, who took the over, and I finally got their inside joke.

The next morning, I fueled up for the physical day ahead by taking down a double helping of scrambled eggs, sausage, toast, and sweet Hawaiian Punch. Oh, that Hawaiian Punch was a big mistake because my uneasiness increased with each jumping jack, sit-up, and push-up in the hot morning warm-up. My nausea reached a terrible climax about twenty minutes in when Coach Clark hollered from the backfield, "Let's go! On the hop. Get across the field for sled work."

I began to run, and—"*RAAALLLPPPHHH.*" I stopped in my tracks and uncontrollably projectile-vomited dark-red Hawaiian Punch, scrambled eggs, sausage, and stomach acid across the 40-yard line.

"NEWMANNNN!" Coach Clark yelled at me, "Do that on the run."

Holy shit. He wants me to puke on the trot? I complied, but not gracefully. Soon several others joined me in the club of the "physically distressed." One guy fainted from the heat; another was bowed over with the wind knocked out of him; and my roommate, second-round draft pick Chuck Bradly, was getting his injured ankle taped on the field by our team trainer. Clearly, camp was not for the weak.

"To the barn!" Coach Clark howled once practice wrapped. After a shower, a lighter meal, and a brief rest, I returned to the gridiron refreshed and ready for the afternoon scrimmage. The cameras in the tower were humming, and the vets took the field determined to educate us rookies. I planned to do some schooling myself.

About fifteen minutes in, the strong, serious, and stately veteran right guard, Larry Little, motioned for me to take his place on the field. I nodded at the All-Pro and joined the huddle, where I listened to our fair-haired quarterback Bob Griese announce, "P-10 on two."

While P-10 referred to a short trap play where the left guard kicked out the defensive tackle on the other side of the center, I was so juiced up on making an impression that I got confused and—*crap!*—I pulled in the wrong direction and slammed straight into a startled Kuechenberg.

"What the fuck, you rookie idiot!" Kuech tore off his helmet and got all lathered up in outrage. "You could have broken my fuckin' neck!"

"Come on, man!" berated Langer.

Shula threw his clipboard to the ground, swiped at his nose, and piled on from the backfield, "God damn it." He hesitated while searching for the name on my helmet. Then, through gritted teeth, he spat, "God damn it, Newman. Damn mental mistakes!"

"I'll take care of this," Coach Clark interjected. He waved at Jenkins and told me to step back. I couldn't get small enough as I came to terms with the fact that this mishap could land me at the top of the cut list.

A bead of sweat ran down my brow later that evening during film review when Shula's eyes fixed on mine, his face got all screwed up, and he cued my P-10 mishap on the silver screen. With a red laser beam, Coach repeatedly circled the calamity, rewound, and replayed the scene as if it were on a loop. Over the uncomfortable titters of my teammates, Shula seethed, "Newman, you must be a twin because no one person could be that bad."

Picking up on my humiliation, Coach Clark met me after film review and confided that even though Shula would never admit it, he saw me as a go-getter but was worried about my inexperience. Coach Clark explained how Shula needed a competent backup guard whom he could rely on to sub in whenever Kuech or Little needed it. My mind flashed to Jenkins, but Coach Clark brought it back to me. "If you run your assignments perfectly, avoid penalties, and stop making these damn mistakes, that backup player could be you, Ed. But," he elaborated, "you need to do better, and you need to find a way to stand out right now." Coach Clark concluded, "You can do that on the special teams."

What? Special teams? My face dropped. *Coach Clark wants me to play point on kickoffs and punt returns?* This didn't sit right. I considered special teams beneath me. At Duke, Coach McGee would never play me on the special teams. But deep inside, I knew I couldn't entertain such thoughts, especially when I was fighting to break into a team that was stacked with talent.

The following morning, I gathered with the others in the locker room and waited for Coach Taseff, a.k.a. "the Turk," reminiscent of the festooned Turkish executioner wielding a head-detaching scimitar, to inform the unfortunates that their time had come. Most looked uneasy, even some of the long-tenured vets, because no one had a guarantee.

The room hushed when the Turk entered. My heart rate increased, and my stomach turned. I looked toward the exit. I wanted to get out because a childish part of my brain believed I wouldn't get cut if the Turk didn't see me. I uneasily watched as the Turk limped around on his bad knee, glanced at his clipboard, and without making eye contact, tapped a dozen or so guys on the shoulder. He advised them, "Shula wants to see you in his office. Bring your playbook."

My stomach dropped for the fallen as they rummaged through their lockers with rounded shoulders, mentally preparing for the imminent rejection. I felt so bad for them. What a shame to be on the cusp of greatness and have nothing to show for it.

A few long minutes later, the Turk turned to leave. Finally, I was able to breathe again. I inhaled deeply, cleared my head, and stood a little taller because, by some miracle, the roster limit had been reached. For the moment, my job was safe, and I could play another day. While that felt good, I knew this wasn't over. I still had to prove myself, one practice at a time, and there were many more to go.

CHAPTER 8

INNOVATIONS

Ed...breathe. I desperately pressed down on my diaphragm and tried to manually restart my lungs, but nothing came in.

Just seconds earlier, I had fantasized about blasting first-team, All-AFC defensive end Vern Den Herder over the fence to open an oversized lane for our running back to charge through. But unbeknownst to me, Vern had a superior ability to ram his shoulder into the trapping guard's face mask. When our quarterback signaled the start of the trap play, I accelerated to full speed—foolishly with my core a little too loose and my spine a little too slack—because five steps in, the 6-foot-6, 250-pound stalwart veteran gave me a first-hand introduction to his patented "Den Herder Ram." *BAM!* Our bodies collided, and all my momentum suddenly snapped.

Ed...breathe... I tried to will air into my body. *Ed...breathe... PLEASE!* I started to panic. *Oh no...I'm suffocating.*

Panting like an overheated puppy, I managed to stand tall, fake a smile, and trot to the sideline, where Shula approved with a "Good hit there. Now," he directed, "go run gassers." Already in respiratory crisis, I barely maintained consciousness as I ran across the field for the wind sprints.

I could have died. The unsettling thought swirled in my brain as I lay awake well past lights out that evening. I asked myself if I really wanted to do this. I loved football way too much to entertain the thought of quitting, but playing in the pros was precarious. I told myself that the only way to proceed down this path was by developing techniques that would safeguard me against future injury. Anything short of that would be foolish.

Next day—*WHACK!*—I hit defensive tackle Manny Fernandez with a strong right cross to his ribcage while raising my left forearm to ward off his formidable swat at my temple. I held my fists, elbows, backbone, and legs in perfect position for maximum leverage when I slapped the inner forearm of the lanky, super-talented defensive end Bill "Stretch" Stanfill and punched him in the face. I pulled my core in tight and girded my spine straight to avoid suffering the consequences of another Den Herder Ram in a follow-up trap play.

My innovations worked. By operating with speed, precision, and an awareness of safety, I hit hard, and the Dolphins "No-Name Defense" hit back even harder. I increased my intensity, and some of the vets started to lash out. All-Pro Manny Fernandez, for example, took cheap shots at my solar plexus and regularly provoked, "You gonna jump offsides, rookie?" I considered his hazing a compliment.

***

Four weeks and two preseason games into camp, Coach Clark squared me against the determined, stiff, and lumbering veteran defensive tackle Maulty Moore, who was also working hard to make the team. As nice as he was strong, the 6-foot-5, 265-pound man stammered with a gentle smile. "Ha...how ya doing, Ed?"

Before I could answer, our senior superstar backup quarterback Earl Morrall started his cadence for a pass play, and I exploded backward to protect him. Immediately, my efforts were thwarted by Maulty, who placed his gigantic paws under my armpits and forklifted all 250 pounds of me upward. *Holy shit.* My feet dangled an inch off the turf, my cleats couldn't gain any traction, and Maulty bulled me straight into Morrall! I felt embarrassed. I felt even worse when it happened again.

After practice, I asked Coach Clark for guidance on how to neutralize Maulty. I waited as Coach Clark sagaciously stroked his chin. Oh, how I expected a fountain of wisdom to pour out from my guru. Yet after several pregnant moments, he simply advised, "Don't let him do that."

What? That's all? I couldn't understand Coach Clark's lack of guidance. I thought about it for a while. Eventually, it clicked that Coach Clark wanted me to learn how to solve problems like this on my own.

I took the note and replayed the action in my head. I watched the films and broke down each of Maulty's movements. In doing so, I identified some vulnerabilities to capitalize on. The next time Maulty's enormous hands reached for my armpits, I punched his Adam's apple and forced him to release his hold. The time after, I crouched below Maulty's outstretched arms and chopped him at the shins. *TIMBER!* The large man toppled like an axed tree.

"Good," Coach Clark complimented my progress and began to pay closer attention to me. After practice, he'd invite me to walk off the field with him and would report on the number of mistakes I made that day. Albeit blunt and brutal, Coach Clark's attention was like heroin to an addict. It fanned my determination to get ahead.

Coach Clark continued with the lessons. One day he gave me Dr. Maxwell Maltz's self-help book *Psycho-Cybernetics* and suggested I employ the self-correction strategies in my game. On another, he handed me a spiral-bound notebook and instructed me to grade every single play I was in. "If you do that," he elaborated with a punch to his palm, "you'll be able to identify your mistakes and avoid making them again." He also reminded me to shine on the special teams.

I still wasn't enamored with the idea of special teams. This sentiment must have been written all over my face because when I sat in the mess hall for lunch later that day, offensive tackle Wayne Moore probed, "What's got your goat, rookie?"

With a slight frown, I shared how I had hardly played any special teams at Duke and how I didn't want to do it now either.

"Don't fight it, young blood," counseled the warm and friendly Texas native. With his eyebrows lifted and a slight smile, he explained, "The coaches will keep the players who bring the most value, and there's real value in special teams." Shooting a knowing look across the table at Larry Little, Wayne added, "Even the greats start on the special teams. Right, Chicken?"

In no rush to respond, Little slowly chewed his meal. He took a big gulp of Pepsi and answered in a deep baritone, "That's right." He looked from his plate to Wayne and grumbled, "But you ain't taking my job, rookie."

"Now, now, Larry. Be nice to the new guy," tempered Wayne as if he were assuming the role of Jiminy Cricket for his buddy Pinocchio.

"Nah, man," I respectfully clarified, "I'm not gunning for your job, but," alluding to the fact that Al Jenkins was my man to beat, I asked, "what do you guys think about Jenkins? He seems pretty talented."

"Ha!" Wayne rubbed at his long legs and explained, "Al is good. He tells everybody he's the 'third-best O-line player in the league' behind Chicken and Kuech. The way I see it, though"—Wayne silently laughed—"talk is cheap."

I bobbed my head in understanding. In a meritocracy like the NFL, it was all about performance. If I proved myself as the better man, that was all that mattered. As I thought about it, the special teams gave me an advantage over Jenkins. While the vet had the physical abilities to fill in at guard, he wasn't lean enough to cover a punt or a kickoff like I could. I finished my meal, feeling optimistic when—

"Roooooookieeee!" Manny's voice carried loudly across the cafeteria. I tentatively turned and found my constant tormentor pointing at me. He wiped some soup from his thick dark mustache and, with a mischievous smirk, demanded, "Sing for us."

I glanced at Wayne, who tipped his Dolphins baseball hat and prophesized, "This could go easy, or this could go hard. It's up to you, rookie."

Easy. Please. "What do you want me to sing?" I asked Manny.

"Your college fight song. Who the fuck cares? Just sing something," Manny urged with cunning eyes.

All right, here we go. I opened my mouth and belted in an intentionally off-tune and pitchy voice, "Fight! Fight, Blue Devils. Fight for Duke and the Blue and White—"

"GET THE HOOK!" catcalled Bill Stanfill over a resounding chorus of boos.

When I persisted, Manny bared his teeth and shouted, "Enough! Shut the fuck up, rookie. And never sing again!"

I smiled as I left the mess hall because I got them.

***

The Miami Dolphins special teams coach, Tom Keane, instructed me to take out two or three of the New Orleans Saints wedge guys on the kickoff during our August 11 preseason game. I bit my tongue at the absurd idea of throwing 250 pounds of me into 750 pounds of them.

As I trotted to the huddle, I considered a better way. Luckily, Garo Yepremian revealed, "I kick the ball to left." Guided by that information, I realized I could fake out the blockers and complete the tackle on my own. I set up to the right of Garo and looked down at the perfectly manicured gridiron. I felt like nothing was beyond my reach. The crowd was screaming. There was urgency in the moment. Everything concentrated in my brain to getting it done.

When the official's whistle warbled, my teammates sauntered in tandem with Garo. Yet I intentionally held back. Then, at the exact moment that Garo's foot pelted the pigskin, I leaped across the line of scrimmage, and—*whoosh!*—took the lead on a field of moving parts. I faded to the right, knowing the ball was going left. *Yes!* My feign successfully drew the wedge guys in the wrong direction. Then, at the perfect instant, I cut clean inside and ran at full velocity toward my left, where, by design, I slammed my helmet directly into the ball as the Saints receiver tried to deliver a big return.

"Fumble!" some anonymous player yelled. The zebra stepped in for a closer look, and I scrambled for the ball, which a Saints receiver got to first. I skipped to the sideline feeling pleased with myself. However, those feelings shifted to concern when I met a hard-faced Keane.

"That was not your assignment," he deadpanned.

I stood silent, hoping that Keane valued my results over how they were achieved.

He continued, "While that wasn't what was asked of you, Shula liked it." Now donning a softer face, he stated, "I'm going to recommend you for special teams captain next week."

The corners of my lips turned upward. I dipped my head in appreciation and proceeded to a nearby bench, where I sat next to Wayne Moore. Wayne pushed a solid fist into my shoulder pad and complimented, "Nice job, rookie. See," he reminded, "you're making a name for yourself on the special teams, after all."

"Maybe so," I said with a smile, realizing that my innovations might actually be my ticket to making the team.

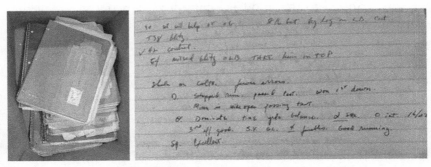

Ed Newman's grading notebooks along with a sample excerpt

CHAPTER 9

THE BROTHERHOOD

Shula gave us a much-needed night off, and everyone scattered. Bob Kuechenberg and Jim Langer went to the disco, Larry Csonka and Jim Kiick to a nightclub, and Jake Scott and Jim Mandich set off for Miami Beach. Some of the married men returned home to their wives. Others went out looking for "strange." Even the rookies had a place to go—well, that is, most of the rookies, except for me. With no family, no girlfriend, no car, little money, and very few friends in the unfamiliar town of Miami, I was painfully lonely.

I stood by myself in Biscayne College's dark and empty parking lot and watched as the last of the players drove off. Desperate for something to do, I walked to the drive-in movie theater about a half-mile down the road. But the ticket teller turned me away, saying something like, "No car, no entry." So instead, I listened to the feature film from the tinny sounds emitted from an errant window speaker outside the chain-linked fence, all while bloodthirsty no-see-ums made a meal out of me.

When every day was the same thing—hard hits, broken bodies, heartless hazing, critical coaching, and cuts that kept on coming—I needed a friend, a companion, anything to help me find joy within the spartan reality of camp. Heck, I needed to find a way to break into the brotherhood.

Luckily, I found an in with Bob Matheson, a friendly linebacker who was also a Duke grad. One day, I engaged Bob about Blue Devil football. Despite my lowly rookie status, the unpresumptuous and witty player shared a few stories. Sensing I was hungry for friends, he took me under his wing.

"I'm not sure Coach trusts me," I confided to Bob one evening over drinks. Bob listened quietly as I rambled on. "How will the coaches decide? I mean, there's Jenkins. He's battle-tested. And there are higher picks in Bradley and Gray. I think it all comes down to a flip of a coin. Heads, I stay. Tails..." my voice trailed off because I didn't want to say it out loud.

"Don't worry so much," Bob put down his beer, rubbed at his strong chin, and predicted in a mild Southern accent, "If you don't make this team, you'll get traded to play for another." With a flash of his perfect season Super Bowl ring, Bob added, "That's what happened to me, and I'd say it worked out all right."

My heart soared at the compliment embedded in Bob's words, but I didn't like the idea of playing for another team, in another town, without Shula. Coach was a brilliant strategist who got the most out of his players. I yearned to make it through preseason wearing orange and aqua.

I knew I had to prove myself to make it happen. This opportunity presented itself on a harsh August day when the sun was broiling our asses, and Shula was toughening us up on the field with no water. The starters and subs were rotating in and out, offering each group a little rest, when Kuech pointed at me and commanded, "Get in there, rookie!"

"You too," said Larry Little to Al Jenkins.

My friendly rival and I trotted to the 35-yard line and squared off against the No-Name Defense in a series of plays. Five minutes in, we were wilting under the heat when Jenkins asked Little for a break. Little declined.

Once we finished the drills, Shoes shouted, "Good. Now do Flow 38."

Jenkins and I launched into our next play and huffed it 30 yards to the right in a wide two-guard sweep. After that, Shula swiped at his nose and commanded, "Now do Flow 39." We did as we were told, but man, we were heaving for air. Shoes did not let up. He continued to run the plays in rapid succession, denying us sufficient time to recover.

Jenkins eyed Little, pressed his hands together as if in prayer, and quietly implored, "Come on, Chick! Give me a break. Please, spell me."

Little folded his arms across his chest and turned his dark brown eyes to the sky.

Noting the drama, Shula adjusted his groin and whispered something to Coach Clark. He shouted, "Again, Flow 38!" Thirty seconds later, "Okay, Flow 39!" Half a minute later, "Get to the huddle, Flow 38!"

While the others got their standard breathers, Jenkins and I did not. It was insane. Coach was running us ragged, but then I realized this was a test. Shula was using this practice to see what Jenkins and I were made of. This gave me a little rise because I needed the opportunity to show him.

When we completed the drill, Coach thundered, "Good effort. Now everyone, go do gassers." Dangerously oxygen-deprived, Jenkins and I jogged across the field, where Coach Clark blew his whistle and started the sprints. Off we leaped. Back! The colors of my vision faded to black. Forth! Every fiber in my body demanded I stop. Back! I precariously listed forward. Forth! I depleted my last reserve and crossed the finish line.

Practically dying from the exertion, I bent over with glazed eyes and stared at the ground, inhaling the O2 like a Hoover vacuum cleaner. Jenkins didn't look so good either. Thirty seconds later, Coach Clark blew his whistle. Recovery time was over. I powered through despite being nearly unconscious.

By the third round, I concentrated on putting the pain out of my mind. That's when, almost as if I were having an out-of-body experience, my rubbery legs began to move on their own. It was crazy. When I got to the finish line, I turned to see what was up with Jenkins. I couldn't believe it…my worthy rival was writhing on the ground, struggling for air.

Coach Clark called for the team trainer to help Jenkins off the field. He ordered the rest of us, "To the barn!" I dragged my body to the swimming pool where, way outside of accepted protocol, I flopped in fully clothed—shoulder pads and all—to cool off.

When I returned to the locker room, I overheard Wayne Moore talking to Larry Little. "Did you see Jenkins go down?" Wayne slapped his hand across his thigh and exclaimed, "*BAM!* The man took a nosedive!"

Little laughed as he worked a tape cutter through his wrist wrap and answered, "Oh yeah, I saw it." Then, spying me sporting a Mona Lisa grin, Little gave a broad, toothy smile and teased, "Get that smirk off your face, rookie. 'Cause, boy, you looked like you were one step from falling out yourself."

I placed my helmet into my locker and confidently responded, "Larry, you wouldn't be talking to me right now if that were the case." I puffed my chest and finished the thought, "Because I'd rather die than give up."

"Did ya hear that, Big Sol?" Little raised his voice and returned his attention to Wayne. "This Newman guy," he replayed my words verbatim, "he'd rather die than give up." Wayne laughed, and the two of them echoed my braggadocio back and forth.

***

"Am I missing something here?" I asked Coach Clark the day after the penultimate roster cut when Jenkins had been picked up by Houston, Gray by the Patriots, and Shoes had acquired Irv Goode, a highly regarded offensive guard from the Bills, to serve as a backup guard. "Is my job safe?" I asked.

"Well, you're still a project," Coach Clark explained. "Coach needs to trust you. He trusts Goode."

My stomach roiled because nothing is certain in the NFL, especially when supply exceeds demand. Feeling charged, I suited up and stormed onto the field for hitting practice, where I was confronted by high temperatures, hot temperaments, and a handful of contenders viciously clawing their way for one of the remaining roster spots. There was also that son-of-a-bitch Manny Fernandez tormenting me.

"On two!" Morrall called for a long pass, and we broke with a clap. I planted my right hand two inches behind the line of scrimmage and stood motionless, waiting to explode backward when—*What the fuck?*—a thick, clear, and aerated mucus-like substance splattered onto my hand.

I looked around and saw that it was Manny—hocking loogies at me! I glowered across the line. "Stop it."

Manny smirked back.

Oh, how I wanted to attack, but too much was at stake. I talked myself down. *Control yourself. Shula is watching.* I inhaled deeply and remained stationary while more mucus mocked me.

Manny provoked with a residue of spit still lingering on his mustache, "What you going to do about it, you pussy?"

I growled in a soft, menacing monotone, "You better cut it out, you motherfucker."

Manny laughed.

Forgive me, for I must plead "temporary insanity," but at that moment, I saw red.

"Hut! Hut!" Langer snapped the ball, and I unexpectedly exploded forward and gave Manny a good pop in his jaw. This startled Manny. He turned his back toward me, and I took the opportunity to wrap my arms around his body and pull him up in a bear hug. I prepared to throw him over the perimeter fence and made it about three steps before Manny managed to neutralize my assault by, I kid you not, securely grasping my balls.

"How about we call it a draw?" he suggested.

I assessed the scene and realized that erratically throwing a teammate probably wouldn't help my chances of making the roster, nor would it help my nuts. So I carefully lowered Manny to the ground. When his feet touched turf, he let go of my family jewels and extended the same hand outward for a shake in friendship.

***

"Rookie!" Manny pounded on my door forty-five minutes before bed check and hollered in from the hallway. "Stretch and I are thirsty. Go get us some beers."

I poked my head out and timidly explained there wasn't enough time.

"No excuses," Manny retorted while prying my door open to reinforce his request.

"But I don't have a car."

Manny rolled his eyes and tossed me his keys.

"I don't know where to get the beer or how to pay for it," I protested once more.

"Come on, rookie," Manny impatiently ruffled his long dark hair and directed me to the 7-Eleven at the college's entrance. "Use your bonus money to pay for the damn beer." With a tap on his watch, he reminded, "Time's a-ticking. Better get going."

I shook my head in disbelief.

God damn you, Manny! I returned to Biscayne College ten minutes too late. It irritated me that this beer run would cost me $50 in fines and potentially the wrath of Shula. I tiptoed to the base of the stairs, trying to sneak up undetected and spied the Turk, who was making his bed check rounds on the floor above. I hid with my back against the wall. A second peek upward revealed that the Turk was lingering at Manny's door. Realizing this was my chance, I backtracked and darted over to a stairwell on the other side of the building and, by some miracle, managed to slip into my room undetected.

"You lucky piece of shit." My roommate, Chuck Bradley, looked up from his *Sports Illustrated* and threw a pillow at me. Nearly a second later, the Turk rapped at our door. I innocently answered as if I had been there all along. Once the Turk checked me in, I snuck over to Manny and Bill Stanfill's room to deliver the spoils.

"Lookie here. It's Dukie, an' with cold brew!" Stanfill said in a slow Georgian drawl as he stepped back to let me in. Stanfill extended his extraordinarily long arms, grabbed a red Solo cup, and hawked black spit into it. He scooped the remaining chew from his lower lip and flicked it into the cup before happily explaining, "Got to get ready for the beer."

"Stretch, there's no need to remove the chew," Manny sarcastically stated. "You use that stuff so often it wouldn't affect you even if you swallowed it. By the way," Manny shifted his attention to me and boasted, "Stretch and I saved you from getting busted by the Turk."

"Thanks, you son of a bitch," I jabbed. "Least you could do for getting me into the predicament in the first place."

"Come on, Taco. It's time you tell him," Stanfill suggested.

"Tell me what?" I asked.

Stanfill gave Manny a purposeful look. "Come on, tell him."

After some prodding, Manny revealed that the coaches had urged him to mess with me.

"What?" I asked.

"It's a stress test, rookie." Stanfill ran his hand through his long flaccid brown hair and clarified, "Ya know. The coaches gotta check the goods before they buy 'em."

Manny clarified, "Ed, you're just..." He looked for the right word. "You're a little hyper. The coaches have never seen anyone so wound up before. They're worried you'll be easily provoked to jump offsides during a game." He expanded, "The worst is having a first down or touchdown called back because some jerk drew a penalty. The coaches wanted me to goad you to make sure that jerk wouldn't be you."

I processed what Manny was saying. I knew I was intense. I was surprised the coaches would test me this way, but I guess I understood why.

Rescuing me from my thoughts, Manny complimented me on how I "kept my cool" during his spit storm.

"Cool? You kiddin'?" Stanfill interjected with exaggerated movements. "Eddy here was about as cool as Wahoo McDaniel slamming another wrestler onto the mat." Stanfill elaborated with a point at

Manny, "If his jewels weren't in your hand, Eddy woulda tossed you five yards through the air."

"Ah, Stretch, you just don't know how to street fight," Manny joked.

I smiled and decided to let it go.

Stanfill finished the last of the beers. He pulled another pinch of tobacco from his Copenhagen tin and lit a Marlboro cigarette on top of the dip. Stanfill parted his lips between puffs and proudly revealed a mouthful of nicotine-stained teeth. "I went to the dentist yesterday and got me a good cleaning," he kidded. "Shiny bright, don't you think?"

Before long, Stanfill had filled the Solo cup to the brim. He raised the rancid saliva/tobacco infusion toward my face and asked in a Georgia boy twang, "Do you wanna drink a little of my Coca-Cola?"

I used the opportunity to say good night.

***

It sounded like a shot from a .22-caliber rifle. *Pop!* My hamstring exploded upon a sudden change of direction as I ran down a ball carrier on a kickoff in the last game of the preseason. I didn't know what was worse, the pain of the rupture or the fear that this injury could end everything. The team's orthopedic surgeon assured me that I'd be good to go in three weeks with therapy. Shula, meanwhile, must have considered his options. Presumably motivated by his inability to cut an injured player, he designated me "physically unable to perform" or "PUP."

Coach Clark found me at physical therapy and reported, "You're on PUP. This means you're on the team as long as you heal nicely."

The excruciatingly sharp pain in my actively stressed hamstring disappeared, and all the blood in my body pumped to my head as I processed Coach Clark's words. *I made the team? YES! I MADE THE TEAM!* All my effort paid off. I was officially in. I nearly jumped off the table, but the team trainer encouraged me to take it easy to avoid further tearing.

Later that evening, I called my folks to share the good news. Mom couldn't help but reiterate her worries that football was too dangerous. She urged me to "make a plan B" and told me to treat every day in the NFL as if it were my last. Dad reminded me that Newman's was waiting for me. I begged off rather quickly because I wanted to celebrate greatness, not wallow in worries.

The next day was team picture day. Some of the guys got rowdy as they squirmed in the hot sun and waited for the photographer to stage us in rows and adjust his light meter.

"Take the picture already!" hollered middle linebacker Nick Buoniconti.

"God damn it, what's the holdup?" bellowed Little as he wiped sweat from his brow. "We should fire this guy and get another photographer for next year."

"Now, now, Larry. Let the man do his job," tempered Wayne.

Kuech, whose cheeks were turning red from the sun, resorted to humor and belted, "Someone get some hats! I'm getting blinded by the sun reflecting off Dick and Garo's bald heads."

Damn, Kuech. The man was just one bad night away from being bald himself.

"That's a good one," laughed Langer.

"Shut up. Let's get this over with," ordered Shula from his seat, front and center beside Joe Robbie.

Click! The historic moment was captured and sealed in the history books.

Shoes next directed us to an area set up for Fan Appreciation Day. We sat in numerical order with Sharpies in hand and waited for a flood of fans to approach with their preprinted team brochures. All were eager to collect signatures from the reigning World Champion 1973 Miami Dolphins.

When the first fan asked for my autograph, I was taken aback to find a large black Magic Marker mustache drawn over the top lip of my image. I pointed toward the inked-in addition and asked the young fan, "Did you do this?"

The boy shook his head no.

The same thing happened with the next fan. Confused, I looked around and tried to figure out what was going on. That's when I noticed that to my left, Bob Matheson was chuckling. I watched as he flipped from his image to mine and drew another mustache onto my clean-shaven face. I smiled as it dawned on me. Not only was I on the team, but I was also recognized by the brotherhood as a "dumb-ass rookie." Hazing and ridicule aside, it was totally worth it.

THE 1972-1973 WORLD CHAMPION MIAMI DOLPHINS

FRONT ROW—(left to right): Stan Taylor, Henry Stuckey, Tim Foley, Larry Seiple, Jake Scott, Garo Yepremian, Dick Anderson, Marlin Briscoe, Hubert Ginn, Lloyd Mumphord, Bo Rather.
SECOND ROW—Joe St. Pierre, Dan Dowe, Jim Kiick, Curtis Johnson, Larry Little, Nick Buoniconti, Don Shula, Joe Robbie, Bob Griese, Earl Morrall, Larry Csonka, Jim Cheever, Larry Gardner.
THIRD ROW—Monty Clark, Bill McPeak, Carl Taseff, Doug Crusan, Manny Fernandez, Mercury Morris, Howard Twilley, Paul Warfield, Norm Evans, Wayne Moore, Mike Scarry, Bill Arnsparger, Tom Keane.
FOURTH ROW—Marv Fleming, Ed Newman, Bob Kuechenberg, Jim Langer, Maulty Moore, Bob Heinz, Charles Leigh, Vern Den Herder.
FIFTH ROW—Ron Berger, Jim Mandich, Doug Swift, Mike Kolen, Bob Matheson, Larry Woods.
SIXTH ROW—Bruce Bannon, Larry Ball, Ron Sellers, Jesse Powel, Charles Babb, Don Strock, Tom Smith, Irv Goode.

Photo credit: Miami Dolphins

CHAPTER 10

MAKE NO MISTAKE

I sat on the sideline and watched my teammates maintain their perfect record in the 1973 home opener against the San Francisco 49ers. With a late-in-the-game touchdown, a pair of field goals, and a safety, we won the match 21–13. It was history in the making. The 17–0 Miami Dolphins were now 18–0. You'd think Shula would celebrate, but no, that wasn't the case.

"Sit down and shut up," Coach ordered when he rushed into the film room, cut the lights, and cued the 49ers footage two days later. As diffused light from the projector emphasized the scowl on his face, Coach announced that we won on Garo's foot, Warfield's big catch in the fourth, and a little luck with how San Fran fared in the heat. "But"—Shoes shook his finger and scolded—"I'm disappointed. You guys are better than you showed."

Shoes shot a menacing glance at Pro Bowl running back Eugene "Mercury" Morris, who had extended himself beyond physical limits to get critical extra yards. He reproached, "We can't afford fumbles of any sort, Merc. You need to do a better job of holding onto the ball."

Mercury's smile softened. He slanted his chiseled face toward the floor and shrank low into his seat. Where generally Mercury and Shula went head-to-head, in this instance, he knew to keep his mouth shut because two turnovers were two too many.

Coach next targeted his red laser beam onto the silver screen and highlighted the moment when defensive tackle Larry Woods jumped offsides. Shula scathed, "Penalties and missed assignments make the difference in a game like this. That penalty," he hissed at Woods, "extended San Francisco's drive." Coach shook his head and fast-forwarded to another play, this one isolating on safety Tim Foley. He raised his voice, "And this penalty for pass interference kept San Francisco's drive alive. We could have stopped the 49ers right then and there, Foley!"

"Didn't we win the game?" Kuech whispered to Langer.

"Mm-hmm," said Langer. "And with only three penalties compared to the 49ers' seven."

"Damn, Shula," Kuech griped. "He's impossible to please."

Langer rubbed at his large forehead and opined, "He's playing mind games with us. He knows that complacency is our worst enemy."

I understood what Langer was getting at. The Dolphins were entering statistical territory where no team had ever gone before. Shula didn't want anything to jeopardize his team's remarkable run.

The boys prepared to deliver a more immaculate show against the Oakland Raiders the following week. There were longer practices, additional meetings, and more in-depth film review sessions. Despite the effort, Coach Madden's strategy of grinding down the clock with a ball-controlled running game worked. And in front of over seventy-four thousand rabid Raiders fans, our formidable opponent knocked us off the mountain.

I watched with the utmost respect as our vulnerable coach walked to the center of the field and congratulated Madden for a good contest. Coach Madden, however, wasn't as honorable. He publicly boasted, "We wanted to play them last year and stop the streak but we didn't get the chance—but now we're the team that did it."[2]

You'd think Shula would tear us apart for the loss. But no, that wasn't the case. "I couldn't be prouder of you guys," Coach said while donning a soft face and cuing the Raiders footage. Jaws dropped at the reverse psychology perfectly played. Coach acknowledged our hurt and warned us against lingering disappointment. "We are winners," he stated with pride. "We've got to continue to play like winners." Shula praised our tremendous fullback Larry "Zonk" Csonka and tight end Jim Mandich for their extraordinary efforts. No doubt those guys would have been heroes had we won. Shoes also recognized Larry Seiple for a good job punting the ball. Then he just stood there. We all felt his pain, and the room got quiet.

"That loss dudn't mean jack shit!" Super Bowl VII MVP Jake Scott spontaneously jumped up from his seat like an offended rooster and rallied the troops. "That loss will just make this team better," Jake vowed. "Because nothin' is going to stop us from winning back-to-back Super Bowls."

I listened, and I believed. We all did. It was a magical moment where the energy shifted, and the team's resolve rebounded. I couldn't wait to heal up and hit the turf after game 3.

Shula worked us harder in the weeks that followed. Despite the consequential bruises, our concentration for crisper hitting and sharper timing paid off. The Dolphins reascended as kings of the mountain and won games 3 through 12, earning 278 points compared to our opponents' 102. Major credit goes to defensive coordinator Bill Arnsparger and his No-Name Defense, who kept our offensive scoring machine on the field and prevented opponents from putting points on the board. Having a future NFL Hall of Famer in Csonka didn't hurt either. He performed like a steamroller and blasted through linebackers and defensive backs, earning us several points. The sheer presence of wide receiver Paul Warfield contributed

---

[2] "1973: Raiders End Miami's Winning Streak," *Today in Pro Football History*, September 23, 2014, https://fs64sports.blogspot.com/2014/09/1973-raiders-end-miamis-winning-streak.html.

much to our running game success. Warfield skillfully stretched the defense and demanded double coverage, catching almost anything Griese sent his way. And whenever the starters secured the win early in the fourth, Shula cleared us backups to sub in. Coach Clark didn't have to ask me twice.

It was an incredible time. The Dolphins were the only professional sports team in the burgeoning town of Miami, and our fans went crazy for us. They'd beg for our autographs and invite us to all sorts of special events—as VIPs. They'd appear by the thousands at Miami International Airport to welcome us back after away games. At home, they'd cheer from the stands, wave their white hankies, and sing at the top of their lungs, "Miami Dolphins! Miami Dolphins! Miami Dolphins number one!" On a couple of occasions, they got so exuberant in our acoustically advantageous Orange Bowl that the refs had to stop the clock and insist that Shula get the "twelfth man on the field" to settle down; otherwise, we'd draw a flag for "delay of game." It was euphoric, especially when we secured a spot in the playoffs.

***

With bellies full and tongues loose, some of the more boisterous players looked toward Shula at Robbie's warm, welcoming, and no-expense-spared Christmas party and started chanting, "Speech! Speech!" Not one to shy away from the limelight, Shoes strutted to the front of the room, and with a smile peeking out from the side of his mouth, he lifted a glass of Champagne and invited everyone to fill up.

The background noise vanished, and all were mesmerized as Coach opened, "We beat Cincinnati in the playoffs, but the march to victory is not even close to over yet. Next is our game against the Raiders." Shoes bristled, "You guys remember they're the team that stopped our perfect string of wins."

Coach folded his arms tight across his chest and continued, "I'm sure Madden wants a repeat, but we're not going to let that happen." Several heads bobbed in agreement, and he continued, "We're the better team. We're going to beat Oakland, and we're going to advance to the goddamn Super Bowl." Coach raised his glass, and with an infectious smile, he declared, "Now that's something I can drink to. Merry Christmas."

"Merry Christmas," a chorus of players sang back.

And I'd add to that a Happy New Year because we seized the momentum at the December 30 Conference Championship and prevented Oakland from lighting up the board. In front of over seventy-five thousand Dol-Fans, we scored 27 points compared to the Raiders' 10 and won the sudden-death match. The Dolphins were Super Bowl bound for an unprecedented third year in a row!

The next day, we flew to Houston to acclimate to the local conditions and prepare for Super Bowl VIII. On the field, Shula put us through lighter-than-normal hitting practices. He enhanced our state of mind by touting confidence, poise, professionalism, 100 percent effort, and, most importantly, flawless execution. Off the field, we studied hours of film and developed strategies to address Minnesota's strengths and weaknesses. We also attended a mandatory session with the press.

What a zoo! I twiddled my thumbs as sports agents, player entourages, and hordes of reporters eagerly waited to meet with guys like Csonka, Griese, Warfield, Langer, Buoniconti, Fernandez, Stanfill, and Scott. As for me, it was rather comical when they'd ask, "Who's this Newman guy?" and pass me by. Eventually, I excused myself so I could get mentally right for the game.

The nerves in my belly bubbled as I whispered to myself in the quiet of my hotel room, "Stay on your toes. Do not make any mistakes. Do not be Shula's scapegoat."

"What you mumbling over there?" my Super Bowl roommate, Garo Yepremian, asked when he came in from his time with the media.

With cheeks flushed, I admitted, "I don't want to do anything that will ruin it for the team."

"I see," said the friendly Armenian. "This is somethin' I know all too well. You saw film for Super Bowl VII?" Garo confirmed.

I nodded, knowing where he was going with this. A year earlier, the Dolphins were up 14–0 in the Super Bowl with less than two and a half minutes on the clock when the Redskins stopped them at the 25-yard line. Shula called for a field goal. It was a mere chip shot that, if successful, would have resulted in a final score of 17–0—perfectly matching the season's 17–0 perfect record. But Washington blocked the attempt, and the batted ball tumbled toward Garo. Rather than falling to ground the ball, our kicker comically flubbed it into the hands of Redskins' cornerback Mike Bass, who scored a touchdown and ended the game 14–7.

"I kick the ball good," said a humbled Garo. "I make no excuses, but," he dropped his voice, "thank you very much. I'm a soccer player. My arm didn' develop good, eh." Garo owned up to his gaffe, "I shouldn't thrown the ball. I shoulda fallen on it." With a groan, he added, "It lucky we won."

I recalled how some still shunned the All-Pro for his mistake. It cemented my thinking that we were the masters of our destiny. Make a mistake, and you suffer the fate of that failure forever.

***

GAME DAY

Super Bowl VIII
January 13, 1974
50 °F, overcast
Rice Stadium (Houston, Texas)
Miami Dolphins vs. Minnesota Vikings

I needed to pace to release my increasing tension, but the space in that cramped Rice Stadium locker room was just too limited. I hopped up and down from my metal folding chair and loudly panted, "Huh! Huh! Huh!"

Larry Little, who was sitting next to me and quietly calming himself, opened an eye to see what was going on. With the strangest look on his face, he asked, "Newman, what's wrong with you?"

"Chicken," I answered, "I'm psyched out of my mind."

"Well, just shut up," Little cut me off. "Hell"—he shook his head—"you're making me nervous."

Stop, Ed! STOP! I tried to quiet down and keep my cool. But man, I was exploding like a keg of TNT.

"It's time." A referee popped open our locker room door and advised Shula to bring us onto the field.

The hair on the back of my neck stood straight up as I ran onto the turf and adjusted to the daylight. In awe, I watched as our team captains Nick Buoniconti, Bob Griese, and Larry Little proceeded to the center of the field—heck, to the center of the sporting world—for the ceremonial flip of the coin. Super Bowl VIII was officially here.

What followed was the most impressive game ever. The extreme preparation of the coaches, the top-notch level of talent, the coordinated effort, and the overflowing energy from the fans was epic. Competing against the Minnesota Vikings, we did as Shula taught and launched into a nearly flawless game. There was only one penalty, one fumble, and—well, one dumb-headed mistake.

"Kickoff return unit—in!" yelled one of the assistant coaches about four minutes into the fourth quarter after Minnesota scored their first touchdown and made the score 24-7. The pace of the game picked up. I jogged onto the field and positioned myself as an immovable barrier between the ball carrier and my assigned cover guy. After a physical hand-to-hand battle, I made a beeline to the oxygen tank.

While I sucked in air, Manny Fernandez strutted over and started chatting about some bombshell cheerleader with "big tits" down the field. He mimed holding two large coconuts in front of his chest and pointed for me to take a look as he reached for his helmet. I couldn't understand why a defensive player was grabbing for his gear when our offense was on the gridiron.

I looked around, trying to put the pieces together and realized that somehow, within the past forty-five seconds, the Vikings had forced us to punt. *Crap.* The offense was on the sideline, and I was supposed to be on the field with the punt team. I cupped my face in dread because I couldn't take to the turf without drawing a penalty.

"Ten fucking men on the field!" Shula covered his mouth with his clipboard and screamed into his headgear, "Who the fuck is missing?"[3]

My mortification extended as Shula's lieutenant, Nick Buoniconti, pointed at each of the special teams players and tried to identify which of us hadn't taken the field. I wanted to hide, but there was no getting out of this one. I stepped up and meekly admitted, "It's me, Coach. I'm so sorry."

The Don didn't need to react because Buoniconti took care of that. With sheer madness in his eyes, he grabbed my facemask and shook my head from side to side. He threatened, "If this mistake causes us to lose this game, we're going to kill you."

My face whitened. I started to pray. *Please, God, let us win.* I feared that the shadow of my single letdown would cascade and tank the campaign for the entire team. I'd never hear the end of it.

Luckily, the Vikings didn't react to the missing man, and Seiple got off a booming punt. Even so, I hunkered down for the remainder of the game. Time dilated during those last few minutes. Each second felt like an eternity. I held my breath and counted with the digital dial: *Nineteen…eighteen…it's not over till it's over. Ten…nine… eight… almost there. Four…three…two…one—YES!!*

"Twenty-four–seven, FINAL," the Super Bowl scoreboard screamed, "Dolphins WIN!"

It was otherworldly. Hats and confetti flew in the air, fireworks pierced the waning daylight, and my teammates hugged. Shula got doused with a bucket of orange Gatorade. When his game-day face finally relaxed, I stopped worrying about my mishap. Instead, I allowed myself a moment—just one—to celebrate the fact that I was part of a World Champion team. A Super Bowl–winning team! It was like I had tasted the nectars of immortals. Every player in a winning Super Bowl is inscribed in the sports books as a world champion—forever.

---

[3] "Super Bowl VII - Minnesota Vikings vs Miami Dolphins: Second Half," *Golden Football Magazine*, https://goldenrankings.com/SuperBowl8-C.html.

The celebration lasted into the early morning and continued through our return home. We were heroes and major Miami celebrities. When the dust settled, I reflected on how less than a year earlier, I was a dopey college student who barely knew anything about the pros. Then I got drafted by Shoes and the Miami Dolphins, survived camp, made the team's roster, recovered from injury, and even started in one game. Holy shit, it dawned on me once more. I competed in a Super Bowl—a winning Super Bowl! There was no other place in the world I'd rather be.

CHAPTER 11

HUNGRY FOR MORE

Now that the Dolphins had advanced from perfect to back-to-back World Champions, fan support skyrocketed, and everybody wanted access to the players. There were booster clubs, team events, celebrations, as well as girls, girls, and more girls. While many took a moment to bask in the glory, I couldn't because I was preoccupied with a few things. For starters, my Dolphins contract needed to be renewed. And, in a broader context, thorny labor issues between players and management had to be hashed out because the NFL/Player Collective Bargaining Agreement (CBA) was expiring.

Brushing over the details, management wanted to keep the players' salaries low and prevent movement across teams. Conversely, we wanted a fairer and more competitive marketplace. As discord rose, management threatened to shut down football and lock us out, without pay, unless we submitted to their terms. It wasn't fair, especially when the NFL's gross revenue was swelling rapidly on the backs of our labor.

I shared this perspective with defensive safety Dick Anderson at a postseason event. The talented athlete with a knack for business explained that if things weren't resolved soon, we'd likely strike at the start of the 1974 preseason.

Preseason? No! I waved my hands in protest at the timing. I believed we could exert a lot more pressure on the owners if we waited for a regular season strike when league revenues poured in from multiple sources, like radio, television, ticket sales, concessions, and apparel. I explained, "The owners are more likely to budge on CBA terms if we time this right. They'll do anything to protect their cash cow."

Anderson seemed impressed by my passion for union matters. He looked me straight in the eye and elucidated, "If we want to have bargaining power, we need to strike when it works for the players, and that's during the preseason. Otherwise," he continued with a defeatist lift of his shoulders, "they'll cross the picket line when the big bills come in and the big paychecks don't. It's simple psychology, Ed." Anderson concluded, "Most are worried they'll never be able to recoup their lost wages."

"I don't know," I countered. But the room hushed before I could say anything more. Coach Shula had taken the mic.

For the next few minutes, an unusually lighthearted Shula extolled our '73 season accomplishments. There were broad smiles and a lot of laughter. However, the happy moment was eclipsed when, right before our eyes, Shula morphed into something else. Almost beyond human, he became the maniacal perfectionist I had come to fear.

The Don stepped back, crossed his arms, and directed a serious mug at the players. He rebuked, "A few of you are starting to look a little soft." Over the nervous titters of the captivated crowd, Shula reminded, "It's never too soon to start training. If you thought you were training hard enough last season, then you're deluding yourself."

A patina of sweat formed on my brow. It was January. We were only weeks into the postseason, and I still felt like I was held together with spit and wax. My right shoulder was swollen from blunt trauma. Three fingers on one hand and two on the other were healing from strains and breaks. The medial collateral ligaments in both knees were stretched and wobbling in ways they shouldn't. Despite needing downtime to recoup, I knew Coach was right. I was a professional ball player—a Miami Dolphin. If I wanted to stay that way, I had to get into top shape now.

Ironically, the Dolphins organization wouldn't make it easy. Outside of an old, beat-up, and clunky universal machine located in a concrete, un-air-conditioned box near Biscayne College's swimming pool, there was nothing more, not even a weight trainer, to oversee our strength gain. In the absence of options, I put pen to paper and designed an incremental weight training program which I launched into right away.

***

Grandma Pauline was the first to greet me when I arrived in Long Island for a short visit that winter. "*Tatala*"—she opened her arms and pulled me in for a big hug—"it's so good to see you." Grandma gushed, "I've been watching you and kissing the TV when you're on the screen. Do you feel it?"

I smiled.

"Oh, did I tell you?" she continued. "I've been clipping out all the newspaper articles you're in. I've made a book! I'm so proud, Eddy." Grandma stepped back and, with deep adoration, gave me a once-over. "You look grea—" Grandma stopped midsentence because something caught her eye. "Eddy," her voice wavered, "what's that on your neck?"

"What?" I squinted my eyes and felt around my Adam's apple.

"Come here," Grandma said. She guided me to the hallway mirror to look. Immediately, I noticed the asymmetrical goiter bulging out from the right side of my neck. *Oh my God.* For a second, I couldn't breathe. *How could I have missed this?*

"You need to get that checked out right away," Grandma Pauline advised.

"Um…don't worry, Grandma," I said with a synthetic smile. "It's probably just a swollen muscle from all the weightlifting I've been doing. I'll ice it tonight and have the team doctor look at it when I'm back in Miami."

"Honey, you're here!" Mom, Dad, and my youngest sibling, Larry, entered the room.

Naturally, the subject shifted to everything about my life in Miami – from the girls I was seeing to my offseason work. Eventually, the conversation turned to a more serious subject: my future. Mom reiterated her fears that I'd get hurt on the field. She begged me to become a dentist, like her brother Lenny. Dad urged me to train up north so I could be closer to Newman's during the offseason. I deferentially deflected on both accounts.

***

I stupidly put off that thing that was trespassing on my neck when I returned to Miami because other things, like weight training, a part-time gig as a laborer with a tree surgeon, and some courses at Miami-Dade Community College, stole my attention. I was busy. I was young. I was distracted, naive, and, how shall I put it…horny.

"I'm ready to play the field," I told my neighbor Lee Sinoff one afternoon after a parade of beautiful Delta, Eastern, Pan Am, and TWA bikini-clad babes seductively swayed their hips by our poolside lounges. Lucky for me, our apartment complex was home to many of Miami's young and single flight attendants. I peeked over the rims of my aviators and admitted to Lee, "I haven't dated much outside of my high school sweetheart. But the girls here seem very approachable. Like that redhead." I pointed toward the curvy beauty's residence on the far side of the building and shared, "She was waiting by my door last night to cook me dinner. I couldn't believe it."

"Of course!" Lee punched my arm. "What do you expect, Ed? She wants you!" My friend looked away and elaborated with a little envy and a lot of admiration, "Don't you think, even for a moment, that the girls here are doing anything like that for me." When I remained clueless, he spelled it out, "You're fit, attractive, and a member of the best football team in the world. You're a desirable bachelor."

My ears reddened. I had never thought of myself in that way before.

"On that," Lee added, "I've got a girl for you. She's tall, attractive, and Jewish. Want me to set you up? We can go on a double date?"

Nothing ventured, nothing gained. I agreed, and plans were made. But the day of, Lee called and canceled. No matter. I went about my business as usual until my phone rang later that evening.

"Are you Ed Newman?" a female voice blared through the receiver.

"Yes," I answered.

"With the Miami Dolphins?" she pressed.

"That's right." I felt a little drawn to the amplified attitude coming through the phone. "Can I help you?" I asked.

"Where are you?" the woman impatiently inquired. "We have a date!"

"I'm sorry, who is this? And how did you get my number?"

The woman explained that she was Lee's friend Cathy Leinoff. She had called 411 to get the numbers for each "Ed Newman" listed in the directory and rang ten of us before reaching me.

I was impressed. This Cathy had sass. So when she told me to pick her up and take her to the traveling carnival passing through the University of Miami, I capitulated for the woman who'd come to change my life for the better.

Gary Glitter's new release "Hey" boomed in the background as I strategically steered the beautiful brown-haired Cathy toward the games of skill because amusement rides made me sick. Over the smell of cotton candy and popcorn, I threw darts and popped balloons to win her a giant teddy bear. Once the victor's siren sounded, Cathy grabbed the bear with one hand and my hand with the other and made a beeline toward the largest ride in the park. I couldn't deny her. With each loop, I became more ill. I closed my eyes and tried to control my gag reflex; but by the time our cart rolled to a stop, I was green, shaky, and weak.

Unaware of how sick I was, Cathy begged, "Let's go again!" But I resisted, whimpering that I needed to sit down. A now-concerned Cathy sat beside me and gently rubbed the back of my neck. Her touch was soft and genuine—different. My heart skipped a beat, and I started to feel better.

"I like your shirt," I told her. I read the words off the front, "Virtue is its own reward," and leaned in for our first kiss.

***

Cathy and I spent much time together over the next few months. Come May, I invited her to join me at the Dolphins' annual awards banquet. This was the same grandiose event I had attended a year earlier as a draftee. However, this time, a whole new cohort of uncomfortable and nervous-looking rookies was standing in our shadows. And this time, I had a beautiful Cathy by my side.

Everyone was on their feet, clapping wildly as Shula took the stage and congratulated us for our back-to-back wins. "We did it again!" he boasted to the sea of aqua and orange banquet tables encircled by wealthy fans. "Most assumed we couldn't, but we proved them wrong." Coach met the eyes of a few MVPs and added, "I think we can do it again. Let's go for a three-peat!" The excitement built in his voice, and he flicked his nose.

"That's one," I joked to Kuech and Langer.

Langer approved. With a nod at Kuech, he commented, "Look at our rookie here. I mean," he corrected himself, "I guess Ed is officially one of the vets now."

The energy grew when Shula began to present our winning Super Bowl rings. One by one, he took a box from a stack of fifty, perfectly arranged in a pyramid on top of a Dolphins-branded table, and called for each of the '73 Miami Dolphins to come up. I was so emotionally eager to collect my prize that I could barely sit still. My heart raced. My stomach turned. Then finally, Coach invited me up.

Cathy squeezed my arm and whispered, "Open it," the second I returned to our table with the highly embellished cedar box that alone could have been a collector's item. I took in a deep breath and slowly flipped the lid. *Whoa!* Instantly, the high-quality piece featuring two diamonds set side-by-side on a gold band with "Newman" and "64" cast on one side and back-to-back Super Bowl symbolism on the other transfixed me.

Ed Newman's well-worn Super Bowl VIII Ring (2022)

I placed the ostentatious large ring on my finger and moved my hand back and forth to initiate blue and green refractions off the perfect stones. Like Tolkien's Sméagol, the sparkle entranced me. *My precious*. This was a ring of power.

Yet I didn't want it to limit me. The ring represented the past. If I wanted another, which I did immensely, then I couldn't dwell on what was. I needed to focus on what could be: a solid contract, a secure spot on the 1974 team, and an opportunity to overtake Kuech or Little—one of the most accomplished starting guards in the league. Feeling hungry for so much more, I indulged in the ring's brilliance for one week. Then I went to the bank, rented a safety deposit box, and placed my coveted prize within for safekeeping before I drove off with a ravenous rumble in my soul.

CHAPTER 12

GAME OF CHICKEN

I was twenty-three years old, very strong, and busting my ass in the gym, getting ready for the '74 season. And then there was that deformity on my neck that I needed to deal with but didn't want to. I mean, what if it was cancer? Nothing good would come from Coach Shula learning about that, so I leaned into blissful ignorance.

But my Grandma Pauline wouldn't have it. She repeatedly pressed, "What's going on with your neck?" When I had no answer, she urged, "You've got to look into that right away."

I tried to appease her. "I will soon…when camp opens." But that was a white lie coming from a dark place because with the imminent strike, who knew when I'd return? It could be July, August, or maybe even September. And when delay could prove foolhardy, it was like I was playing a game of chicken with my life. Taking control of what I could, I initiated a meeting with Pat Peppler, the Dolphins' director of player personnel, to discuss my contract.

"Tell me, Ed," the all-business company man casually opened, "whom do you best compare to in the league?"

"Joe DeLamielleure of the Buffalo Bills," I answered without delay.

"DeLamielleure!" Peppler's eyes focused. He assumed a sour face and retorted, "You're a backup guard! A second-year, sixth-round draft pick for God's sake, and DeLamielleure is a starting first rounder. You have no right to compare yourself to him!"

I shrugged because I really felt I was at DeLamielleure's caliber of play. I just wasn't getting the airtime to prove it. "Haven't you watched the films?" I asked. "Can't you see what I'm doing when Coach subs me in?"

"I think you ought to get an agent," Peppler cut me short. "Because"—his words hung in midair, and in a softer voice, he elaborated—"I want to be delicate here, but telling you to your face that 'you're not as good as you think you are' might seem harsh."

This was not a great start, so I hired the well-regarded sports agent Bob Woolf and scheduled a meeting with Coach Shula to move the needle.

There was a lot of mahogany with red and gold accents, notable photographs, and magnificent trophies adorning Shula's austere office. The space spoke of greatness. His eminence sat in the center of it all on a gigantic brown leather cushioned chair situated behind a large desk, with countrywide sports pages scattered across every surface.

Coach looked up from his black notebook, jutted his chin, and directed me to take one of the two smaller seats opposite him. "What's up?" he asked.

Sitting a step lower than Shula, I looked down at the floor and explained my dilemma. "Don't get me wrong, Coach. I'm happy in Miami. But..." I hesitated. "I got this idea in my head that if I were playing for another team, I'd be starting by now."

Coach gave me an intimidating stare, so I got straight to it. "You know, I'm in talks with Peppler. He's treating me as a 'typical' second-year, sixth-round backup guard. The trouble is, I'm not typical." I met Shula's eyes and expanded, "I think it would take a second-round pick to replace me."

Shula's intimidating stare intensified into a glare. He scorched me for a few painful seconds before retorting, "I don't get involved in player contract negotiations. Direct your concerns to Peppler."

"Coach, it's not fair!" I protested. "Peppler is disregarding what I bring to the team. He's treating me like I haven't grown over the past year when he should negotiate with me as a potential starter."

Shula folded his arms before reluctantly divulging, "I agree. You are worth more today than when we first drafted you. But," hewing to Peppler's party line, Coach stated, "you're not as good as you think you are."

I desperately entreated, "When you talk to Peppler, would you please advise him that I am playing at a higher level now because," I emotionally blurted, "because I'm not going to play for less than I'm worth!"

Tensions palpably rose on that last comment. Coach clenched his jaw and slowed his words, "I thought I made it clear, Newman. I don't get involved in negotiations."

My back stiffened. I knew to hold off. I sat there in silence for a good twenty seconds.

After a while, Shula backpedaled. "You're an asset. I'm glad you're on our team. If you keep improving," he admitted, "you'll be a fine starter one day. But for now, you must be patient." Shula wrung his hands and spelled it out, "I've got Little. He's All-Pro. I've got Kuech. He's on the cusp. And you, well, you're here just in case one of those guys can't step up." Coach scratched his chin and concluded, "It's plain and simple. Little and Kuech have established themselves as effective and dependable guards. You've got to pay your dues and prove yourself."

***

The National Football League Players Association (NFLPA) declared a preseason strike at midnight on June 30, 1974. A week later, about twenty established Dolphins gathered at Biscayne College to demonstrate. It was history in the making because never before had football players identified with labor. "No Freedom, No

Football!" we loudly chanted as we walked in an elongated loop across the school's entrance road, holding red, white, and blue NFLPA-branded picket signs.

I couldn't have been prouder of our public show of solidarity. But then, *Whoa damn!* Mercury Morris skittered his red Corvette around us pedestrians, jammed hard on his brakes, and barked out the window, "Get back to work, you suckers!"

"SCAB!" some guy from the NFLPA hollered at Mercury. We were only one day into this, and things were already getting ugly. In the days that followed, they got worse. The press spun stories suggesting that the strike was the fault of the "greedy players." The fans bellyached that we were depriving them of their football.

Pressure rose across the league, and tensions were particularly skewed in Miami because, by winning the prior year's Super Bowl, we expected an extra payday for competing in a special perennial preseason opener called the Chicago College All-Star Game. But with the strike, taking to the turf was a no-no. Even so, some players wavered at the allure of an extra paycheck and crossed the picket line. What started as a trickle soon became a stream and then a flood.

While I continued to hold out as a union-faithful, most of my teammates were dressed and ready to compete in early August. Clearly, management had broken the back of union solidarity, and the strike was basically over.

Around that time, my agent called to explain that the Dolphins had sweetened the pot to motivate my return to camp. They were now offering me a three-year contract with $25,000 for this season, $37,500 for the next, and $50,000 for the third. "It's a good offer," Woolf explained, "right in line with a player of your ability." He encouraged, "You should take it."

With an even coldness in my voice, I responded, "I'm worth more." Woolf pushed back, but I refused to hear it. I demanded that he tell Peppler I wouldn't return to camp for a penny less than $35,000. "And enough with this multiyear-contract bullshit," I expanded. "I don't want to be locked into a long-term contract, especially when the team is offering me such low wages. Mark my words,"

I prophesied, "I'll be a starting guard by next season, and I should be paid accordingly."

Woolf sighed but did as I asked. Minutes later, he reported back, "You've got a good handle on your value, Ed. Peppler just upped the Dolphins' offer to $32,000 for a one-year contract." He encouraged, "You ought to head to corporate headquarters to sign the papers. They want you in team uniform for tomorrow's game. With Little, Kuech, and Goode still out, they'll likely start you against New Orleans next Saturday."

Holy shit. My face flushed. I felt relieved because this was one less problem to deal with. I also felt energized that Coach would let me show my stuff. However, I had a lot of toughening up to do in the span of one week. It would be a major shock to my body to engage in heavy hitting so soon after the offseason. But I was up to it, and I'd take it any way I could get it.

***

This was the moment I had been waiting for ever since Grandma Pauline first noticed that mass on my neck seven months earlier. I kept my cool as Dr. Virgin carefully traced the egg-sized goiter with his thumbs and pronounced, "There's nothing to be concerned about. It's probably an inactive virus that's caused your thyroid to grow. I'll prescribe some pills to dissolve the lump." While I much preferred this diagnosis over a more morbid one, a tiny voice in the back of my mind nagged that he got it wrong. *Stop playing chicken!*

For the rest of the day and onto the next, Coach tested our fitness. Eyes popped when word got out that I had bench-pressed 385 pounds in the strength test. Though that challenge was a piece of cake compared to Shula's infamous "twelve-minute run."

Rivulets of sweat poured down my neck as I prepared to launch into my paces. I removed my shirt, kicked off my shoes, and calculated that if I ran the mandatory five laps at two minutes and forty seconds per lap, I'd complete the 1.33-mile course within the required timeframe. At Coach Clark's cue, I bolted out—way too fast. The only guys in front of me were first-round draft pick defensive end

Don Reese and sixth-round defensive tackle Randy Crowder, who each progressed like competitive Clydesdales.

In the first lap, my heart pounded painfully against my rib cage. In the second, I slowed and gulped for air. By the third, my mind got the better of me. I feared I wouldn't finish on time. In agony and trailing behind everyone else, I bargained with myself: *Keep going. Just one hundred yards more.* I must have looked pathetic with my slack face, glazed eyes, and bare feet chugging along, but I managed to drag my sorry ass across the finish line just as Coach Clark shouted, "Time!"

Feeling completely depleted, I returned to my locker and found the thyroid pills Dr. Virgin had prescribed. I took the first one, and the effects came on gradually. Within a week, I got hungry—really hungry. I ate so much that Shula announced to the team that the food budget had nearly doubled since last year. With a point in my direction, he stated, "The chef is telling me you go for triples every meal. Nobody can have triples without permission from the trainer first." I shrank in my seat, and my belly rumbled.

I also started to sweat a lot. I had to drink gallons of water to replenish the fourteen pounds of water weight I lost in each practice. Add to that hyperactivity and the onset of mild paranoia. Inherently, I was high-strung, anxious, and nervous. But now those feelings were amplified. The Turk lurked. The pressure of preseason cuts overwhelmed me. Subtle, insignificant tells from Coach Clark put me in a tailspin. And one time, when Larry Little and Wayne Moore neglected to say hello, my mind raced. *What did I do to piss them off?* Clearly, something wasn't right. I wasn't right.

Thankfully, I had Cathy. My savior. My love. My cheerleader was at every home game rooting me on. I'd find her in the stands, point at her with two fingers, form my hand into a fist, and pound my chest two times over my heart to signify my deep devotion. This routine took on a life of its own, and a few weeks in, about a hundred fans sitting around Cathy repeated the same gestures back at me. It was funny. Even more amusing was when the action heated up, I could hear Cathy's voice carry through the Orange Bowl, "Come on,

Snookums! GET HIM! Get your man!" Then one day, the nameplate over my locker magically changed from *Newman* to *Snookums*.

***

The 1974 regular season began with an away game against the New England Patriots. Compromised by the hardship of travel, the intense desire of the Patriots to vindicate themselves after a dismal '73 season, and the strained knee of our starting offensive tackle Wayne Moore, the Patriots took control and won.

On the home front, Shula did his reverse psychology thing. Sure, he was firm and didn't make light of the defeat, but he encouraged us to shake it off because we were a heck of a team. "Starting now," Shoes suggested, "let's treat it one game at a time." We all agreed because stumbling right out of the gate would be ridiculous.

In the following games, Coach shored up our offense by moving Kuech to start at left tackle and me to start at left guard. You hear that? By treating the O-line as interchangeable parts, Shula gave me the golden opportunity to shine, and I made the most of it! Between September 22 to October 13, our offensive machine purred without missing a beat, and we won three of those four games.

An ecstatic Grandma Pauline called to congratulate me. As expected, she asked about my neck. Her question forced me to confront reality. For the first time, I answered honestly, "It's not good. That thing is still there."

Grandma begged me to do something about it. "I know of a reputable neck tumor specialist," she said. "His name is Max Som, and he is at Mt. Sinai Hospital. Please see him the next time you're in New York."

"Okay, Grandma. I'll talk to the team doctor about it," I promised.

The next day, I met with Dr. Virgin, whose eyelids stretched wide when he saw the lump was still there. He agreed that it needed to be diagnosed straight away, so I scheduled an appointment with Dr. Som for the day after we played the Jets in the Big Apple, about six weeks later.

I'm not sure if Dr. Virgin ever discussed my case with Shula. What I do know is that Coach did what was best for the team when he returned Kuech to his sweet spot at guard, used other talents to fill in at tackle, and returned me to the special teams.

Over the next several weeks, the '74 Dolphins continued on their march to victory with wins stringing together like pearls on a necklace. But our five-game winning streak was punctured when we lost to the Jets on November 24. While my teammates mentally replayed their performance on the flight home to Miami, I stayed in New York and actively cleared my mind in preparation for my appointment with Dr. Som.

After a battery of tests, Dr. Som declared that the mass needed to be surgically analyzed—as soon as possible. He proposed December. I found myself debating between football and health because my 8–3 Miami Dolphins were playoff bound. I didn't want to miss a shot at the Super Bowl. "Can't we wait just a few more weeks?" I desperately pleaded. "Because we might go to the Super Bowl." Understanding the unique opportunity hanging in the balance, Dr. Som agreed to operate in mid-January.

As bizarre as it may sound, the Ed Newman who returned to Miami was a robot. There was no fear or emotion—just football. I kept my medical condition private because I didn't want to distract my teammates, especially as we closed out the 11–3 season and prepared to face John Madden and his Raiders for the sudden-death AFC divisional playoff in Oakland.

Remember, every owner, coach, and player in the league wanted to prevent the back-to-back Dolphins from clinching a third championship title. Undoubtedly, Oakland also wanted revenge for the last time we beat them in '73. As expected, they showed strong on December 21, 1974, and went toe-to-toe with us until the final minute of the playoff game, when they scored a touchdown and ended our run with a two-point lead. That was it. Our season was over.

At that moment, all the deeply repressed tension within my soul broke through. I felt vulnerable for the first time because the game of chicken was finally over. I no longer needed to race toward danger. I could now veer toward health. And all I could do was hope that it wasn't too late.

CHAPTER 13

THE REALITY OF MORTALITY

Dr. Som appeared at the foot of my hospital bed, muttering something about stitches. Through a handheld mirror, I watched as he removed the last of my bandages. *Oh my God.* I gasped at the sight. This was not the picture of a healthy, vibrant football player. No, not at all. This collage of crusty blood and thick black sutures, with rubber drains leaking fluid from a six-inch gash cut beneath my Adam's apple, looked a lot more like Frankenstein's monster.

I tried to hold the thread of Dr. Som's words as he explained how he had found and removed a cancerous lesion on my thyroid. *Cancer.* My eyes rolled. *I knew it was cancer. Fucking game of chicken.*

"Di ye ged e all?" I garbled through the fog of waning anesthesia.

"I believe so," Dr. Som answered. He explained how he had removed the northern, diseased portions of my thyroid and collected some tissue samples from the remaining portions simply to dispel the need for further surgery. In a rush to make his rounds, he turned toward the door and encouraged me to take it easy while we waited for the lab results to come in.

Take it easy? I didn't know how to do that. I was restless and believed you went stale if you didn't move. I also trusted that a mildly stressful physical routine was just the ticket for a quicker rehab. So, I dragged my sorry ass out of bed the following morning and did push-ups, sit-ups, leg raises, deep knee bends, and other floor exercises. The day after, I took it up a notch and walked twenty circuits through the hospital wing in my powder blue cotton robe. Three days in, I was well enough to get down with Cathy. As I progressed through days four, five, six, and seven, I neared full recovery and expected to be discharged from the ward where most were languishing with terminal illness. But on that ninth day, Mom, Dad, and Cathy filed into my room and awkwardly stood there, silent, with puffy, tear-filled eyes.

"What's wrong?" I asked.

Mom opened her mouth. But before she could say anything, Dr. Som slipped into the room, adjusted his reading glasses, and dropped the bomb. "The lab analysis came back positive for cancer. The remainder of your thyroid needs to come out—tomorrow."

Wait? Tomorrow? What? Cancer? My eyes bugged out from the enormity of it all. *No! No, no, no. I thought he got it all!* This time, the weight of the C-word knocked me into a tailspin. I looked to Dad for emotional support, but the sadness in his eyes only made it worse. *Ohhhhhh. No, no, no.* Just a few weeks earlier, I was at the crest as an active Miami Dolphins player, feeling like Superman, working toward my second run at a Super Bowl. And now the foundations of my life—health, football, Miami, and Cathy—were starting to disintegrate. Cancer could be the end of everything. I could be dreadfully sick. My joyful days as an athlete could be over. And surgery? Tomorrow? I wasn't ready for that! I needed to mentally prepare. *No! No, no, no.* I was desperate for a safe place. Cathy instinctively took my hand. And somehow I managed to slow my mind, ask questions, and listen up.

I progressively glazed in and out of shock as Dr. Som dismissed my first concern of serious illness. He informed me that my type of thyroid cancer, when treated, was nearly 100 percent curable. As for football, the surgeon clarified that my lack of a thyroid had nothing to do with my prospects. Whether I'd rebound and meet the challenge of making the '75 season cut was totally up to me. As for my last concern about having surgery the next day, Dr. Som insisted that we couldn't delay—not anymore—due to the risk of metastasis.

That was it. All I could do was go with it. I went under the knife for a second time the following morning. After a successful procedure and another dreadful week and a half of recovery, Dr. Som discharged me with a reminder to allow my body time to recover.

Yeah, right. I wouldn't let cancer slow me down. On the contrary, I'd use it to fuel me forward. Already delayed a month, there was no time for anything but dedication. I needed to get with the program. I needed to renegotiate the terms for the '75 season. And now that I was a "cancer survivor," I needed to find a way to overcome the doubt and negative biases that would likely emerge from the coaches.

Knowing that the path to success for offensive linemen was getting stronger, I committed to a 10 percent strength gain over the prior year. If I did that, I'd enter the preseason in the best shape of my life. I'd dominate on the field and position myself as an unquestionable asset. It would be hard for the coaches to waive me with such power.

The fire in my belly burned white hot as I returned to my weightlifting routines. I ground rep after rep as if tomorrow would never come because cancer taught the great truth that tomorrow might actually never come. And despite the searing discomfort in my neck and ribcage from the recent surgery, I refused to let pain control me. Instead, I increasingly added weight to the stack. By mid-February, I was humming. By May, I hit my prior year's max. By July, I achieved a new bench press goal of 390 pounds. Cancer schmancer, I was strong, confident, and ready to meet with the powers that be to get the player contract I deserved.

I first met with Shula, who, to his credit, made no reference to the large bubbly-pink keloid scar gracing my throat like a ruby-studded necklace. Subsequent conversations with George Young, the team's new director of player personnel, also went well; and the Dolphins made me a compelling offer. Perhaps I deserved it, or maybe the team's real objective was to staunch what could become a talent drain to the newly formed, higher-paying World Football League (WFL). Whatever it was, I accepted their terms and signed on the dotted line.

***

Coach was also on a mission to overcome the unfortunate hand he'd been dealt. After the WFL snatched up three of his best players in Kiick, Warfield, and Csonka, Shula used the '75 preseason to assess his talent and adjust his roster. He decided to draw heavily upon the well-tenured and reliable running back Mercury Morris and tap into two lesser-known commodities: fullback Don Nottingham and wide receiver Nat Moore. Shula hoped that this lineup—along with the usual O-line suspects of Wayne Moore, Bob Kuechenberg, Jim Langer, Larry Little, and right tackle Norm Evans—would enable the Dolphins to sustain the dynastic success recently enjoyed.

Coach was relatively right. After losing to the Raiders in the home opener, we prevailed against the Patriots in game 2 and substantially improved by game 3. In the latter, we handled Green Bay right out of the gate and logged 31 unrivaled points by the end of the third quarter. With such a strong lead, I knew Coach was considering substitutions. I stared at him from the sideline and tried to will him to play me. *Let me sub in. Please! It's time.* Finally, Shula gave Coach Clark the go-ahead, who roared, "NEWMAN! Get in there. Little, take a rest."

I darted onto the field, and my adrenal glands did their thing. Time compressed. My focus intensified. *Win the war.* The ball snapped, and before the Packers' left defensive tackle even knew it, my face mask crashed into his numbers. With my legs pumping powerfully, I thrust my fists into his ribcage and drove him back. This allowed Mercury and Nottingham to cut off my block and gain additional yards. By this hardnosed performance, we maintained possession for fifteen plays and ate up over eight minutes in the final quarter.

Coach must have liked what he saw because he had me spell either Little or Kuech in the next set of games. With my great strength gained from all those extra hours pumping iron, I emerged as a highly respected reliever for our superb starters. I also maintained my dominance on the special teams, where occasionally, I'd slam my helmet on the ball and cause the kick return specialist to fumble. Coach Shula rewarded that quality play by naming me "special teams captain" and allowing me to go to the center of the field for the coin toss during select games. It was cool.

***

"The guy with the most kickoff tackles gets treated to dinner," wagered rookie and special teams compadre Bruce Elia from the huddle during our fifth game of the season against the Jets. "What say you?"

"You kidding?" I eagerly accepted.

When the huddle broke, I did my thing with a little extra kick. I glided past the defenders, neared the wedge, and looked for the ball carrier. My stomach knotted when I noted that making the tackle would require exquisite timing. We're talking microseconds for me to cut under the giant and dart into the gap formed next to the Jets' 300-pound wedge guy. I picked up speed and threw my total weight into the ball carrier's frame just as the wedge guy put a pretty powerful punch through the right ear hole of my helmet. *WHACK!*

Everything exploded to black.

There was nothing. No sound. No physical sensation. All I knew was that I existed as I lay there on my back, staring up at the sky, wondering what all that light blue stuff was.

"Great tackle!" Elia congratulated me from his upright stance over my traumatized body. "You really want a free meal, don't you?"

"Uh…yuh…" I blinked a few times, sat up, and tried to make sense of things. "Where our sidelin?" I slurred.

"You okay?" Elia arched a brow and extended an arm to help me up.

"Uh. Yuh. Jus' ne a lil smellin' sal," I mumbled while shaking my head to get rid of the tweedy birds.

Once at the Dolphins' sideline, I asked the team trainer for some ammonia salts. I snapped the bean-sized, fiber-meshed capsule and inhaled deeply through my nose. The ammonia vapors stabbed like a knife through my brain. Immediately, the birdies were gone. I was alert and ready. I jumped up and started to pace while keeping an eye on Shula, hoping he'd sub me in, which he did.

Sure enough, I won the bet. When Elia later treated me to dinner, we discussed life after football. I shared with the fourth-round linebacker out of Ohio State my dilemma that football wasn't forever but that I was so invested in the sport that I had to be careful not to neglect laying the foundation for another future now. I admitted, "I don't want to leave the NFL with nothing but a broken body to show for it."

"I hear you," Elia agreed. "I think most of us want a fall-back plan."

I shared how I had been thinking about setting up a business I could run alongside football – something like a turnkey franchise. Upon hearing this, the Ohio State luminary bragged about having an in with Dave Thomas, the owner of the newly established Wendy's franchise. With thumbs pointing inward, he explained that Mr. Thomas was a major Buckeyes fan who might be interested in helping a star alum. Elia suggested we fly to Wendy's headquarters after the season to explore purchasing a franchise territory together. I liked the idea.

But first things first, we still had games to win. Shula's coaching shined brilliantly for the remaining six games of the '75 season. Don Nottingham logged his personal best with twelve touchdowns. Nat Moore emerged as a premier wide receiver, and Mercury performed quite well. Personally, I did my part and played in almost every game. But I started in none.

With a 10-win, 4-loss record, I expected this edition of the Miami Dolphins to be in the hunt for a playoff berth. But it was a numbers game. Pittsburgh and Oakland edged us out with better stats. That was it. The clock stopped, and our season ended after we beat Denver on December 20.

It was disappointing, but that's the reality of mortality. Our days are numbered. When you realize that, whether through a sudden death loss or a bout of cancer, you have a choice. You can either wallow or rise up. It's your next move that defines you. Personally, with that scar on my neck reminding me that I could have died, I vowed to no longer be casual about things. While '75 was all about healing and rebounding, now was the time for me to step up and make the sacrifices necessary to reap the rewards of tomorrow.

CHAPTER 14

THE MAN IN THE MIRROR

I stared at my reflection and studied the image. I was 6-foot-2, 257 pounds, and lean with only 4 percent body fat. Buff with solid muscle, even my eyebrows seemed to bulge. And outside of that jagged scar on my twenty-inch neck, I appeared happy and healthy. However, a deeper look into my dark-blue eyes revealed a certain heaviness lingering from within. *Three years. Three long years as a backup.* With my chin jutted, I audibly lamented, "You're getting ripe on the vine there, old fella." That zing triggered my twenty-four-year-old heart to beat faster, and I wondered why. Why was I still a backup? Why wasn't I realizing my NFL destiny?

I gazed deeper into my soul and plumbed for answers. I knew Kuechenberg and Little were formidable rivals. I knew breaking into their elite club would take time, but I was getting restless already. Physically, they were slightly larger and heavier, but I was stronger. On the field, they were measured and skilled, but I was faster and more flexible. Despite being evenly talented (in my admittedly biased opinion), Shula started Kuechenberg and Little over me. *Why?*

The more I thought about it, the more I realized the answer was obvious. It was trust. The '72 season greats had earned the trust of Don Shula. By reliably performing at All-Pro levels in Super Bowls VI, VII, and VIII, Coach had their back. He would not swap them without evident cause to do so.

But the clock was ticking. And when a whole new cohort of young, fresh, and ravenous rookies was entering the arena, hungry to seize the start, now was my moment. I felt frustrated. Coach knew it. He'd often repeat, "Be patient. Your time will come." Easy for him to say when he was fulfilling his NFL dreams. His contract covered his lifestyle. Mine didn't! I wanted to marry Cathy and buy her a beautiful home. I wanted to have kids and set them up for success. But all that cost money – money I did not have.

I stood there motionless for a long time and frowned at my reflection. I was at a crossroad. I could either continue on this NFL path and hope to reap the rewards or slip into oblivion and do God knows what? Maybe Wendy's? Maybe something else? *Ahhhhhhhhhhhh.*

I leaned in closer, and a voice from within nudged me. *What are you doing, you idiot? Just standing there? You're a professional football player. A Miami Dolphin! Stop wasting time. Get to the gym. Get stronger and faster. Work harder. Use the tools you have to make it happen. Do it. Do it now!*

"Okay," I promised, vowing to control what I could. With six months leading up to the '76 season, I could train like a beast and attain another 10 percent strength gain. If I did that, I'd be the most physically fit player on the line. Shoes would have to see me as the best choice for the starting position. And if he didn't, well, then at least I'd be able to look at the man in the mirror, knowing I gave it my all.

***

My great strength was born from all those years of wrestling, and I only resorted to weightlifting after my rookie season. In other words, I was a beginner, making things up as I went along. In that vacuum, and without the aid of a strength coach, I did my best to map out a plan to achieve several weightlifting goals, including a single maximum bench press of 425 pounds in twenty-six weeks. In phase I, "shock week," I'd blow out the old and frayed muscle fibers throughout my body with a combination of high reps and low weights. In phase II, "strength building," I'd spur the development of new muscles with a flipped model of low reps and high weights. With limited time, every second mattered.

I arrived at Biscayne College to commence shock week. I loaded 155 pounds onto the bench press bar, took a deep breath, and punched out as many reps as possible. The first ten were easy. My triceps, deltoids, and pectorals warmed. The following ten got progressively more challenging. My face reddened, my pace slowed, and my upper body spasmed and tightened like a rock. As sweat poured off my body, I became aware of the accumulating lactic acid wreaking havoc within. Blood pumped through my veins, my chest billowed, and I heaved for air. I tried to detach myself from the pain by labeling it as a mere distraction. *Ignore it. It's good pain.* Though, at twenty-one reps, my bloodshot eyes began to bug out. At twenty-two, I roared like an injured animal. By twenty-seven, I could barely take it. Yet the drill sergeant within berated me. *Stop being a pussy.* Twenty-eight. *Complete each lift you attempt!* Twenty-nine. *Don't you dare falter.* Thirty. *Good!* I shakily returned the bar to the saddle and lay on the bench with nothing more to give.

I repeated the same exercise at a reduced weight of 125 pounds a few minutes later. My muscles protested even more, but I gritted my teeth and pushed through. I toweled off, downed some Gatorade, and removed another 30 pounds to suffer the same exercise at 95 pounds, then at 60 pounds, and ultimately down to the naked bar of 45 pounds. *Oh my God.* I couldn't believe how challenging it was to lift the low weight, and this was only the beginning! I still had twelve more stations to go.

Next up: arm flies followed by lat pull-downs, dips, biceps, and triceps. When I transitioned to my lower body, my upper body was mush. I underwent the same tortuous routine for each major muscle group below my waist.

After three hours of pushing steel, I stumbled toward the gym's exit with heat radiating from the cartilage in my knees. I felt satisfied because I knew my efforts would translate into a significant advantage on the gridiron. Shoes would have to notice.

But maybe it was too much? That night, my muscles spasmed as if they had a mind of their own. The following day, they went on strike. I was so locked with pain and stiffness that I couldn't bring my fork to my mouth to eat. I grimaced at my breakfast, puzzling how I could down the necessary calories with immovable arms.

"What's wrong?" a genuinely worried Cathy asked. But her gentle disposition shifted to outrage when she saw me dip my face toward the plate and suck the scrambled eggs up into my mouth. "Eddy!" she scolded. "Don't eat like an animal."

When Cathy finally understood my distress, she suggested I take a day off from the weights. I recoiled at the idea and explained, "This is the time for me to work harder. If I stop now, all my effort will be for naught."

Though, as I drove to Biscayne College, my body fired unequivocal bolts of pain. I wondered if Cathy was right. Maybe this was bad pain? The kind that was associated with injury.

I loosened my locked muscles with a spell in the team's 101.5-degree Jacuzzi and some light stretching. When I felt human again, I returned to the bench-press station and launched into the same high-rep, low-weight shock routine again. As before, my body cried for mercy, but I followed through that day, the next, and all the way to Friday.

By the end of the first week, I was a mess. I looked broken, wobbly, and bone-weary. But I could feel my biochemistry kicking in. My flabby muscles were sloughing off and making way for stronger, newer, and more resilient tissue growth.

After a weekend of rest, I returned to the gym and launched into phase II: "strength building"—with much heavier weights lifted fewer times. Given the risk of injury associated with handling such heavy loads, I sought a spotter. Serendipitously, I found it in my friend and aspiring business partner, Bruce Elia, who was also lifting at Biscayne College that day.

As we rotated through warm-ups, I asked Elia if he had any updates on Wendy's. After all, we had an encouraging meeting with Mr. Thomas.

"Not really," Elia answered. "I think Wendy's is pitting us against a wealthy and experienced franchiser."

This upset me. I didn't want to be a backup in another arena. So I chalked my hands, loaded the steel bar, and uttered, "Let's push a little harder, and if this deal doesn't progress, let's cut bait before we waste any more time."

"Okay," Elia said as he positioned himself to spot me and confirmed I was ready.

"Yup," I answered. I grasped the steel bar's scored handholds, lifted the 210-pound weight off the holder, and rapidly exploded ten warm-up lifts. With each return, the crossbar bounced off my chest like a kid jumping on a trampoline.

After a brief rest, I increased the load to 250 pounds and, as before, recruited a concert of muscle fibers to blast the weight up to the reach of my arm seven times. From there, I added another 25 pounds and worked with and against gravity to move the 275-pound load through a complete cycle. ONE! My movements were fast, efficient, and effortless. TWO! The forced rebound off my chest resembled a piston. THREE! The bar pounded my sternum and depressed my ribcage two inches. FOUR! My heart was literally squeezed.

I returned the bar to the holder and added another 25 pounds, bringing the total weight to 300 pounds for my inaugural single maximum bench press of the year. Elia stood at the ready, but I wouldn't allow myself to falter.

I followed a similar warm-up to maximum lift approach with the incline bench, decline bench, and other upper body groups each Monday, Wednesday, and Friday. I focused on legs on Tuesdays and Thursdays. In doing so, I gave each muscle group at least one full day to rest before my next workout.

Week over week, the weight of my single maximum lifts steadily increased. This made me feel good, especially when my Plan B with

Wendy's floundered. Then, in late March, the newly formed Tampa Bay Buccaneers acquired Elia in the NFL's 1976 expansion draft, and my hope for the turnkey restaurant dissolved.

Feeling frustrated, I enrolled in a real estate sales course at Miami-Dade Community College. I earned the credential, joined a firm, and began showing commercial properties just southwest of Miami International Airport. While I learned the market value and began cultivating a handful of leads, it became clear that I needed a much longer lead time to close deals than the NFL's offseason allowed. This prompted me to elevate my license from sales to brokerage to expand my options.

***

Hopping from one foot to the next, Cathy shared that I'd been invited to vacation on a Sitmar Cruise as a celebrity guest. "Let's go!" she begged. "We'll have the best time!"

"No way!" I reproved. I had only fifteen weeks to attain my 425-pound bench press target and couldn't afford any time away from the gym. But my girl...she doesn't give up easy. She pushed, and she pushed, and she pushed again. Eventually, seeing that the path of least resistance was to yield to Cathy's wishes, I reluctantly capitulated.

Bon voyage. Seven days at sea. All-you-can-eat food. Exceptional entertainment. Fun memories sailing the Caribbean with my teammates and my girl. The cruise was wonderful. And despite my sincerest efforts to work out, my strength training fell behind schedule.

Once back on solid ground, I relaunched into phase I: shock week. However, I added 40 pounds onto the initial 155-pound stack to make up for lost time. *Ready?* I exploded out as many reps as possible at 195 pounds. *Manageable.* I decreased the load, and the pain intensified. My mind protested, *This hurts!* I felt nauseous. I wanted to quit, but I assured myself that I was suffering from a mental limit, not a physical one. *This is good pain.* Even when dull dog-tired aches warned that I was overdoing it, I pushed through because I believed it was better to pay the small price of fleeting discomfort than risk the enduring agony of getting injured or cut from the team.

Well, look at that. I stared in surprise at the bright-red pee streaming into the white toilet bowl later that day. "CATHY! Come here!" I screamed across our apartment. "You got to see this."

"Oh no, Eddy." A startled Cathy demanded we go to the emergency room right away. I tempered her concerns by explaining that the red color was probably muscle pigment leaking into my bloodstream from bruised tissues. Even so, Cathy insisted I call Dr. Virgin to verify it wasn't something else.

With my history of thyroid cancer, Dr. Virgin wanted to rule out any metastasis in my kidneys or bladder, so he referred me to a urologist. While I wasn't keen on wasting any time at the hospital, I also wasn't willing to play chicken with my life again.

A hospital stayover confirmed I had overdone it and broken through a physical limit, causing tens of thousands of micro-fissures in my exhausted muscles to release myoglobin into my bloodstream. While not ideal, at worst, the red pigment could lead to kidney dysfunction. Luckily, it was already clearing my system with no sign of ill effect.

I proceeded with caution when I returned to the gym because I now knew that bad pain was a real thing that could lead to injury if not avoided. This prompted me to abandon shock week and return to phase II: strength building, with a more substantial ten-pound increase for two weeks. Holy crap. Those weeks were a slow-moving hell. However, this time, I correctly recognized my suffering as good pain—a mental limit that I, as a pro athlete, needed to push through.

***

Camp opened for the '76 season, and word got out that Kuech had made team history by bench pressing the most weight ever lifted by a Miami Dolphin: 415 pounds, to be exact. I found my place in line behind second-year linebacker Steve Towle and waited for my strength assessment. Towle turned and remarked, "Sheesh, Ed. You got big! I think I'll call you 'Lead Head.'" I nodded in appreciation because Lead Head sounded a lot better than Snookums.

When it was my turn, our team trainer, Bob Lundy, invited me to take the station. After a brief warmup, I loaded the bar with 425 pounds.

"Ready?" Lundy asked.

I looked to the right and noticed Kuech and Langer staring at me in disbelief. "I am," I answered. My adrenaline pumped. My clarity increased as I internally initiated the start. *Ready, set*—I wanted to explode—*GO!* Every fiber inside me compressed, and I rapidly lifted the bar off the stand and elevated it to the full extent of my arms. The bench beneath me groaned. I pulled the bar down toward my chest. Upon contact, my heart stopped, and my blood pressure spiked. Feeling like one with the bar, I rocketed all 425 pounds upward off my ribcage. It accelerated nicely up until the last two inches of my extension, when I really had to apply myself.

"Holy shit," the peanut gallery marveled when I returned the bar to the saddle and sat up as if it were nothing.

Kuech stepped up and congratulated me, "You know what this means, Ed? You're officially the strongest man on the team."

"Good job," praised Langer.

I smiled but dared not gloat. This was just one test of many. For goodness' sake, I still needed to get past Shula's twelve-minute run the next day. But I can assure you one thing: the next time I looked at the man in the mirror, I liked what I saw.

CHAPTER 15

MATTERS THAT MATTER

My priorities remained with the team as we progressed through the '76 preseason. Not only was I gunning for the start, but I was also seeking stability through job security because I had just asked Cathy to marry me. I needed to get the most out of camp and impress the coaches. I snuck extra calisthenic reps into my warmups, kept my feet moving throughout practice, ran wind sprints, and hit the weights late into the evening.

Shoes seemed to appreciate my effort. But Coach Clark's replacement, John Sandusky, didn't. For some reason, the early-fifties, old-time tackle and good friend of Shula's, liked to bust my balls. He berated me when I slogged through the twelve-minute run and got chummy with everyone else while kind of just looking through me. I found this irritating. But I trusted that Sandusky would eventually see that I was the real deal—a solid player who gave his all for matters that mattered.

In any event, with all the extra effort, I was more voracious than ever. I ate a lot, and in rapidly consuming such large quantities of food, I experienced some unwanted byproducts, specifically… gas.

Everyone farts, and ball players are anything but reserved when it comes to bodily functions. There I was, resting in my dorm room, watching a group of talented Soviet Union gymnasts compete in the Montreal Summer Olympics when my stomach rumbled. I ignored it because these things always seem to work themselves out. Instead, I kept my attention on the tube where the judges flashed a handful of *8* and *9* scores, signifying their positive appraisal of the gymnasts' performance.

The pressure in my belly passed the point of no return during Shula's evening meeting. Out of respect, I held it until Coach finished his first agenda point. But then, I had no other choice—*holy mackerel*. I sheepishly looked around and saw Kuech and Langer cracking up. I wondered if they were laughing at me but dismissed the idea and returned my attention to Coach. In my periphery, I saw Langer write something on his spiral-bound Miami Dolphins notebook.

"Hey! Ed!" Langer threw a hand towel at me and raised a piece of paper with a large "5" scribbled on the front. "Not even a contender on a ten-point scale," he quietly taunted.

Sitting a foot closer to me, Kuech followed suit with a "6."

My face reddened, and my eyebrows lifted.

"No issue, Hump and Rump," interjected a playful Sandusky from the side of the room. With a charming smile set on his beefy face, he said, "A farting horse will never tire, and a farting man is the man to hire!"

I couldn't believe it. These guys were talking about me and the quality of my fart. They were scoring it, Olympics-style. This gave me a slight rise. I could do better than a 5 or 6! *Nadia Comaneci, step aside. I also want a perfect 10.*

For grins, I gathered with Kuech and Langer in the locker room and asked, "What do you guys think about making a competition of this? We can have categories like volume, timing, and zone of death. We can have individual and group challenges, judges, and medal ceremonies."

"Yeah," Langer laughed. "Let's do it."

Kuech slighted with a smirk, "You won't have a chance of winning with anything like that last submission."

"You sure about that?" I confidently countered. "Because I'm in it to win it."

While proposed in jest, word of the "Fart Olympics" spread like wildfire. Most got into the spirit because it was a contest, and we were all so darn competitive. The running backs and linebackers featured a staccato machine-gun style, while the receivers and defensive backs were more silent but deadly. The quarterbacks were precise with timing, but they quickly lost steam because gas was not what they were paid to pass. Besides, they couldn't match the power of us linemen.

About a week into the games, the meeting room's concentration of hydrogen sulfide was elevated when Shoes took the podium. Personally primed to compete on a steady diet of milk products, beans, garlic, onions, and my secret weapon of mangos, I respected the man way too much to flagrantly disrupt his flow. Yet another O-lineman, we'll call him "Dirty Wally," showed less restraint. Just as Shula neared the climax of his coaching point, Dirty Wally ripped the loudest blast for what seemed like two seconds. Everyone nearby fanned their noses, bit their fists to stifle a chuckle, and raised their score sheets for the timing category: 9, 10, 9.

Sotto voce, "Whoa."

I turned to see how Shula would react to the meeting room disturbance, but the man continued as if nothing had happened.

A few minutes later, the receivers, positioned at the front of the room, screeched their desks across the terrazzo floor and yelped for mercy while vacating a six-foot diameter to escape ground zero, where another stink bomb went off. The score sheets for the zone of death shot up: 8, 7, 9.

I looked past my teammates at Shula and noted that, outside of a swipe to his nose, Coach did not flinch. It was unbelievable. Only ten feet from the action, the man would not dignify such crudeness. His focus remained on the upcoming game and his plan to get the most out of his players.

The following morning, Kuech sat on that stinky brown couch set off to the side of the locker room and waved his hands to gather the O-linemen. Nine of us stepped up. Kuech asked, "Do you know why they call us the Mushrooms?" He waited a few seconds before answering his question, "It's because they keep us in the dark and feed us shit." Coach Kuech continued, "Our performance is lagging behind the D-lineman. Let's show them what the Mushrooms can do by winning the overall scoring category."

Feeling more competitive than ever, we filed into Shula's next meeting and listened as Coach went through his usual topics. With a shift of his hips, Shoes folded his arms and told us to pay attention. With piercing eyes, he announced, "The assistant coaches are extremely upset about their work conditions. They say that your 'gas competition' is creating an untenable environmental hazard." With a straight face, he concluded, "The public release of flatulence is to be avoided whenever possible, and any 'fart of consequence' is a punishable offense."

What? Necks turned. Eyes met eyes. What was a fart of consequence? Simply by mentioning it, our leader made it a thing. We wanted to—no, we needed to know exactly what it was and who'd establish the standard. The energy built. The locker room was abuzz with conjecture. And then, our champion, Dirty Wally, stepped up and delivered a magnificent sample during Sandusky's film review.

A disgusted and disturbed Sandusky abruptly shut off the projector, cut the lights, and stormed out of the meeting room. He slammed the door behind him, so the entire O-line was forced to stew in the dark, in the stench.

If Dirty Wally's performance wasn't so funny, I would have been a little turned off by the funk. But man, he made the 'Shrooms proud that day. And with that, the Fart Olympics ended, the flatulence teams disbanded, and the NFL's preseason concluded. With the regular season upon us, it was time to leave the horsing around behind because those of us who had survived the final roster cut were there to play good ball—and win.

***

Yet winning wouldn't be easy because we were down some significant talent. In addition to Elia, linebacker Doug Swift and offensive tackle Norm Evans were picked up in the expansion draft. Coach Shula also had to shore up for Mercury Morris, who was traded to San Diego, Jake Scott, who went to the Redskins, and Manny Fernandez, who reluctantly retired with a bad knee. On top of that, others, like Bill Stanfill and Earl Morrall, were aging out of the game. All this, combined with the previous loss of Kiick, Warfield, and Csonka, compounded the Dolphins' deficits.

Narrowing in on my orbit, Shula played musical chairs with the offensive linemen he had. He played the '75 season first-round draft pick, right tackle Darryl Carlton, in place of Norm Evans while keeping Wayne Moore at left tackle, Kuech at left guard, Langer at center, and Little at right guard. While much stock was placed in the University of Tampa grad, Carlton had a hard time adjusting to the pressures of the big league, and our opposition quickly exploited his weaknesses.

In mid-October, our season went sideways with a .500 record. Shoes swapped offensive tackle Tom Drougas in for Carlton. But this didn't work either, primarily due to Drougas's gimpy left shoulder. We lost our fifth and sixth games, making our record 2–4.

Palpable pain permeated the locker room. Tempers flared, fingers pointed, and the Shula bomb detonated on Drougas. He stripped the journeyman of his status, along with the start. In Drougas's stead, the Don moved Larry Little to right tackle and tapped me to start at right guard.

From October 24 through November 14, Little and I played side by side and did the job the way it was supposed to be done. Shoes seemed satisfied, especially when we won three of those four games. But when Kuech was knocked out with a minor injury, Shula moved Little back to right guard, returned Carlton to right tackle, and shifted me to start at left guard. Unfortunately, we couldn't pull it off in this new lineup, and we lost games 11 and 12, making our record a pathetic 5–7.

Almost overnight, something shifted in Shula. His intensity went way down, and he stopped hounding us so sharply. It was surreal going through film review with a leader who was apathetic to his own standards. Sure, Shula maintained his focus on perfection, but he spoke without gusto. He let critical penalties and mental mistakes slide. He stopped calling us out for lack of effort. And he acted as if it was pointless to beat this already dead horse. I found myself longing for the days of constant screaming because that meant we were winning.

With no hope of making it to the playoffs, a few guys disengaged. They were like zombies going through the motions. I, however, kept my head down and went full force. Where they put in half the effort, I doubled mine. When they began to pack their things, I considered buying a Miami residence. And as they prepared to hang up their jerseys, I vowed to wear mine out. I knew the soul of Don Shula. The man was already placing a bullseye on half a dozen players for the '77 season. I didn't want to give him any reason to put a target on my back.

When the season concluded with a 6–8 record, I went to Shula's office for an end-of-year check-in. To my delight, Coach admitted that he noticed my extra effort and stated that if I kept up my conditioning, I'd be a "core member of the future Miami Dolphins."

Then Coach's face got very serious. He shifted in his seat and jutted his chin toward the door. "Now," he ordered, "get out of here." My face dropped. I didn't know what was going on. But then Shula's expression softened. He expanded, "I understand you're getting married, and that bride of yours is a tough one. You don't want to keep her waiting." I smiled because Shula was right. I thanked him and darted home to focus on another matter that mattered.

CHAPTER 16

HERE, THERE, AND EVERYWHERE

I guided Cathy to the dance floor for our first dance as husband and wife. As we swayed to the Beatles' ballad, "Here, There and Everywhere," I listened to the lyrics because they spoke my truth: "To lead a better life, I need my love to be here."

Cathy was the healer of my mind, body, and soul. She brought me peace and psychological safety and steered me toward the light in a world where many temptations threatened to pull me into the dark. As Cathy gently cupped the back of my head, I thought of the stark contrast between my two worlds of war and peace. Take just a few weeks earlier when Minnesota's All-Pro defensive tackle Alan Page was roughly cuffing at my collar, trying to detach my head from my torso. Brutal. But now, here, my caring bride was massaging my neck. She was giving me the unconditional love and stability I needed to stay on track.

"I want her everywhere. And if she's beside me, I know I need never care." The band faithfully carried the tune, and I playfully twirled my wife. With each revolution, I thought about how Cathy also needed stability. She was ready to start a family and was looking to me to provide for whatever little blessings may follow. I couldn't let her down.

The final verse sealed the message in my heart: "I will be there. And everywhere. Here, there and everywhere." I dipped my bride, kissed her, and planned to do all I could to ensure her happiness.

After a round of applause, Cathy and I greeted our guests. When we arrived at my parents' table, Dad pulled me in and offered counsel. "Son," he said, "you have a wife to care for now. It's time to figure out something beyond football."

Of course, Dad was right. Real estate brokerage was falling flat. And while I was fully focused on football, it would be selfish of me to neglect paving the way for another future, especially when football would likely end by injury or waiver within just a few short years.

Cathy tugged at my arm, but Dad had more to say, so I hung back. With a twinkle in his eye, he boasted, "Newman's is expanding. Now is the perfect time for you to join the family business. You can open a radiator distributorship in South Florida, somewhere near the team."

"Dad," my latent reservations persisted, "you know I can't nurture a business during the season. It's impossible with Shula's schedule."

To my surprise, Dad countered with details about a former business partner of his who could run the business when I couldn't. My heart swelled. Dad was trying so hard to make this happen. Though in truth, I wanted to land higher than Newman's. But with nothing else, I had to give it a go.

"Sure," I said. "It's worth a try." I then shook Dad's hand and looked him full in the face before returning to my bride.

Cathy and Ed Newman on their wedding night (1977)

***

"Is that Richard?" Cathy asked when a long dark-haired man wearing a bright-yellow polyester polo and a thick garish gold chain, complete with a dangling three-quarter-inch penis pendant, appeared at our doorstep.

"I guess so." I lifted my shoulders and opened the door to greet Dad's proposed business partner. Despite my unsavory first impression, I remained cordial and looked for Richard's merit. Yet it soon became clear that this guy wasn't a good fit. Insular and narrow-minded, he refused to work out of Miami-Dade County, complaining that it was "Cuban-owned territory."

"So what?" I countered. What Richard saw as a disadvantage, I considered a huge advantage. Miami was becoming more Cuban, and the Cuban community was full of savvy and high-integrity people who had great industry. I proposed that we learn Spanish or hire a Spanish-speaking salesperson. Yet Richard was unwilling to budge.

When I informed Dad of the chasm forming between us, he told me not to worry.

"Even if you fail in partnering with Richard," Dad encouraged, "you'll learn a lot. And there's great value in that."

"I don't want to fail!" I retorted in anger. "That's not how I do things."

Dad got quiet. As did I. The silence hurt because the implicit was becoming explicit. My heart wasn't in it. The logistics didn't make sense, and this Richard guy was a major mismatch. Dad's dream for me to join the family business was essentially evaporating, and I had to accept that I was back at square one when it came to my plan B.

***

I swirled for a while. Then on a tip from Shoes, I joined the NFL Player Management Training Program at Ryder Trucks, where I worked alongside Cincinnati Bengals' linebacker Glenn Cameron. Fun as it was to pal around with that crew, I could see that the whole thing was a showboat situation, offering little future.

I vented on my plan B challenges to Cathy's older brother, Andy Leinoff, while on a camping trip. The intelligent, take-charge, and budding legal maestro inquired what other careers I had in mind.

"Dentistry, maybe?" I answered as I gathered some kindling to start a fire. I expanded, "Two of my uncles are dentists."

"Dentistry? With those hands?" Andy shut his dark brown eyes, shook his head, and chuckled. "No. I don't see it."

"What do you mean?" I asked.

"Look at your hands, Ed."

I put down the wood and examined my hands. *Oh no.* I could see what Andy was getting at. My very large and injury-deformed hands were less than appealing. Few would want them in their mouths. I could only imagine what they'd say: "Ed Newman—from jaw crusher to jaw repairer."

Andy sat on a large rock, rested a finger on his brow, and considered an alternate path. In a eureka moment, he jumped up and proposed, "Law! Have you ever considered becoming a lawyer?"

121

Me? A lawyer. I squinted.

"Yes," Andy said. "You'd be a great lawyer!"

My lips widened in disbelief. "You're joking, right?"

"No," answered Andy. "Think about it, Ed. You did well at Duke. You take classes during the offseason. You're always reading. You pretty much negotiate your own NFL contracts, and you enjoy taking a leadership role in union matters." Andy stretched out his long legs and encouraged, "I think you could do it."

I didn't know what to say, so we left the discussion there.

***

Word of it was all over the newswire—Dolphins Don Reese and Randy Crowder were arrested for trying to sell a pound of cocaine to undercover officers. Miami was becoming the "drug capital of the world," and those two got swept up in it. The newspapers even suggested that other teammates might be involved. I was disturbed. Who'd want to mess around with drugs and dealers?

I assumed Shoes would be apoplectic. We already had a lousy roster and were now down two more talents. But a little part of me hoped that this development would give Coach good cause to talk me up in my upcoming contract discussions with George Young.

Still, Young had a job to do. Predictably, he stalled and made lowball offers when I pressed for a fair and lucrative multi-year agreement. Our negotiations entered impasse when we couldn't see eye to eye. It was awful, especially when the 1977 preseason approached, and I still needed to work out without pay and without the certainty of a contract.

Young and I met once more a few days before camp opened. While we made some headway, we remained hung up on the duration of my contract. I wanted three years. George wanted four. I proposed a workaround: a contract option that would allow me to terminate my contract's fourth and final year if I had a stellar third year and, from that posture, could negotiate for more pay. George hesitated but said he'd float the idea by management.

I left the discussion feeling optimistic. But my certainty receded when camp opened with no follow-up from George. The pressure built each day, and I started to weigh my options: I could cave in and accept the Dolphins' subpar terms, or I could hold out and not return to camp, hoping they'd accept mine.

Nearly a week into the power play, I worried that I'd be out of the NFL before even having my moment to make it. And despite my efforts to establish a career outside of football, there still was no viable plan B. Feeling depressed, I crawled into bed and yelped for the support of my bride.

Cathy came in from the next room over and lay beside me. She listened closely as I explained how if the Dolphins and I couldn't come to terms, they could keep me locked up as a reserved player indefinitely. Understanding my deep anguish, Cathy embraced me as she did on our wedding night. She ran her hands through my hair, gently rubbed my temples, and assured me that everything would be okay. In time, my cares melted away, and I slipped into sleep.

A few days later, the phone rang.

"It's George Young," Cathy said with a heartening smile. She mouthed, "You got this."

I grabbed the phone, took a deep breath, and listened as Young updated how it was tough, but he got me the clause I wanted. "Come in and sign the papers straight away," he insisted.

Delight overcame me upon realizing that my holdout worked. I hung up the phone, shared the good news with Cathy, and went to our bedroom to pack up for camp. But as I gathered my things, I slowed a little because it dawned on me that I was off to Biscayne College for the next month and a half. I'd only be able to see my girl a couple of days each week. The absence hurt; I didn't want to be away from her.

I walked over to Cathy and wrapped my arms around her waist. "Dance with me," I requested.

Cathy took my hand. For a few precious moments, we swayed while I softly sang the words of our wedding song in her ear. "To lead a better life, I need my love to be here." I then gave Cathy a peck on the cheek, told her I loved her, and set off to camp for my 1977 tour of duty.

CHAPTER 17

TWO THUMBS UP

The atmosphere in the locker room was melancholy because Shula was cutting the underperformers from the '76 season. Some, like my roommate, Tom Drougas, expected it. Others didn't. Those of us who survived to play another day gathered to give our comrades a proper sendoff. Surrounded by my teammates, old and new, I raised a mug to the fallen and declared to the room, "We went to war with you guys. Our brotherhood is forever."

"Here, here," the troops responded in unison.

Feeling unsettled, I snuck off to my empty dorm room, where I met my reflection with worried eyes. Shaking my head as if to ward off bad juju, I listened to the tiny voice within nag about the inevitability of my football finale. *You're not too far behind those guys.* I tried to blink the negative thoughts away and whispered, "No! I'm not going anywhere." But the realities of the NFL could not be denied. Time was ticking away. Who knew how much longer I could go?

I unlocked my eyes from the image, flopped on my bed, and distracted myself with thoughts about the next six weeks. There'd be the traditional alpha dog trials, the drama of who would and would not make the club, and the coaches' constant critiques. My mind spun, and my eyes focused on a solitary cockroach climbing up the wall, burrowing into a small crack. *Lonely*. I felt lonely. I missed Cathy. It didn't sit right that I was a twenty-six-year-old newlywed holed up in this grungy sleepaway camp.

Yearning for the softness of my bride, I went to a payphone and called Cathy. "Honey," I pled, "some of the guys have jumped the wall to be with the ones they love. I want to come home and see you tonight."

"Ohhhhh. No, Eddy." Cathy seductively sighed. "Coach would find out. You'd get in trouble." She continued, "I'm sure he'd fine you, and I'm afraid he'd scream at me."

I chuckled because even Cathy tiptoed around the man. Once back in my room, I noticed another cockroach, this time a smaller one, climbing into the same crack to join its companion. Even the darn pests had someone to go home to! I resolved that if busting curfew to be with my girl wasn't an option, then I needed something to brighten my dreary dorm room because the basic accommodations of the "Biscayne Hilton" were bringing me down.

On our next day off, I went to the supermarket and bought a "potted pet," a corn plant, to keep me company and add a little color to my room. While I didn't talk about it, I saw the shrub as a symbolic metaphor. Nothing major, just a sign of life. *It's surviving Biscayne College, and so am I*. I watered the plant daily and rotated it to give it the right amount of sunlight. In time, my plant thrived.

Dirty Wally noticed my affinity for the greenery. With his big old black-beard, gutter mouth, and crude ways, he saw it as an opportunity to mess with me. He snuck into my room and peed in the pot when I wasn't around. At first, I had no clue. But after several deposits, there was that urine smell. And then my plant withered and died.

I was disappointed. Yet Dirty Wally was proud of himself. Outside of my presence, he bragged about it—even to Sandusky, who surprisingly was not amused. Fearing that the loss of my talisman would impact my play, Sandusky demanded that Dirty Wally come clean.

There we were, sitting in the locker room, wrapping our wrists before the morning practice, when Dirty Wally lowered his gaze and impishly admitted what he had done. More curious than anything else, I asked why he fessed up. The man explained that Sandusky was worried about me because he had seen other players "go mental" over disruptions to their superstitious beliefs. He didn't want me to "lose it."

"Anyway, you okay?" Dirty Wally asked with genuine concern.

You kidding? I found it hard to believe that these guys thought I was so fragile. I mean, a dead plant was nothing compared to a punch in the face or a busted knee. With a slight frown, I answered, "Don't sweat it. There are much more important things to worry about, like winning the next game."

"Mmm," mumbled Dirty Wally, who got up and offered me his hand out of respect.

***

Shula proved his genius right out of the gate when we kicked off the '77 season with three consecutive wins, two of which I started in place of Kuech, and four wins in the next six games, one in which I covered for Little. Mike Current filled in nicely at right tackle. And three newer talents—linebacker Kim Bokamper, defensive end A. J. Duhe, and nose tackle Bob Baumhower—started in every game at near All-Pro caliber.

Even though our solid performance earned us the accolade of playoff contenders, there was some debate about who would win the Thanksgiving Day match against the Cardinals in St. Louis. Betting against us, our hometown sports reporter Ed Plaisted of the *Hollywood Sun-Tattler* had the temerity to suggest that the Dolphins would be the "turkey special" served for dinner.

Shula wouldn't let Plaisted's offensive write-up distract us. "Your fates are entirely in your hands," he counseled during a team meeting. "You've worked so damn hard. Don't let reporters like Plaisted get in the way of your performance." With an encouraging gaze, Coach predicted, "You guys are going to take this victory right where the Cardinals live."

A few days later, we were waiting on a plane to depart for St. Louis when, lo and behold, Plaisted appeared. The extremely over-sized man, who happened to be shaped a lot like a plucked turkey, waddled his wide waist down the airplane's narrow aisle. The cabin filled with hisses and boos. One player even chucked his copy of the *Sun-Tattler* at the reporter. But Plaisted remained placid. He softly excused himself as he bumped several shoulders along the way. Once seated, Plaisted hid behind a magazine. A quick read of the room revealed this wasn't over.

The following day, I headed to the hotel dining room for a large breakfast of steak, eggs, and coffee. That's where I found Kuech and Langer bantering about faith in football.

"It's good to see you, Ed." Kuech looked up from the table and shared, "Langer and I were just talking about how we needed members because we're underrepresented."

"What?" I clarified.

Kuech pointed across the hall and explained, "A good number of our teammates are in that conference room over there, having a prayer meeting with the Fellowship of Christian Athletes. Anyway," Kuech earnestly suggested, "you should join our club. I've named it the Fellowship of Pagan Athletes. What do you think?"

I uncomfortably smiled and decided to hold my tongue because there are some things that a Jewish fellow ought to let slide.

When my silence lingered, Langer changed the subject. He tapped his finger hard on Plaisted's article and growled, "This son of a bitch is going to pay."

Kuech bobbed his head.

I squinted, wondering what these guys were up to.

A short while later, we checked out of the hotel and boarded the bus for Busch Memorial Stadium. The energy was buzzing at a high hum—all systems go. I sucked in the cool air and started to get mentally right.

Once settled in the locker room, I launched into my pregame rituals. Seeking solitude, I ventured to the shower area, where I began several choreographed yoga-like stretches. In, I inhaled. One. Two. Three. Out, I exhaled. One. Two. Three. Four. By degrees, I got centered and ready. I felt no pain from torn ligaments, stretched tendons, or broken fingers of games past. Instead, I was connected to the euphoria of purpose. All was right in that state of supreme power and well-being.

As I glided back to the lockers, I caught a glimpse of my reflection and did a double take. The man in the mirror was the picture of solemnity and determination. I entertained myself with visions of domination over my opponent as I fitted pads into my football pants and pulled them on. From there, I went to see Lundy. While our trainer rapidly wrapped my ankles, he offered good conversation. However, I was in no state of mind for chitchat. You see, this Newman was very different from the rookie who was nearly exploding like a keg of TNT back in '73. With time and experience, I found more effective ways to channel my energy, and silence helped.

Next, I headed to the other side of the room to get my B-12 shot. As I waited in line, I overheard our robust running back Benny Malone nervously chattering about how he was "brave enough to do this." *Brave enough to do what?* I didn't understand. The 193-pound Malone was fearless on the football field as he pumped out the yards and bobbed and weaved through 300-pound defensive tackles trying to slam into him.

"Benny hates needles. His talk is to boost his courage," explained tight end Andre Tillman from his seat on an examination table about five yards away.

When Dr. Herbert Virgin called Malone up and prepared the injection site, Malone began to hyperventilate. With his lips in the shape of an *O*, he audibly huffed, "Ohh. Ohh. Ohh." Dr. Virgin held his arm tight and plunged the needle deep into his flesh. I kid you not: Malone's eyes rolled. I leaned in to grab him if he fell over, but Malone willed himself to take it like a man. Then, like a banty rooster, he bounded off on his extraordinarily muscular legs as if it were nothing.

After I got my shot, I glanced back at Andre and saw that the starter's knee was the size of a volleyball. There was no way he could play without treatment.

"Andre," I overheard Dr. Charles Virgin, son of Herbert Virgin, explain, "the damage to your meniscus is triggering an overproduction of synovial fluid, and the pressure is restricting your range of motion." With a subtle purse of his lips, he stated, "We can treat it all by draining the fluid and leaving a shot of Xylocaine to manage the pain."

I shook my head, feeling unsettled by this standard of medicine. Indeed, any doctor in any other setting would not clear a civilian to return to work with an injury like Andre's. But this was the NFL.

Like a good soldier, Andre responded, "Do what you need to do." He remarkably tolerated the procedure as his doctor jabbed a three-inch draining needle into the center of his knee and removed at least a cup and a half of light golden fluid.

"Does it hurt?" I asked.

Andre answered in a low, soulful rasp, "I've been here before. I'll suffer the prick of a needle to be free of pain in a game anytime." But with two fists raised, Andre predicted, "I'll be hurting by the end of the second quarter."

"Andre," Charles cut in, "come back at halftime for another shot if you need it."

I grimaced. I didn't want to think about the consequences Andre would face later in life with this repeated trauma on his injured knee. But Andre was a warrior. He wasn't thinking about any of that now.

The game-day clock ticked down. With less than an hour to go, I checked my equipment and began to wrap my hands. Tired of suffering broken digits, I used a combination of half-mitted boxing gloves, webbing, and tape to protect my fingers from snapping like twigs when they caught an opponent's shoulder pad. Once my hands were wrapped, I stopped by equipment man Dan Dowe to inflate the air cushions in my helmet to perfect pressure.

"Round it up!" Shoes trumpeted from the front of the room forty-five minutes before kickoff. We hustled onto the field for warmups. My heart pounded furiously as the PA system blared, the fans piled into the stadium, and the energy built. I was absolutely psyched because an all-out war was coming. Asses and elbows were about to fly.

With only twenty minutes remaining on the countdown clock, Shula thundered, "Everybody into the locker room!" We stormed in and divided into our offensive and defensive teams to hear the coaches review play adjustments. As Shoes and Sandusky went through their spiel, I fumbled through my equipment bag and located a couple of NoDoz caffeine supplements, which I popped to ward off the post-adrenaline letdown I knew was coming in the second quarter of the game.

When the meeting adjourned, I went to the head to empty my bladder. There was no other opportunity outside of halftime, and I didn't want to leave it on the field.

T-minus ten. Shoes gathered everyone for the team prayer.

As Father Walker launched into his sermon, I thought of my late Nana Anna. I hurt when she passed, so much so that I regularly summoned her spirit before athletic events and—

"Jesus Christ," said Father Walker.

The words stood out. I never specifically mentioned Jesus in my prayers. I knew some gained strength with communion. Others inspiration. Heck, a bunch of players prayed to Jesus for his protection. I looked to God for guidance on how to be the best I could be. My thoughts returned to Anna. I prayed to her. *Please, be my guardian angel. I dedicate my performance to you.* In unison with the rest, I said, "Amen."

"—Jesus Christ," Father Walker said it again.

My thoughts of Anna vanished. I looked around and noticed that my teammates appeared at peace. If prayer to Jesus was good for the team, it was good for me.

Five minutes to kickoff, we charged from the air-conditioned locker room onto the battlefield. Goose bumps erupted over the back of my neck. It was the best place to be—with the screaming fans, enthusiastic announcers, spirited cheerleaders, and overwhelming intensity. Glowing with superior strength and vitality, I felt nothing but the high of adrenaline.

From the start, we dominated the Cardinals. Sporting a new pair of unbreakable Clark Kent–style dark-rimmed corrective eyeglasses, Bob Griese had no problem seeing his receivers. He registered four touchdowns within the first two quarters of the game! Three of them were caught by Nat Moore. And after getting his second shot of Xylocaine, Andre pulled in Griese's record-breaking sixth touchdown pass of the day.

It was amazing. We were conquering the favored Cardinals in their house. However, as we neared the end of the game, defensive end Vern Den Herder suffered a season-ending knee sprain. When Bob Matheson went to help him up, Vern accused, "It was Dobler."

Known as an NFL goon, Cardinals' offensive guard Conrad Dobler was one of those players who'd hit to cripple. His techniques included spitting, poking people in the eye, and cold-clocking players from their blindside just because. No matter whether Dobler was responsible for Vern's injury, the man was pissed. He gave Matheson some lip. Fists were thrown, and when an official tried to intervene, Dobler pushed the referee. Next thing, both sidelines emptied to the center of the field for a full-blown melee. Despite my preference to avoid physical altercations, I couldn't sidestep an opportunity to defend a teammate who'd been abused, so I jumped right in.

"God damn it! Stop fighting!" a red-faced Shula screamed from the sideline as yellow flags dappled the field. The clock stopped. The officials solicited help from the coaches. And Dobler was ejected for unsportsmanlike conduct.

We eventually finished the game with another two touchdowns, one of which was scored by Vitamin B-12 Malone. The proof was in the stuffing. With 55 points compared to the Cardinals' 14, 503 yards, 8 touchdowns, and 34 first downs, nobody in their right mind could call the Dolphins turkeys!

After a follow-up prayer and a quick shower, Shula opened the locker room for a cadre of reporters to swamp in. In strutted Plaisted. At first sight, Kuech and Langer pounced. They grabbed the reporter by his collar and pulled him to the ground. Plaisted flailed and screamed for help while a cackling Kuech and Langer recklessly dragged his large body across the floor and into the shower area.

I averted my eyes as Plaisted flopped like a big fat fish out of water. Seeing a grown man being handled in such a way wasn't right. And while I didn't think the reporter deserved it, I understood why he got it.

As my teammates proceeded to dump Plaisted upside down and headfirst into the cold running shower, I thought lawsuits would follow. But lucky for Plaisted, someone tipped off the coaches, and they sprinted over to break things up. Shoes nearly crashed into me. Sandusky yelped at Kuech, "Put him down!"

A few days later, Coach stomped into film review and cut us to shreds with his beady laser eyes. From his pedestal, Shula growled, "Commissioner Rozelle saw that drama on the field, and he sent me this letter." Shoes opened the memo, and affecting disdain, he read the names of each player involved in the cardinal sin along with the associated penitence.

Little got a $3,000 fine because he threw a few punches. Matheson was charged $2,000 for, among other things, kicking Dobler in the ass. Then Shula called my name. "Newman"—he scowled—"$500."

I nodded in approval because I'd do anything to protect my brothers.

When Shula finished reading the excerpt, he told us, "This is intolerable behavior, and I want you to know how I really feel about it." Without saying anything more, Coach put down the letter, turned his scowl into a big grin, and held two thumbs up.

***

The 1977 season ended abruptly on December 17 with a 10–4 record when our great nemesis, John Madden and his Oakland Raiders, edged us out of a wildcard shot at the playoffs with their superior 11–3 record. It was ironic that we didn't even face Oakland head-to-head that year. And it was unfortunate because this edition of the Miami Dolphins had merit. But the win-loss record was a stubborn thing. Had we been given a go at the playoffs, who knows? I guess it doesn't matter. As Shula would say, "It's history."

With a serene smile, I stood before my locker at Biscayne College after an end-of-year check-in with Shula and tapped on the plastic Snookums nameplate that was becoming a more permanent fixture. I felt pleased about the season. I had made major strides, played in every game, was injury-free, and had no reason to doubt that next year would be even better. Now it was time to go home. Time to relax and be with my girl. But to be honest, a little part of me was already dreaming about the season ahead.

CHAPTER 18

WHEELS UP, WHEELS DOWN

Now that I was a well-established veteran, I enjoyed watching the young blood find their way through the brave new NFL world. I noted that one guy in particular—the 1978 fourth-round pick, offensive tackle Eric Laakso—was proving himself as a quality player on the field and a quality person off it. Packing 270 pounds of muscle into a 6-foot-4 frame, Laakso was physically equipped to handle his assignments. He also had a strong work ethic and an ease about him.

From my locker, I overheard Kuech school the pale and flaxen Tulane geology grad on one of his favorite chestnuts: why they call us the Mushrooms. Laakso chuckled and tried to get comfortable through Kuech's abstract teach. But eventually, he interrupted and asked Kuech if he'd ever seen a mushroom rock before.

"A what?" Kuech winced. "What are you talking about, rookie?"

Appreciating the deeper discussion, I jumped in and ventured a guess. "Isn't that an eroded rock that resembles a mushroom?"

"That's right!" Laakso affirmed with a genuine smile. "Rocks for jocks," he boasted.

"Rocks for jocks," I echoed back.

Laakso later invited me to grab a beer with him before the evening meeting. While we sat at our pizza dive, I asked him why he chose to study at Tulane.

"Fill up," Laakso said with a motion toward my mug, "and I'll tell you."

I flagged the waiter down and ordered a pitcher of beer for us to share.

With a spark in his eye, Laakso launched into his tale. "Well, Ed, you need to know that I'm Scandinavian, and we Nordic folk love the sauna." Laakso licked his lips, took a sip of beer, and continued. "We love it so much that we use it socially. Anyway"—he arced his hands wide across the air as if to paint a vista and explained— "it was the winter of my senior year at Killingly High School in Connecticut, and the colleges were visiting my house trying to sell me on their schools. I didn't care where I went, so my old man and I decided to have a little fun with them."

Laakso closed his eyes and swayed his large rounded head while happily recalling the events. "When those recruiters showed up at my door, Pops would invite them to our backyard sauna, set fifteen yards off the house, to discuss their offers. You see," he explained, "it was below freezing, so some flat-out refused to hike through four inches of snow to get there." Laakso gave a belly laugh and continued, "Pops and I knew those guys weren't worth our time. But for those who took the challenge…"

Laakso drained his mug and asked, "Would you believe it if I told you that we'd strip down, wrap a towel around our waists, and get into the sauna with them?" He laughed. "Because we did! We'd turn up the heat to like 120 degrees. Before long, everyone would be sweating and feeling very uncomfortable. When it got intolerable"—Laakso paused to replenish his drink—"my dad and I would go outside, butt naked, and flop around in the snow with a dare to the recruiter to hit the powder too."

He slapped his knee. "Whoa, damn! The instant temperature change was invigorating, let me tell you."

My eyes widened, and Laakso picked up the tale.

"All those recruiters must have thought that Pops and I were crazy, but the Tulane recruiter was different." Laakso smacked his lips and concluded, "He got into the snow! He acted like it didn't bother him and just rolled around. So that's why I went to Tulane."

I joined Laakso in laughter. The rookie ordered a second pitcher of beer and encouraged me to drink up and drink a lot. It didn't take long for us to polish off the draft. After that, we returned to camp for the evening meeting. But listening to Sandusky go over basic rookie assignments was wasted on me. My time would have been much better spent in the gym. At least with the Budweiser in my belly and a bit of a buzz, I felt better. I turned to Laakso and, with an arched eyebrow, suggested, "Drinks tomorrow?"

With that, a pattern was set, and I acquired a taste for beer and a very good friend.

***

Faster. Go faster! I parked my car at Miami International and hustled to make our chartered flight to New Orleans for the third game of the 1978 preseason. I boarded the plane with just a minute to spare and met Shula's death stare. The heat radiating from Coach's impatient eyes sent a shiver down my spine. With my carry-on bag hoisted over my shoulder, I trotted past Robbie, the assistant coaches, a few reporters, and the ranking veterans seated in the first-class cabin before grabbing a seat next to Laakso.

"Almost missed the flight there," Laakso joked.

"For good reason," I answered while unveiling a bag of treats. "I made a stop along the way."

"Damn skippy! Is that what I think it is?" Laakso asked while appraising the bag of Jewish delicatessen I had picked up. There was an abundance of bagels, cream cheese, lox, tomato, onion, pickled herring, smoked whitefish, caviar, and super sour dill pickles. Laakso rubbed his hands together and celebrated, "That's Scandinavian soul food!" Before I could respond, disgruntled noises from the back of the plane stole our attention.

"Thank you very much!" sang a delighted Garo Yepremian.

"Come on, Garo!" one player yelped. "That's almost $100!"

Laakso and I craned our necks and saw that Garo and backup quarterback Don Strock were in the middle of a high-stakes black-jack game. Garo had just cleared the pot, and a few players were loudly protesting from their section of hacked seats.

"If Garo ever invites you to play," I cautioned Laakso, "you ought to make up an excuse to bow out unless you want to pay for his lunch." I elaborated, "Garo always plays the house and almost always wins."

Just then, a very attractive and professionally dressed Eastern Airlines stewardess descended through the aisle. She kindly asked the card players to return the plane to its original configuration with all seats facing forward and buckle up for takeoff. Admirably, the flight attendant remained composed despite the players' resistance. She redirected her attention to distributing drinks and small bags of Planters peanuts.

I took a few bags, rested my head against the seat's cushion, and popped a handful of peanuts into my mouth when—*whoosh!*—three peanuts soared through the air. Then another two! Almost instantly, the projectile peanuts multiplied into hundreds, and the air dark-ened. Several teammates were now engaged in a new game, "Hit the Reporter," with all missiles directed at the journalists.

This tipped the scale. The stewardess became apoplectic. She hid her face behind her hand, covered her head with the inflight magazine, and took refuge in the galley near the bathroom. "Stop! Please stop!" she begged. "We're about to take off."

The writers and broadcasters tried to practice indifference. But when I beaned Ed Plaisted on the top of his noggin, the man had enough. He jumped out of his seat, turned toward the players, and with his fingers balled in a fist, shouted indignantly, "Who did that?" I dipped below the line of sight, downed the rest of my peanuts, and tucked the foil packet into my seat's storage compartment to lose the smoking gun.

We all settled when the pilot began his take-off script. Soon enough, it was wheels up and, by my standards, a good time to feast. I set up our spread, and two nice men from the South, second-year defensive back Charles Cornelius and rookie cornerback Gerald Small, came over and asked about the unfamiliar food.

"What the he' is that?" Cornelius asked with wide eyes.

"Bagels and lox," I explained while licking my fingers clean of cream cheese. "Want to try?"

Small looked confused. He questioned, "Which is the bagel, and which is the lox?"

Appreciating their interest, I walked them through the various items and offered some samples. With mock bravado, Small popped a bite-sized portion of smoked salmon into his mouth. He grinned and asked for more.

Cornelius crimped his nose and tentatively smelled the salted salmon. "It's good," he said after taking a bite. But the scowl on his face indicated that he felt otherwise.

When we landed in Louisiana a couple of hours later, Laakso boasted, "I know all the best places on Bourbon Street. Want me to show you around my college town?"

"Of course!" I took him up on his offer.

But before we left the hotel lobby, Shula swiped at his nose, wagged a finger, and warned, "Don't eat the oysters. If you have a bad one, you'll end up in the hospital with stomach problems."

Coach should have known better. Telling a group of man-children not to do something is the best way to get them to do it. Case in point, Laakso winked at me and whispered, "We'll start by getting raw oysters at Felix's."

Over the next several hours, we scampered from restaurant to restaurant and scarfed down an abundance of food and buckets of beer. We capped it all off with coffee and doughnuts at Café du Monde. As for Coach's big no-no, we ate raw oysters on the half-shell, fried oysters, baked oysters, and chargrilled oysters. Laakso had fun teaching me how to layer an oyster with lemon juice, cocktail sauce, and horseradish on top of a cracker. He also introduced me to the best fried oyster po'boy in town. With our bellies full, we walked the length of Bourbon Street, got into the jazz vibe, watched piano players belt out old-time singalongs, and took in some of the Creole supernatural feel. It was a good time with a great friend.

Laakso and I returned to the hotel for more beers, food, camaraderie, and a few official announcements during Shula's 9:00 p.m. meeting. When we all settled in, I quietly asked my brothers, "Anyone eat the oysters?"

Several looked around. After confirming that no coach was within earshot, they acknowledged that the forbidden fruit was "so damn good."

The next day, we played the Saints and won the game. Just as quickly as we arrived in the Big Easy, we boarded the jet to return home. But for some reason, we sat on the tarmac for an unaccountably long time. I shouted toward the front of the plane and asked Griese if he knew what was causing the holdup. Griese shrugged and said it had something to do with Robbie.

I stared out the plane's window and reflected on the good trip and the great game. Based on my observations, the '78 Dolphins were flush with talent and primed to go far.

Just then, an unbelievable scene unfolded before me. Almost as if it were staged on a movie set, Robbie's limo pulled to a painfully slow stop beside our plane. A chauffeur appeared from stage left and reluctantly opened the back passenger door to reveal a cardinal in full scarlet regalia! I rubbed my eyes when the religious figure bolted from the limo, vigorously fanning his nose as if to ward off an evil smell. The chauffeur then peered into the back seat and, with a disapproving shake of his head, summoned for help.

"Look it! Come 'ere! You gotta see this!" Garo pointed his finger at the tarmac and yelped, "Robbie is shitfaced drunk!"

Over a hundred eyes looked portside and fixated in disbelief at what appeared to be an inebriated Robbie being horizontally carted up the gangway and onto the plane.

"I guess he ate the oysters," Laakso kidded with a wink.

Wheels up. Wheels down. We landed in Miami, and I dashed to my car to get home to my girl. I didn't want to be late. I missed her and wanted to tell her about my New Orleans adventure. But

139

before I could share any news, a beaming Cathy opened the door and greeted me with some news of her own.

"Eddy, guess what?" she said with a glow on her face and a hand on her belly. Before I could answer, Cathy revealed, "I'm pregnant! We're going to have a baby."

Whoa. This time, it was chills of excitement that ran down my spine. In less than nine months, I'd be a dad. The way I saw it, nothing was more important than raising a child. I was all in.

CHAPTER 19

RELEVANCE

"'Bout time you got rid of that piece of shit Karmann Ghia," joked Wayne Moore in his slow Southern drawl as he negotiated his 6-foot-7 frame into the front passenger seat of my new Mercedes-Benz on a carpool ride to Biscayne College. Wayne rubbed at his left knee and continued, "You looked like a canned sardine in that old two-seater."

I smiled and felt pleased that I was commanding a great enough salary with the team to afford a modest upgrade.

"Look at that!" boomed Larry Little when we pulled into his driveway. He complimented with a bright, toothy smile, "Now that's a respectable ride for an NFL player. Well done, Ed."

"Thanks, brother." I glowed at his words.

Little settled his 6-foot-3, 265-pound body into the backseat of my new ride, scratched at his freakishly large lats, and pulled out a pack of Marlboro cigarettes. "Want one?" he asked.

Wayne and I took him up on his offer, and we shot the shit through the smoke while motoring north on the Palmetto Expressway. After discussing family, religion, politics, Shoes, and the season ahead, the subject shifted to Wayne's recent knee injury. With genuine regret, he disclosed that the doctor ordered him to sit out until the next game. My heart broke for my friend, who was desperately trying to play another day. No doubt, his superhuman efforts of days past had come at a price.

Little patted Wayne on his back and, almost as if he were a blood brother, encouraged, "Don't worry, Big Sol. Work with the doc, and you'll be at full speed in no time."

"Thanks, Chick," said Wayne.

Trying to keep things light, I interjected, "Hey, Little. What's this 'Chicken' all about? Are you like Chicken Little and afraid the sky is falling?"

"Ed." Little smacked his knee and roared with exaggerated guttural overtones. "It's a damn lie." He lit another cigarette, rubbed his hands together, and explained, "I did and still do love chicken. And when I was with the Chargers, we played a game in Buffalo. You know, Buffalo is known for their chicken wings, so the night before the game, I got a big bucket of chicken and ate a few pieces."

"Fifty…fifty pieces," chirped Wayne.

"No, Big Sol. It wasn't fifty!" Chicken grumbled.

"Mm-hmm," mocked Wayne.

Little shook his head and finished, "Anyway, that's how I got the name, and it's stayed with me ever since."

Now feeling familiar with these guys, I met Little's eyes in my rear-view mirror and confided, "You know, Chicken, Shula has regularly started me to cover for you and Kuech, but I'm looking for a more permanent gig."

Little laughed and sat tall with well-deserved confidence. "I welcome the competition, but you be dreaming if you think you'd ever take my job."

I was dreaming. Larry Little was one of the best, and the future Hall of Famer wasn't going anywhere. Shula made this perfectly clear a week earlier when he admitted that he would bench neither Little nor Kuech unless things changed.

My second-class status remained prominently on my mind as we proceeded through the '78 season. It wasn't until after our fourth game, when Shula told Wayne to rest his knee, that things really opened for me. Pulling a page out of the '74 season playbook, the coaches had Kuech cover for Wayne at left tackle and had me start at left guard. It was ironic that I got the opportunity I so desperately needed through my good friend's injury.

Fortunately, the Kuechenberg/Newman formula worked very well. For the first time, the masses noticed that I was filling in competently at guard. Various media types sought me out after games for quotes. Fans recognized me outside of my uniform and adorned me with great respect. And numerous charities asked if I'd speak at their events. I made myself available to pretty much any community service organization that asked because I liked doing good.

***

In early November, George Young presented an entertaining and informative scouting report about our upcoming match against the Dallas Cowboys. "Listen up," Young advised with a look in my direction. "The Cowboys' down defensive linemen are like 'ponderous pachyderms,' though their All-Pro defensive tackle Randy White is the exception." Young licked his lips and continued, "White is fast and aggressive. Unless otherwise controlled, he is a major disrupter of offenses around the league. Take my word for it, Newman," Young motioned like he was swinging at a punching bag and concluded, "The guy just doesn't quit."

Fast-forward to a few hours after the game when I had the pleasure of watching the prerecorded match off my Sony Betamax in the comfort of my home. With a big pan of buttery Jiffy Pop and a bottle of beer, I reclined on my cushy brown Barcalounger and listened as the big boys in the broadcasting booth brazenly boasted their bias toward Big DALLAS.

I increased the volume when an announcer introduced a "critical matchup" on the O-line and started talking about—well, I'll be damned—he was talking about me! It went something like this: "We have a key lineup today with Ed Newman, a brand-new entry, and Randy White, 'The Manster.' Let's zero in on a couple of plays and see how this half-man, half-monster Pro Bowler welcomes Newman into the league."

I didn't love how more than five years of NFL play was being boiled down to "a brand-new entry." But I felt a tickle in my belly knowing I'd have the last laugh. I leaned forward as the camera frame zoomed in and featured my televised self getting the jump and gaining six inches of explosive momentum before White could even react. I watched as he went for my shoulder pads, and I ducked low and slammed my face mask into the 4 of his #54 jersey. Like a sledgehammer, my right fist pounded into the left side of White's rib cage. Pow! Pow! Pow! Wow! Wow! Wow! In the now, energy coursed through my veins as I watched our ball carrier slip through the opening I had created and register a first down—right over White.

"Cathy! You got to see this!" I yelled for her to join me in the TV room. I excitedly explained, "The broadcasters keep talking about how Randy White is going to dominate me, and I keep proving them wrong."

I rewound the footage. Together we watched as I manhandled White in that play and several others, giving our quarterback the pass protection he needed and our running backs the space they needed to score. I soared with satisfaction six points at a time because I was becoming relevant in front of millions on national television.

***

But nothing lasts forever, certainly not in the NFL. Football is a game of Russian roulette. Anything can happen on the bounce of a ball. Even with talent and precaution, there's a lot of unpredictable action on the gridiron. Add to that Chaos. Chaos is always lurking, and it reigns supreme in the pros. More playtime means more opportunities to get knocked out, and in a random instant, a lifetime pursuit of success and fame can end—abruptly.

Take our November 20 away game against Houston, when the Oilers' running back Earl Campbell refused to let a loss happen in his house, and he scored two touchdowns with less than five minutes on the clock. The drama could not have been more intense as we had twelve points to post in less than a minute and a half. We marched down the field on a do-or-die mission. If ever there was a time for 110 percent effort, this was it. I pulled my belt in a few notches and resolved to be perfect. The sentiment was shared. Griese tried to pull off a miracle with a "hurry-up offense," calling audibles on the run. We scrambled as the seconds ticked away.

Falling back into pass protection, I focused on stopping the Oilers' linebacker Gregg Bingham if he blitzed. But Bingham smelled the pass and pivoted into coverage. I turned to help Kuech, who was fighting Elvin Bethea, a tough and savvy All-Pro defensive end. Bethea sensed my double team from the inside and ran outside. I then turned to assist Langer, who had his hands full with nose tackle Curley Culp. That's when Bethea unexpectedly changed direction and advanced inside toward Griese. Bethea's sudden shift collapsed Kuech. His body arched, stumbled and—*shit!*—crashed can first onto the fleshy part of my left calf.

POP! It was as loud as a cherry bomb. While adrenaline masked the pain, I knew I was seriously hurt because a healthy knee bends only front to back, though mine had the otherworldly power of moving left to right. Instantly, the sweat beading off my body increased tenfold.

With worried eyes, I looked at Little and saw that he was also on the ground, moaning in pain, asking for help off the field with a twisted and hyperextended ankle. The timing could not have been worse. The Dolphins were down two guards in one play.

I knew I should call for help. But with an extreme desire to win and the real fear that no backup guards were available to sub in, I decided to gut it out. *Only a few seconds to go,* I coaxed myself. *Play today. Heal tomorrow.* In my mind, this was the most important game ever. I would not let my team down.

As I stood on the field and watched 265 pounds of Curley Culp come my way, I thought, *This is insane. Nobody plays on a busted knee.* Still, I hid my injury and favored my good leg. I hoped for pass protections because, with my superior upper body strength, I could at least assist Griese. But if Griese called a run play, or if I needed to do a pull, a sweep, a screen, or a trap—then, well, I'd have to excuse myself because any amount of lateral stress would tear the connective tissue of my knee to shreds.

Somehow I managed to stay in through the end of the game, which we lost. After the final whistle warbled, I ambled to Dr. Herbert Virgin, pretending as if nothing was wrong. Dr. Virgin sat me down and manipulated my left knee joint. Trying to be gentle, he confirmed that my medial collateral ligament had ruptured and needed to be operated on.

I kept to myself on the flight back to Miami. Wrapped in silence and several ice packs, I didn't want to face reality. When I got home in the middle of the night, I told Cathy I was seriously injured. Cathy patted me on my shoulder, and in a semi-dream state, she softly said, "It's okay, honey. Take two aspirins, and you'll be fine in the morning."

Oh, how I wished that were the case. As I lay in bed, I thought about how things were just starting to get good. I was finally getting into my groove and gaining prestige. But now…I wallowed in the reality of how quickly relevance fades. Nobody would remember me if this was it. While I hated the negative thinking, it was very hard to remain optimistic.

CHAPTER 20

THE WARRIOR'S WAY

In a swirl, my consciousness flickered. *Where am I? What's going on? Oh, that's right. My knee...the surgery.* As I lay in my post-op recovery room, under the bright fluorescent lights, I tried to focus on my mended limb. All I could feel was a dull pain on the right side of my left knee. *Not too bad.* But when my eyes scanned the length of my body, they were startled to find an oversized plaster of Paris cast, swallowing my leg from hip to toe. *Whoa.* The sheer size of the monster would present some problems.

I tried to contort within the narrow restraints, just the slightest amount to stretch the tissues and see how they felt, when—*OH MY GOD!*—my eyes shot open wide like saucers. That minuscule movement generated the most severe and sustained stabs of pain I had ever felt. *OH MY!* The intense pain cascaded out of control. It brought me to the verge of panic just as Dr. Charles Virgin appeared in my hospital room and mercifully jabbed a dose of morphine into my IV line. "That will help," he assured.

Ahhhhhhhhhhhhhhhhhhh. The opioid provided instant relief, followed by a dopey head. "Hoa looon?" I drunkenly garbled with my finger pointing toward the cast.

Dr. Virgin hesitated. He explained how he had reattached the ruptured ends of my medial collateral ligament and how my tissues were especially vulnerable during this recovery time. "That's why," he finally answered, "you need to be off that leg for eight weeks."

Eight weeks? My eyes rolled. I had responsibilities. A new house, a new car, a baby on the way. How could I sit out for eight weeks? The whole thing was unbelievable, especially when just forty-eight hours earlier, I was at the top of my game, feeling invincible as I expertly coordinated with my O-line brothers to pound the Oilers defense. But now I couldn't even get out of bed to pee. Worst of all, I'd be relegated to the Injured Reserve (IR) roster for the remaining four games of the season. It was so depressing.

Fighting distress, I promised myself that this was not the beginning of my end. Instead, I began to contemplate a recovery plan. I'd lift weights. I'd work my core. I'd—and then that opioid that Dr. Virgin had administered slowed me down. I lost my train of thought and fell asleep.

***

"The body wants to maintain its symmetry," explained Lundy when I asked for advice on how to best bounce back. Our team trainer expounded, "If you work the rest of your muscles, especially your good leg, like there's no tomorrow, the power in your surgically repaired knee will snap right back once that cast comes off."

I looked around and motioned over to the team's stationary bike and asked Lundy if he'd help me get set up. Lundy appeared surprised. "Sure." He sucked in a big gulp of air and confirmed, "You want to bike with one leg?" When I affirmed, he studied the apparatus and declared, "All right. We'll make it work with some athletic tape." Lundy escorted me to the bike and secured my casted leg onto the steering column with the adhesive.

After enduring a painful hour of single-leg cycling, I shouted to Lundy to cut me loose. Next up were hundreds of sit-ups and leg raises, followed by my time-tested routine of shock week. I took everything in stride, but I was hurting badly about ninety minutes in when Sandusky peeked his head into the weight room and incredulously asked, "What are you doing here, Newman? You just had surgery!"

When I explained my plan to rebound quickly, Sandusky gave me a skeptical look and asked if I could talk. I followed him to his office, where a 16 mm film projector loaded with the Houston game reel sat on his desk. "It doesn't make sense." Sandusky scratched the back of his head and expanded, "I've looked at the footage dozens of times. You played until the end of the game. Wh…where did you get hurt?" he sputtered in frustration.

I opened my mouth to explain, but Sandusky raised his hand and instructed, "Just show me." He cut the lights and cued the film to the last few seconds of the match.

"Rewind a few plays," I directed.

Sandusky puffed a little air out of his fleshy cheeks, fiddled with the forward/backward switch, and advanced the footage to a minute earlier. Together, we watched the low-grade film.

"There! Right there." I pointed to the mishap involving Bethea and Kuech, describing the trauma as it occurred.

Sandusky's jaw dropped. "But you got up! You don't look injured."

I assured him that that was the moment.

"Why did you do that?" Sandusky stammered with genuine dismay. "You should have come out right then!" Sandusky pounded his desk in anger and raised his voice, "Your knee was blown out, for Christ's sake!"

I tried to explain that I stayed in for the good of the team.

"You can't do that!" An exasperated Sandusky shook his head. "You've got to protect your health. By staying in, you risked permanently ruining your knee. I wouldn't ask that of anybody."

Coach Sandusky was right. But I was a warrior. This was the warrior's way. I would quit only if it were for the good of the team, and at that moment, staying in seemed like the best course of action.

***

I sat in the mini stands on a hot December day and watched the team practice alongside Dolphins' publicist Charlie Callahan. Desperate for distraction as a quart of perspiration accumulated in my itchy cast, I asked Callahan about an upcoming interview. With the mild scent of Scope still lingering on his breath, the seventy-year-old chronic alcoholic muttered a few indecipherable words. He retrieved a white handkerchief from his pocket, wiped the beading sweat from his pasty, parchment-like skin, and scribbled a few notes into his little black book. He then stared into the distance, and we sat silently for a while.

"—Ha gaaaah um um," Callahan started sputtering nonsense. His body convulsed. His eyes rolled back, and he began to choke on his tongue.

I reached for Callahan. Despite my overwhelming desire to assist him, I couldn't because my ginormous waterlogged cast acted like an anchor and made it impossible for me to move quickly within the confines of the bleachers. It was horrible. I felt deficient, incredibly impotent in this critical moment. "HELP!" I screamed at the top of my lungs for our team trainer. "HELP! Lundy! Please!"

Lundy darted over with his medical kit. He used a nylon screw to lever Callahan's top and bottom jaw apart, preventing him from biting his tongue off before the ambulance arrived. It was later conveyed that Callahan had suffered an alcohol-induced seizure.

The whole thing freaked me out. I hated how I couldn't do more for someone who was in such a state of distress. It caused me to think about my life differently. I considered something Dad regularly said: "A successful life is one that leaves the world a better place." I wondered, How successful was my life when measured by these standards?

I made a list of all my do-good efforts. This included each charity, fundraiser, and televised experience I engaged in. While it amounted to much time and effort, it no longer seemed sufficient. At that moment, I vowed to use my celebrity status to make a more significant impact on the world.

***

Back on the gridiron, I felt insecure as my teammates won game after game. While they celebrated their admittance into the '78 season playoffs, I moped around because my IR routine was less than exciting. All I could do was stay out of the way because sitting there, in that awkward cast, made me a living symbol of vulnerability.

And then finally, it was eight weeks post-op. Dr. Herbert Virgin arrived at the Dolphins' training room with a saw in hand. *Bzzzzzzzzzzzz!* Puffs of white powder mingled with the most putrid, tear-inducing stench you can imagine as he split my cast open and unveiled my surgically repaired limb. *Oh no.* I was mortified by the skeletal leg resting on the examination table.

Dr. Virgin saw the fear in my eyes. He assured, "The atrophy will pass, and your leg musculature will increase by 50 percent when it gets a little blood flowing through it." Moments later, he wrapped his hands around my arm and prompted me to bear the total weight of my body onto my repaired knee. "Ready to give it a go?" he asked.

With butterflies in my belly, I looked over the red vinyl bench toward the floor and felt like a novice skydiver, hanging out the side of an airplane, with legs dangling ten thousand feet above the ground, hoping the chute would open. I slowly shifted my weight forward and brought my feet to the ground. *Oh my God.* I felt unsteady and in pain. Instantly, a terrible nightmare flashed before me that I'd never be able to walk correctly again.

"Doc, I'm all locked up," I begged for an explanation.

Dr. Virgin pinched his lips and explained how several adhesions had formed while I was in the cast. "You need to break them," he stated. "That's the only way to regain full mobility." With a slight frown, he added, "It'll be painful, but with effort, you'll get it done."

With the '79 preseason less than six months away, I had no time to waste. I wobbled over to the team's Jacuzzi, where I cranked up the water temperature to just north of bearable and immersed myself, hip down. In the near-scalding tub, I did thousands of leg extensions and contractions. The heat and repetition outlasted the discomfort, and I started to break through the adhesions.

A daily pattern was established. Before long, the tissues were healing, and I was getting stronger and increasing my range of motion. I began to walk hundreds of laps in the pool. I commenced roadwork and engaged in full-body weightlifting workouts. I repeatedly pushed through the pain because I knew I couldn't make excuses in the NFL—not when survival went to the fittest.

***

Cathy awoke me with a jab in the middle of the night in late March because we needed to get to the hospital—this time, for a very happy reason. "The baby is coming!" she urged. Through heavy eyelids, I rushed my wife to Mercy Hospital.

When we got to the waiting room, I thought about my child and the person he or she would become. While I had never told Cathy this, I hoped for a daughter because I feared the dilemma any son of mine would face. I didn't want him to feel pressured to meet the athletic standards I set. I didn't want him to risk perpetual injury as I did. I'd encourage him to follow his own path, whatever it may be.

Three and a half hours later, the doctor announced, "It's a girl!"

A girl? A girl! I had a daughter, not a son. Delight overcame me. I felt most blessed to have a healthy child—a perfect eight-pound, eight-ounce Stephani Anne. As I uneasily ambled to meet my baby, I dreamed about her future. I promised myself I'd do everything possible to make her dreams come true. Instantly, my resolve to rebound skyrocketed. Becoming a father was just the elixir I needed to kick my ass into high gear.

CHAPTER 21

GOT MAN

The great circle had run its course, and I hearkened to Shula's call for my seventh campaign to make the team as a starting guard in July of '79. I crossed Biscayne College's half-full parking lot and felt confident that I was strong, steady, and structurally sound. But I wasn't naive. I knew there was danger with every step in the NFL. Most opponents looked for weakness—like a vulnerable knee—to gain an edge. Others hurt just to hurt. Even the coaches rewarded ferocious hits and doled out instructions to "get your man" at all costs. With Chaos thriving in this brutal context, I had to protect myself. Lost in my thoughts, I turned into the locker room, where a familiar voice snapped me back.

"—ENOUGH! Out with this old, disgusting couch!" ranted friend and former teammate Larry Csonka while glaring at that same crappy, brown sofa that had been there ever since my rookie year. The corners of my lips turned upward. *Zonk's back!* After one season with the WFL and three with the Giants, Csonka had returned home. Lucky for us, the shining star was synonymous with success.

"Hi, Zonk," I interrupted. "Welcome back, brother."

"Oh, hey, Snookums," Csonka replied with a quick look from the couch to me. "It's good to be back. But man…this piece-of-shit couch." Csonka pinched his severely crooked nose and emphasized, "It reeks so bad. Why hasn't Robbie replaced the goddamn thing? It's covered in the sweat of over ten thousand naked asses, for Christ's sake."

I scanned the low-rent locker room. Outside of the individual metal folding chairs in front of each player's locker, that filthy couch, with its unwashed cloth, was the only place to sit. It really was time for Robbie to spruce things up.

But that was a matter for another day because Shula made it clear that talent assessment was top of mind. Naturally, I considered my competition. Kuech and Little were so damn durable, but I hoped that with Wayne Moore's recent retirement, the coaches would start me at left guard, with Kuech at left tackle, just as they had done before my injury. However, versatility and depth on the O-line would impact everything. For example, rookie offensive tackles Cleveland Green and Jon Giesler were turning heads. Either one could take the start. It was also hard to overlook the fact that the Dolphins had dedicated their second-round draft pick to offensive guard Jeff Toews, who seemed to have a little bear blood coursing through his veins. But I wasn't going to let that distract me. I mean, sure, Toews was a heck of a lot younger; and sure, he came to camp with sound knees, but…*that damn rookie don't know shit.*

Naturally, Toews viewed me as his primary rival. He started to size me up. One day, he followed me into the weight room and asked if we could work out together. "Holy shit," he muttered under his breath when I loaded four hundred pounds onto the bar and punched out eight reps as if it was nothing.

Come Toews's turn, he rubbed at the stubble on his chin and took his position. With red face and bulging veins, he strained to complete a single four-hundred-pound rep. Despite his admirable can-do attitude, the guy couldn't muster enough strength. With a spot for safety, he returned the bar to the rack and removed a few plates before pressing a more manageable load.

I respected the young tiger's gumption and invited him to join Laakso and me for buckets of beer. To my astonishment, the rookie entered the rather casual watering hole sporting a pair of James Dean jeans and a remarkably badass leather motorcycle jacket adorned with logos on the back and all the studs and trimmings.

"Damn skippy! That's some outfit," Laakso chuckled. "Where are your regular shorts?" Laakso was referring to a pair of beat-up, military-grade, high-utility Navy Seal shorts that Toews wore every day outside of practice.

Toews deflected, suggesting we get some brew. Holy crap, the rookie drank like a fish. He cussed and bitched about how Shoes forbade him from riding his Harley Davidson. With beer loosening his tongue, Toews slurred, "Dis fine fer 'conduct detrimental' is bullshit." He continued, "I shou' be able to ri' my fuckin' hog anytime I fuckin' wan'."

I was amused. On the field, Toews seemed innocent and reserved. But here, he was acting like an eccentric juvenile—loud, loopy, and like a lush! I concluded that the guy liked to work hard and play hard. No matter. I could support him if he performed on the gridiron.

***

Several players dragged their hungover asses into the locker room after our first night off. Don Strock was holding his head, nursing a hangover after lighting up the town with '78-season tight end entrant Bruce Hardy. Bob Baumhower, A. J. Duhe, and Kim Bokamper were boasting about their wild South Florida party pursuits. Running back Delvin Williams was telling rookie talent Tony "TNT" Nathan that he should "go running with him" and check out a raging nightclub the following week. And Laakso was rubbing at a swollen knot on his forehead that he had earned from taking a nosedive into the edge of a table after one libation too many.

With sleep in his eyes and beer on his breath, Kuech pointed toward a new beige sofa that had magically appeared in the same spot as that old shitty one and exclaimed, "Well, look at that!" He walked over to the sofa and gave a little bounce to its springs.

"Yeah, a new couch," Langer said as he sat next to Kuech and ran his hand over the clean, odor-free fabric. "Zonk had it delivered this morning and asked a few of us to throw the old one into the dumpster. If it were up to me," Langer said with a finger raised, "I would have torched the thing."

"Langer, you just gave me an idea!" Kuech tittered. "Come on, Mushrooms, giddy up." Kuech waved his arms inward, summoning the rest of the O-line to gather.

Laakso, Little, Giesler, Green, Toews, and I circled Kuech and Langer.

"Ahem," Kuech cleared his throat. "You all see that Zonk got rid of that stinky couch." He looked at Toews with a mischievous smile and stated, "Now it's time for our rookie to lose those stinky shorts."

Toews's attention snapped. He raised his hand, and with his face blanching and increasing agitation, he protested, "Not these! Don't you fuckin' touch them! They're my lucky shorts."

Langer arched an eyebrow at Kuech, who subtly nodded and changed the subject. Now directing his attention at Laakso, Kuech referenced the *Saturday Night Live* character played by Dan Aykroyd, who had a deformed head, and said, "And we got 'Conehead' over here. What happened last night?"

Laakso leaned forward, and with a spark in his eye, he launched into his tale. "Let me tell you…"

Our meeting adjourned when the Turk shouted from the hallway that hitting practice would begin in thirty minutes. Dowe distributed protective gear to the rookies, and Lundy took me to get fitted for a state-of-the-art knee brace.

***

"Line up!" ordered Coach Sandusky bright and early the next day. "It's time for the Oklahoma drill." Our assembly of eager and rugged linemen stared at the field with game faces on, waiting for the annual alpha dog test to begin. With a look at my knee brace,

Coach Sandusky said, "Okay, Newman, you're first. Get in there and get your man."

As I walked to the center of the field, it occurred to me that the coaches would want to see how Newman, with his surgically repaired knee, would show in the pass protection drill. I rolled my shoulders, wrung my hands, and waited for our defensive line coach, Mike "Mo" Scarry, to select my counterpart. Mo pinched the stubble on his chin, considered his corral, and designated '78-season entrant, defensive end Doug Betters, to square off against me.

As the super-strong, phenomenally talented 6-foot-7 Star Wars Wookiee-like giant with freakishly long arms and an overgrown auburn beard took his spot opposite me, I got quiet and focused. Betters's objective was to touch an orange traffic cone positioned seven yards behind me. Mine was to prevent him from doing that for four long seconds. At stake was the approval of others, the validation of the coaches, and equally, if not more important, my pride and confidence that I could hold up in the heat of battle.

To the noise of our teammates chanting "Snookums!" and "Chewbacca!" Sandusky barked, "Set!" The din settled. Betters and I took our stances. Not wanting to face the emotional baggage of battling a friend, I mentally transformed Betters into a 270-pound automaton.

"On two. Hut, hut!" Sandusky said and snapped the ball.

I leaped backward and noted that my knee felt good. *Yes!* Betters exploded forward like a charging bull. Our helmets collided. Bright lights flashed, and my entire frame absorbed the collision. For half a second, we were at a stalemate. *My knee still feels good.*

"Three!" Sandusky screamed.

No more than three yards from the target cone, Betters tried to accelerate his assault. He thrust his body forward. But I wouldn't let him. *WHACK! SMACK!* I delivered a neutralizing one-two punch into Betters's ribs and armpit just as Sandusky howled, "FOUR! TIME!"

Betters threw his arms up in defeat. Cheers erupted from the O-line as I sauntered offstage, smiling brightly and feeling great. Well, I felt great except for that pounding headache that Betters had left me as a parting souvenir.

157

Next up was Duhe against Toews. Duhe's chatter slanted toward taunting as he teased, "You ain't gonna stop me, rookie." Toews tightened for the assault. But with fancy arm work and a swimming-like motion, Duhe got to the cone before the deadline. Advantage, defense.

"It's okay, buddy," Conehead encouraged Toews as he kowtowed to the sidelines.

And so went the dance. The Oklahoma drill was as violent as it got. It was like getting hit in the head at full force by a two-by-four multiple times. Players and coaches kept score as man pounded man in this pitiless dogfight.

After several rounds, the competition ended. My score: 4 up, 0 down. Knee: A-OK. I felt exhilarated because, at least in the contrived context of the drill, I had established I was back in business.

Once practice wrapped, I trotted to the locker room to cool down. As I rounded the corner and passed Csonka regally lounging on the replacement couch, I sniffed a new scent. *Smoke? Is that smoke?* I hastily scouted the locker room for the source.

That's when I saw Kuech holding some lighter fluid in one hand and Toews's redolent shorts in the other. With a naughty look on his face, he lit the trunks and thrust them into a metal trash can in front of a greatly amused Langer. *Shit.* I shook my head. This wasn't going to be received well.

Next thing—*whoosh!* Toews rushed in from the field and pushed through the growing crowd of bystanders. Desperate to save his favorite threads, the rookie frantically reached his bare fingers into the flames and flung the fiery shorts to the floor. As red embers crisped the seams, he furiously stomped them out.

But it was too late. Toews's trunks were toast. Kuech and Langer got their man. And Toews—well, he absolutely lost it. The vulnerable rookie fell to the floor and fumed. When the crowd cleared, I remained back because I wanted to make sure that he landed on his feet.

CHAPTER 22

THE CRAZY

The intensity of Toews's reaction gave me pause. This was not just about singed shorts. No. This was about the entire NFL rookie experience. Toews was going mental over the hazing, the constant challenge from rough-hewed players, the stress of a hostile and demanding Shula, and the roster cuts that kept on coming. He was also suffering the unsettling adventure of finding his way in a new town with no support system and no familiar place to kick back and regroup.

I understood what Toews was going through because six seasons earlier, I stood in his shoes and endured my own NFL indoctrination. It was a turbulent, unstable, and dangerous time. Heck, there were moments when I felt like the trauma was too great to bear. Now, perceiving that the rookie was in one of those moments himself, I took a lighter tone and suggested he get showered and grab a spare pair of shorts so we could grub together.

Over lunch, a sullen Toews mushed around his food and barely spoke. Eventually, he looked up from his plate and asked with a pleading expression, "How do you manage to survive this place?"

This was a serious question that deserved a serious answer. I met Toews's eyes and told him, "You need to find a way that works for you to deal with the pain and bullshit. If you do, you'll be better for it. And if you don't," I counseled, "you're in the wrong business."

"Bu...but...," Toews stuttered, "I warned those fuckin' assholes not to touch my shorts. They outright disrespected me."

"Enough, rookie!" I raised my voice. "Forget about those damn shorts. They have no relative importance. You can't dwell on superstitious bullshit like that." I ran the tips of my fingers over the large bumpy keloid scar that endured at the base of my neck and shared, "You know, Jeff, shit happens—shit like cancer. Cancer is real. Not burnt shorts."

Toews got quiet. He gnawed at his cuticles and confided, "I hear ya, but this place is a madhouse. It's nothing like what I expected." He looked at me with such sadness in his eyes and said, "I just don't know how to deal with all the crazy."

I meditated on this. Toews was right. Many things could throw a guy off-kilter in the NFL. Beyond the aggression, violence, and brutality, there was substantial pressure coming from the coaches, the fans, and the media. Numerous nefarious forces—like drugs, bookies, con artists, and gold diggers—also tempted the vulnerable to go to the dark side. I interlaced my fingers and considered how I coped with it all. Then in nearly a whisper, I revealed, "Cathy. Thank God I have her." Speaking more plainly, I explained, "My wife is the key for me. Cathy has kept me from going off my rocker more than once." Toews cracked a smile for the first time and shared how he also had a girl named Kathy.

As preseason waned into the regular season, I noticed that Toews was going through some sort of religious transition. At first, it was subtle. He stopped cussing and put away his leather jacket. But then, it became more apparent when he declined offers for beer at the bar to join his Kathy at Bible study. He even encouraged me to come along. And while I thanked him for the invitation, I declined, explaining that I was Jewish.

"You're Jewish? I had no clue!" Toews looked me up and down with interest piqued and inquired, "What does it mean to be Jewish?"

I responded with a few details about my religious upbringing and explained how I looked to the Jewish tenets for guidance on how to live a better life. I then shared that while I wasn't particularly religious, I was proud to be Jewish.

"But...um...what about Christ?" Toews asked with a furrowed brow.

I answered my truth, "Jesus was an exemplary man. His virtues are worthy of following. But personally, I don't see him as the son of God or the Messiah."

Toews looked pained at this. He asked, "Haven't you seen our fans waving John 3:16 signs during games?" Before I affirmed, Toews recited the psalm verbatim:

"For God so loved the world that he gave his one and only Son, that whoever believes in him shall not perish but have eternal life." With genuine concern, Toews stated, "Do you understand what's at stake here? It's eternal life!" He urged, "Ed, you've got to join me at Bible study so you can learn about eternal life."

I declined Toews's offer and tried to establish some common ground. "When you think about it, Jeff, the moral objectives for Jews and Christians are identical. We all want to live good and virtuous lives."

"But, Ed"—Toews raised his hands as if he were appealing to the Lord and exclaimed—"it's important! You've got to believe. If not"— he looked so worried for me—"if not, then your soul is doomed."

I knew Toews's words weren't mean-spirited or meant to hurt. It was evident that my friend cared about me and was genuinely worried for my soul. But still, we had arrived at a delicate crossroads that could not be smoothed over, so I dropped the subject. Toews, however, persisted by quoting a few sections of the Hebrew Bible.

"Jeff," I countered, "religious figures have been debating this for centuries. Each side is convinced they're right. The truth is, we all see things differently, and that's okay. Come on, man," I encouraged, "let's agree to disagree."

Toews let it go. But a few days later, he approached me in the locker room with a new idea. "I discussed your situation with my minister, and he suggested you become a 'Jew for Jesus.' This way,"

Toews happily concluded, "you can keep your faith and avoid going to hell."

My face fell. *Please! I do not need saving.* I ran my hands through my hair and closed my eyes tight. This conversation needed to stop.

Sensing my extreme irritation, Toews shifted his tactic and delicately warned, "You're my friend. I really want you to go to heaven because that's where I'll be with the other believers."

I slowed my breath to keep my cool and replied, "While I thank you for your concern, Jeff, you don't get to say whether or not I'm going to heaven."

"But, Ed," Toews interrupted.

"No!" I cut him off. "I'm a good person. I'm fairly confident that heaven is where I'll end up." I couldn't believe how this conversation was turning.

An exasperated Toews scanned the locker room for help. He found it in another rookie, a Christian fundamentalist, who reaffirmed the exclusionary rule in a cold, authoritative tone. "Jeff is right," the guy deplored. "If you don't believe in Christ, you're going straight to hell."

Straight to hell? The line had been crossed. I was a good person with laudable values. I ran my ass around South Florida to give back to the community. I didn't mess with drugs. I respected my wife. I led by example. But here, a rookie was telling me I'd end up in hell solely because of my religious beliefs. Damping my ire, I leaned on logic and tried to test Toews's buddy. I asked, "You mean that people like Aristotle, Einstein, Mahatma Gandhi, and Moses are all in hell?"

"Exactly," the guy intractably responded. "You're either with Christ, or you're with the devil."

Seeing that several others were now gawking at the escalating scene, Toews tried to nip the conversation. But another rookie, this one a placekicker of German descent, ignorantly picked at the scab and cackled in an eccentrically high voice, "It's too bad Hitler didn't put all the Jews into the gas chambers when he had the chance."

I couldn't believe the fool was so cavalier about the massacre of six million Jews. Now blinded by rage, I crowded into the placekicker's personal space, and with fists clenched, I growled, "Never say that again in my presence."

The guy lowered his gaze and begged off, stating that it was "just a joke."

"A bad one," I bristled.

Witnessing the whole thing, Tony Nathan, a pretty righteous fellow himself, intervened in a slow Southern drawl. "All right, let's settle down. We can't let differences like these interfere with our success on the field."

A few others seconded Tony's sentiment. Recently acquired linebacker Ralph Ortega cooled the temperatures by telling a "priest, a minister, and a rabbi walk into a bar" type of joke. At this, the ignorant placekicker scurried off. The Christian fundamentalist clammed up, and the others went on their way. As for Toews, he awkwardly lingered to apologize. Perhaps somewhere deep inside, my friend realized that the overt anti-Semitism he had just stirred was one source of my NFL crazy.

"Let it go, Jeff," I responded. "It's time to move on." I said this because, like those damn shorts, it wasn't worth the drama. I wouldn't let hate slow me down, especially when another game was around the corner. Still, I was secretly shaken. To be clear, I wasn't mad at Toews. He was a good guy, and his role was innocent enough. He just got the ball rolling, and the others carried it too far forward. But now that it was over, all I wanted to do was get home and see my girls.

Thirty minutes later, I walked through the front door and heard Cathy softly singing "Where Is Love" from the musical *Oliver!* to our baby girl. *Heaven.* My heart melted. I tiptoed to the nursery and found Stephani cuddled in Cathy's arms. I poked my head in for a kiss, and our six-month-old looked up from her bottle, cooed, and reached for my face. Her delicate small hands softly grazed my cheek. She was so sweet, innocent, and loving—such a counterbalance to the bare knuckles and knuckleheads I braved daily. I felt deep gratitude for my blessings. Cathy and Stephani were my antidotes to the crazy. They were what I needed to deal with the pain and bullshit. And without them, it would have been much harder for me to endure.

CHAPTER 23

PURPLE PATCH

My waiting days were over when Shula converted Kuech to left tackle and started me at left guard for the '79 season. Eager to take control of my destiny, I treated every game like a Super Bowl. With Kuechenberg on my left and projected Hall of Fame center Jim Langer on my right, it wasn't too hard to pave the way for Griese and Csonka to light up the board.

By November 29, the 8–5 Miami Dolphins could visualize a path to the playoffs. But it was a crowded race at the finish line. We needed to get past our divisional adversary, the also 8–5 New England Patriots, to win the battle. This challenge was accentuated by an injured Langer, subbed by Mark Dennard, and the assumption that our thirteen-year veteran quarterback, Bob Griese, was too old to get it done.

It was a cool Thursday night under the bright lights in Miami's weathered Orange Bowl when our supercharged fans stomped their feet so hard that the old lady dropped a few concrete blocks from the rafters near our tunnel. I told Dennard that he better keep his helmet on as we returned to the field after halftime.

On a mission to come back from behind, we received the kick-off and found ourselves in a third-and-twelve situation, where a just subbed-in Griese turned to Tony Nathan and said, "Pull this in and get the first down."

Tony responded with a slow nod.

Griese continued, "Seventy halfback short option. On two. Let's break."

As we walked toward the ball, Kuech said under his breath, "Keep your eye on Lunsford, Ed. He's fast as a cat and can turn the corner quickly. I'll shade him to the outside. But you got to be alert if he decides to slant in."

"Yup," I said.

I took my stance on the line with feet shoulder-width apart, my right foot two inches behind my left, my left forearm on my left thigh, and my right hand extended to the ground, holding myself in a balanced, horizontal position. I swiveled my head from left to right to assess my adversaries while shouting some misleading information to confuse Mel Lunsford, the Patriots' defensive end.

"Set! Hut, hut!" Griese went through the snap count, and Dennard slapped the ball right into our quarterback's waiting hands. Griese masterfully motioned like he was going to hand off to Tony. But Tony ran past the offensive tackle into the secondary, where there were no defenders. I, meanwhile, looked toward the Patriots' perennial All-Pro linebacker Steve Nelson and confirmed he wasn't blitzing. I then turned to Dennard and noted that he had the Patriots' strong-as-a-bear nose tackle Ray Hamilton neutralized. *Good.* I followed that with a glance to Kuech and saw that Lunsford was indeed pressing the edge of the pocket. Kuech needed my help.

Ed Newman pass protects for Bob Griese (−1979)

Photo credit: Miami Dolphins

My anxiety increased, knowing it was going to be close. I had to intercept Lunsford without interfering with Griese. I picked my knees up high, charged four yards, and rammed my shoulder into Kuech's back, transferring double the energy into Lunsford. Thank you very much. The defensive end teetered on a tangent upfield, giving Griese the split second he needed to connect with Nathan. *First down! Momentum change.* The Dolphins completed the drive with a score, and we re-established our dominance.

In the myopic lens of only football, it was a wonderful time. Miami was paradise, and the Dolphins were dynamite. However, a storm in the background clouded the skies. On December 21, 1979, a week after our last regular-season game, four Miami police officers brutally beat black motorcyclist Arthur McDuffie to death on a routine traffic stop. The whole episode was captured on film and repeatedly displayed on the evening news between features of the playoff-bound Miami Dolphins. Tensions rose, and whispers of riots were in the air. But the upcoming game in Pittsburgh seemed to distract the fans, and peace prevailed—at least for the moment.

***

"How's the knee?" inquired Dr. Charles Virgin during my end-of-year medical evaluation after we lost to Pittsburgh. I rubbed at the zipper-like scar running seven inches down the medial side of my left knee and divulged that it hurt a little. "Let's look into that," suggested Dr. Virgin, who called for the technician to take me for x-ray imaging.

As we waited for the tech to arrive, I engaged the doctor about some literature the NFLPA had recently sent, suggesting a correlation between concussions and brain damage. I explained to the doctor that while most didn't think there was much to it, I wasn't so sure.

"What do you think?" I asked.

Dr. Virgin's eyebrows knitted in consternation, and his skin appeared a little whiter than usual as he considered the taboo subject. He got up from his chair, closed the door, and asked in a low voice, "Do you think you have any mental deficits as a result of playing football?"

Me? I recoiled in surprise. I wasn't talking about me! As far as I knew, my brain was totally healthy. I chose my words carefully, almost a little defensively, and said, "No, I'm not experiencing any cognitive issues. Though," I added, "I have my doubts about a couple of the others." I explained how some occasionally went off in a stare, others mumbled nonsense, and a few acted eccentrically wild without cause. My mind flashed to the terrible headaches I suffered each preseason after the Oklahoma drill and stated, "I wouldn't be surprised if all the hitting was taking a toll on some."

The good doctor thinned his lips and confided that he was on the lookout for telltale signs of brain injury. "You've got to be careful, Ed," Dr. Virgin cautioned, "especially with those shots to the temple because head trauma is known to lead to transient brain bleeds and inflammation." Dr. Virgin expanded, "What we don't know is how deep the damage runs." He lowered his voice to almost a whisper and concluded, "There are some studies underway, but until it is proven otherwise, the league will promote NFL football as 'healthy and wholesome.'"

I nodded, and we left the discussion there.

***

"Have you ever thought about using your reputation as the strongest guy on the team to run a business?" asked Alan Wilhelm, the head coach of the charitable Miami Dolphins Basketball Team, at an offseason charity event. The frail man, who remarkably persisted through the handicaps of cerebral palsy, excitedly elaborated, "Because I'd like to open a training center with you, Ed!" Alan managed to face me square on and proposed, "We could call it 'Ed Newman's Fitness Center.'"

I considered the prospect. Alan was a nice man, a good friend of the team, and a go-getter who had the requisite gumption to get it done. His idea was also appealing, but it felt a little too fuzzy to grab my interest. Even so, it reminded me of my desire to use my growing celebrity to do more good in the community.

I contacted Bob Kearney, the Miami Dolphins' Public Relations Director, to solicit his support in connecting me with a worthwhile cause. Kearney was very good at his job. He made a few calls and put me in touch with Dr. Peter Tomasulo, the CEO of the South Florida Blood Service, and their director of public relations, Pam Gadinsky, to discuss a major marketing campaign coined "The Ed Newman Challenge." As described, the campaign would substantially increase the collection of blood donations across South Florida, beginning with eighteen-year-old high schoolers at the start of the 1980 football season. If successful, it would expand into the corporate community.

I was thrilled. This was everything I wanted. By engaging in this charity, I'd make a big difference and play a direct role in saving lives. But the plan hinged on me returning to the team, and that wouldn't happen until I had a satisfactory contract. I shifted gears to get that sorted out.

Back in 1977, I had fought for a contract clause that empowered me to void my fourth and final year of a multi-year contract if I had a stellar season in '79. Serendipitously, I had a terrific year and could now execute that option. Knowing that the Dolphins would fight like hell to keep my compensation low, I asked my brother-in-law Andy to represent me in the negotiations.

"God damn it, Newman! What are you doing?" an irate Shula barged into the weight room after Andy sent the team a certified letter stating my interest to reopen negotiations. Coach swiped at his nose, squinted his eyes, and elucidated, "We consider trades, draft picks, and salary caps year over year. And now, you're asking to advance your contract's expiration date?" Coach glared at me. "This God damn maneuver is screwing up my plans!"

I stared at Shula. Hadn't he repeatedly told me that he didn't get involved in the minutiae of contract negotiations? Wasn't that what Pat Peppler or George Young were there for? And now he was interrupting my workout and yelling at me because I was trying to get paid for the value I brought to the team. My nostrils flared, yet I said not a word. Shula waited for a reaction but stormed off when I gave him nothing.

A few weeks later, Andy and I met with the team's new director of player personnel, William Stonewall, at a neutral location away from Biscayne College and laid out our terms. The diminutive Stonewall dispassionately opened, "You're not as good as you think you are." I rolled my eyes. *Heard that before.* But when Stonewall added, "You're pricing yourself out of the market," Andy and I countered with actual compensation data that proved him wrong.

An unruffled Stonewall rubbed at his beak-like nose, closed his notebook, and reluctantly admitted, "You've reached the limits of my bargaining authority. I have to get back to you."

I had enough of this bullshit posturing. I was no longer a backup. I was one of the team's starting guards and nearing NFL royalty as one of the best in the league. From that posture, I impertinently suggested that I speak directly to the team owner.

A few days later, with head swaying and eyes rolling, a seemingly intoxicated Robbie staggered to the negotiating table. In time, specific terms were offered and accepted; others outright rejected. When both parties were about $50,000 apart on a contract upwards of $200,000, Andy called for a sidebar.

"Ed," he introduced a little self-interest, "if I can get you the terms you want for three years of contract, will you come to Machu Picchu with me?"

Machu Picchu? In Peru? Huh? My face contorted at the curveball.

Andy explained, "I know how hard you work in the offseason. I figured this was the only way to get you to commit. It will be a trip of a lifetime, and we can travel with plenty of time before camp opens." Andy persuaded, "Cathy already gave me the go-ahead."

Despite Cathy's agreement, my instinct remained to say no. I had to train. I couldn't take time off, especially when my bench press minimum had increased to 450 pounds. But then I reasoned that Andy was my friend. He was also about to work some serious compensation magic for me. I ultimately convinced myself that I could make it work if I exerted superhuman effort at the gym before and after the trip, so I agreed.

***

Andy and I took off for Peru a few weeks later and had an adventure rich with highs and many notable lows. For starters, my passport and wallet were stolen within hours of touchdown. Then, after consuming *la especialidad de la casa* from a hole-in-the-wall cantina in Lima, I suffered the worst case of dysentery ever. Three days in, I was down twenty pounds and looking so decrepit that in a country where paupers with one leg were getting money from those passing by, kind people were throwing coins at my feet in pure pity. Drained, dehydrated, and all too familiar with the bathroom, I feared I'd never get back into NFL shape again.

When we crossed district lines a few days later, Andy and I encountered corrupt police officers prowling for a squeeze. They pulled our bus over, took me out of sight, and accused this large gringo of smuggling cocaine. When *la policía* learned that I had neither the money to pay them off nor the papers to support my reason for travel, they threatened to conduct a full body cavity search. My poor ass couldn't take it anymore.

To cap it off, I became faint with altitude sickness when we crossed the highest mountains on the way to Machu Picchu. Upon seeing my distress, a local worker at a rest stop offered me a remedial coca tea that was said to help the body oxygenate. Although I didn't want to mess with anything that had trace amounts of cocaine in it, I labored for air in the thin atmosphere, and—*ahhhhhhhhhhhhh*—the tea opened my lungs. It helped me relax. Finally, I felt comfortable.

I took a seat under a shady tree and drifted off into a dream—a strange and trippy dream. In a world of no color, I wandered the desert for what felt like years. Thirsty, hungry, and yearning for more, I passed the skeletons of dead animals. Each step required so much effort with little payoff. But then, from out of the nothing, appeared Shula. *Coach. My coach.*

I approached him and begged, "Please, help me find some fresh fruit and water. I'm trying so hard. I need it so bad."

With eyes glistening in approval, the Don in my dream pointed off into the distance. "Fly over there," he advised, "over that hill. When you get there, you'll find a purple patch. It will have everything you need."

I lingered. *Purple patch? Isn't that the thread reserved for royalty?*

Shula pointed once more and urged, "Go now. Spend some time there. You'll like it."

With that, I thanked my coach and set off to realize my reward.

CHAPTER 24

WHO'S WHO

A sharp beam of sunlight reflected off my windshield as I turned onto the Palmetto and headed north to Biscayne College for the first day of the 1980 preseason. I was on autopilot in that I knew what was coming and knew what had to be done. However, this season, the status of starter no longer seemed sufficient. I now wanted to become part of NFL royalty and walk among the All-Pros.

As I made my way to the locker room, I recalled how I had stiffened in anticipation last year when Shoes announced the '79-season honorees because I believed I was in the hunt. I held my breath when Shula congratulated second-team selections, wide receiver Nat Moore and cornerback Tim Foley. Time slowed when Coach licked his thumb, turned a page from his clipboard, and called out first-team entrant, defensive tackle Bob "Bama" Baumhower. I closed my eyes and hoped Shula would say my name when he concluded, "And finally…Tony Nathan, first-team kick return specialist." I sighed in disappointment because the selection committee didn't think it was my time. Evidently, I had to work harder to enter my purple patch.

A bouquet of body odors, cigarette smoke, jock-itch spray, and liniment scents wafting from the team's crowded locker room reminded me that my All-Pro ambitions needed to be put to the side because I was one soldier among many. We were all on a mission from the Don, and each Miami Dolphin won and lost together.

I looked around the room and felt an empty pang of sadness because Larry Csonka and Bob Matheson had entered retirement. Even the greatest warriors had a final fight. Jim Langer was also gone—traded to his hometown Minnesota Vikings. The best center in the league and the best friend of Kuech would be hard to replace. But just as the conveyor belt rotated out the old, it brought in the new.

I scanned the names on the freshly assigned lockers and took in the who's who among the entering class. There was "McNeal," "Rose," "Woodley," and right next to my locker, "Stephenson"—referring to Dwight Stephenson, the Dolphins' second-round center from Alabama. Just then, the shadow of a large man crossed behind me. I turned to introduce myself. "Hey, Stephenson. I'm Ed Newman. How you doing?"

The young man with curly dark hair and a receding hairline puckered his lips and barked, "Jus' call me Dwight."

"Hey, Dwight. Where you from?"

Dwight shuffled his feet, averted his clear brown eyes, and answered, "North Carolina."

Even though this guy wasn't big on small talk, I tried again. "How was it playing under Bear Bryant?"

"Was a no-bullshit guy," Dwight grunted.

I opted to ignore Dwight's standoffishness because talent was the currency on the gridiron. Yet I wondered if this behavior had anything to do with the intense friction growing between Miami's white and black communities. After all, deadly riots had flared in Overtown and Liberty City because the McDuffie jury had returned with four acquittals. In this context, it would be reasonable for a new black teammate to be defensive upon first meeting a white teammate.

***

"Did you see what Dwight did to Bama?" I later overheard Coach Sandusky enthusiastically ask Kuech after the rookie repeatedly flipped our 261-pound All-Pro, Bob Baumhower, onto his back multiple times.

My chest tightened in petty jealousy because it took me seven years to emerge from the shadows of Kuech and Little, and within days, Dwight was becoming one of Coach Sandusky's favorites. I threw my hands up in frustration and hissed a few four-letter words.

"You okay?" Little asked from his metal folding chair while holding a bag of ice onto his chronically injured ankle.

"Fuck it. It's nothing." I disciplined myself to keep my priorities straight. As long as Dwight helped the team win, little else mattered.

Though tensions boiled when late July churned into August, and Miami's deadly combination of high heat and humidity came to just south of intolerable. Dwight was getting territorial over his locker space and ordering me to stay on my side. Sure, the space was cramped, but nothing like this had ever played out with a neighbor before. When the pattern persisted, I asked Dwight, "What's really bothering you here?"

He answered, "Jus' don't go anywhere in front of my space."

Wanting to show Dwight how ridiculous he was acting, I got some tape and newspaper and constructed a floor-to-ceiling divide between our chairs.

"What the fuck?" Dwight boomed upon seeing the barrier.

"I made a wall," I explained. "You're so keen on keeping your space. This ought to help."

To my astonishment, Dwight liked it. He raised his cheeks and eyelids in approval and walked off with a skip in his step. However, the moment Coach Sandusky saw my construction, he insisted we take it down. With feigned defeat, I removed the barrier and offered Dwight my hand, which he suitably took. I smiled because, at a minimum, this was a beginning.

***

Personally, one of the more notable things of the '80 season didn't happen on the gridiron. It happened over the airwaves, in advertisements, in high school auditoriums, and at blood donation centers across South Florida, where after hearing my heartfelt pleas to donate blood, thousands joined the Ed Newman Challenge. Within weeks, the South Florida Blood Service celebrated some of its best collection rates ever.

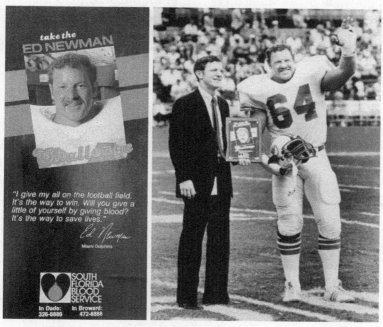

Ed Newman Challenge flyer (left) and promotion with Dr. Tomasulo (right) (–1980)
Photo credits: South Florida Blood Service (left) and Miami Dolphins (right)

As for the Dolphins, it wasn't our best show. We ended the year with an 8–8 record and had no players selected by the All-Pro committee. The silver lining of the mediocre season was that I started in every game—sometimes at left guard, with Kuech at left tackle, and most times at right guard, when our almost-retired Little couldn't play with that bad ankle.

***

I was ready to seize the moment when Shoes called us back for the '81 season. I wasn't getting any younger, and Cathy was pregnant with baby number two. I strutted into the locker room and met Dwight, who barely grumbled a hello. Clearly, we had to do better because precise communication among teammates was critical to superior play.

This became obvious in our first preseason game against the Vikings when Shoes subbed Dwight in for our starting center, Mark Dennard. I hastily instructed Dwight from outside the huddle, "Say 'odd' if you want me to pick up the blitzer or 'even' if you'll get him. Just call it quick enough so I can react in time. Understand?"

"Jus' shut up. I know what to do," Dwight stomped.

Even though his response irritated me, I let it go because I believed he'd do as we discussed. However, as our scrappy and scrambling second-year quarterback David Woodley counted down the snap, Dwight gave me nothing. When milliseconds made the difference between success and failure, Dwight kept me in neutral. Finally, as the blitzer inched toward the line of scrimmage, Dwight shouted, "ODD!" *Too fucking late!* I couldn't shift back and angle to the blitzer fast enough to prevent him from disrupting Woodley's pass, and the ball fell short.

"God damn it! Why didn't you make the call early like we discussed, Dwight?" I shouted as we returned to the huddle.

Dwight mumbled, "It's what we did in Bama to keep the D-line in the dark."

"Bullshit," I scowled. "The only one in the dark was me. Next time, you got to call it sooner."

"Yeah, yeah. Jus' shut up and play football," Dwight brushed me off.

I was infuriated. Preseason was the time to iron out details like these. Yet Dwight was ignoring my input. This disconnect had to be corrected because a breakdown in the heat of battle could actually get a quarterback killed. And then, the same drama played out a few weeks later in our match against Kansas City.

"Come on!" I barked with fists clenched. "Work with me, Dwight!"

"Yeah, yeah." He pouted.

Fortunately, the blitz issue lay dormant for the next several weeks. But when Dennard tore his calf in late November and Dwight got the nod to start, the center refused to do what I told him. I was furious because I couldn't effectively intercept the blitzer, and we were forced to punt in a close game against the Jets.

Finally understanding that he was responsible for the breakdown that killed the play, Dwight tugged at my sleeve and tried to apologize.

"Go fuck yourself," I said as I steamed toward the sideline, shaking off his grasp.

"Newman, you're benched!" a lip-reading Coach Sandusky irrationally exploded on the faulty assumption that my curses were directed at him. My jaw dropped. I tried to explain, but Coach Sandusky cut me off and bristled, "Sit down, NOW!"

I couldn't believe how this bizarre cascade of events was turning. Behind me, Dwight was taking responsibility. In front of me, Coach Sandusky was benching me for insubordination. On the field, the Jets were catching up. My adrenaline was high, but there was no place to vent. For an emotional moment, I considered storming off the field and insisting on a trade, but I calmed myself down enough to sit there and stew. A few minutes later, I made peace with Coach Sandusky, who called me back into the game, which we lost.

Dwight tried to apologize again that evening. "My bad," he groveled. "I'll call it sooner next time."

Dwight's words sounded good, so I agreed to leave it in the past because we really needed to gel to win.

***

With guns blazing, the Miami Dolphins stormed the field for what would turn out to be one of the top playoff games of the decade. Later dubbed the "Epic in Miami," this was a war of attrition played in high heat and high humidity. My counterpart, San Diego's perennial All-Pro defensive tackle Louie Kelcher, measured 6-foot-5 and was forty lean pounds heavier than me. Known to grind offensive linemen like meat at the butcher, Kelcher gave me my share of lumps while I neutralized him throughout the first quarter.

When the Chargers took a stunning 24–0 lead, I tried to shake the thought that this might be a blowout in our house. But Coach wouldn't have it. He ignited a spark in all of us by swapping quarterback Don Strock in for David Woodley with twelve minutes left in the second quarter.

For the remainder of the game, eleven men worked as one. Defensive coordinator Bill Arnsparger blended the brilliance of Baumhower, Betters, Bokamper, Brudzinski, and the Blackwood "Bruise" brothers—collectively known as the Killer Bees—to best benefit. On the other side of the line, Kelcher and I slammed into each other, and the rest of our offense capitalized with scores. Credit goes to tight end Joe Rose, who came through like a superstar with two touchdown receptions that bracketed a legendary hook and lateral play, where Tony Nathan danced twenty-seven yards into the end zone.

"Shit," I overheard Kelcher mutter when we caught up and tied the game with less than a minute on the clock. I was veteran enough to know this was the time to give it my all. As did Don Strock, who showed flashes of genius as he quickly advanced the ball to the Chargers' end zone. When San Diego stopped us on downs, we tried to win by chipping in what should have been an easy forty-three-yard field goal, but the Chargers' tight end Kellen Winslow broke our hearts by deflecting the ball's trajectory. Exhausted and dehydrated, both teams were thrust into overtime.

Despite the breathtaking drama of two missed field goals, neither contender scored for several minutes in the extra period. I pulled my belt in a notch and tried to rally my drained teammates. "Come on, guys!" I encouraged. "These next plays are the most important of our lives. Let's get it right and get out of here with a win."

My brothers responded with grunts.

I don't remember ever being as bone-weary as I was when a TV timeout was called about twelve minutes into the overtime action. The game paused, and the players from both teams unfastened their chin straps and removed their helmets for a break. In a loose huddle,

I rested my hands on my thighs and looked under my arm to check on Kelcher. To my surprise, the superb defensive tackle looked listless as he stared off into space. His depletion gave me what I needed to get my man for the remainder of the game. Even Coach Sandusky recognized my effort with a satisfied "attaboy."

Despite what I did, what we all did—it wasn't enough. After nearly fourteen minutes into overtime, the Chargers scored a field goal that immediately stopped the game and our season. Shula, who had been known for scorching players in times like these, was sympathetic. He called everyone together for a final prayer and gave us an encouraging end-of-season type of talk before inviting the press into the locker room.

Too tired to think straight and too emotionally volatile, I didn't want to be interviewed for fear of saying something I'd later regret. I quickly grabbed my clothes, showered, and snuck toward the back door to slip out undetected. I turned from the exit to catch a final glimpse of the men in the locker room. The 1981 season was over. My teammates would scatter to the four winds. Some I'd never see again. Others, who knew? I felt proud to be a member of this team. And I was confident that the 1982 edition of the Miami Dolphins would be even better.

As I walked toward my car, I felt a season's worth of tension release from my body. A smile crossed my face, and I stood a little taller as I recalled the moment about a month earlier when Shoes announced the 1981 All-Pro honorees. Baumhower had done it again. A. J. Duhe made the cut. And then, Shula said it—he said my name—"Ed Newman, second team."

After eight years of climbing the NFL mountain, I finally reached the summit. At the time, I couldn't celebrate because there were still games to win. But now that the season was over, I allowed the sensations to flood in. Amazing. Number 64 had finally made it into the book of Who's Who and was going to the Pro Bowl in Hawaii to celebrate. No doubt, this was the most significant accomplishment in my football life thus far.

CHAPTER 25

PERSPIRATION AND PERSEVERANCE

"Aloha," greeted the Hawaiian beauty as she placed a string of fragrant lei around my neck and offered Cathy and me a Mai Tai. Cathy, who was in her third trimester, beamed at the first-class treatment. I grinned from ear to ear. *Life is good.* Yet some soreness in my shoulder lingering from the '81 season reminded me that with the good came the bad. Aging and injury were football's twin demons, and both were taking a toll. But I wasn't going to dwell on that, especially when I was at the Pro Bowl, in paradise, with the one I loved.

"Look!" an elated Cathy squeezed my arm and pointed toward a handful of All-Pros whom she recognized from TV, standing in the flesh in our hotel lobby. My brown-eyed girl marveled, "Eddy. See? Over there! It's Dan Fouts!"

Overhearing his name, the Chargers' quarterback waved hello.

Cathy blinked her long lashes and continued, "Ooh! And there, at the reception desk, it's...um, Earl Campbell from the Oilers!" She pointed toward the back of the lobby and stated with a snap, "And that's John Hannah from the Patriots and Joe Klecko from the Jets!" Her voice picked up speed, and my chest swelled because my wife saw these men—my peers whom I regularly competed against—as A-list celebrities.

I guided Cathy to meet Klecko because I wanted her to know one of the best defensive tackles I had ever faced.

"Any tips on playing under Shula?" the thick-bodied, thick-lipped, almost Hulk-like Klecko politely asked after I gave him a well-deserved handshake. He shifted his weight from one foot to the other and added, "It's nice you get to play under him here."

I agreed but clarified, "I would have much preferred advancing to the championship with Shula and playing with another Pro Bowl coach here instead. Anyway," I returned to Klecko's original question and advised, "Shula is a tough son of a bitch. Whatever you do, make sure you're prepared."

Surprisingly, the Shula in Hawaii was different from the Shula in Miami. Relaxed and carefree, he ran light practices and gave us ample time off to explore the island. I'm glad he did because there was much fun to be had.

Take one evening when Cathy and I joined several Pro Bowlers at a traditional luau. Under a full Hawaiian moon, we piled poi and pit-prepared pig onto our plates and watched the Polynesians prance in their grass skirts. On another evening, we took a limo to a night-club and saw the world-renowned Don Ho croon his famous songs. With glasses raised, we sang along: "Tiny bubbles, in the wine, make me happy, make me feel fine."

Bob Baumhower, a Hawaiian representative, Ed Newman,
and Don Shula at the Pro Bowl (1982)
Photo credit: Miami Dolphins

Come game day, I put my best foot forward and slammed into wild warriors like New York Giants' linebacker Lawrence Taylor and Tampa Bay Buccaneers' defensive end Lee Roy Selmon. Though, my primary counterpart, Cowboys' defensive tackle Randy White, a.k.a. the Manster, told me to "chill out" when I popped him in the nose. Pumping his hand to the ground as if to slow me down, the seasoned Pro Bowl vet suggested, "You gotta make a lot of noise, not a lot of hurt in this game. Just have fun. That's what today is all about."

I reluctantly followed the Manster's lead. But when the AFC/NFC teams tied in the fourth, and Shula prodded us for an additional score, I couldn't help but magnify my effort. We all did, and we won the game, 16–13.

"You ballbuster! Couldn't let me have it, could you?" NFC's Tampa Bay coach, John McKay, playfully griped at Shula when they shook hands in the center of the field after the game. I was amused. Even the coaches had their own drama.

***

Gym was the word when I returned to Miami. Each day, I chipped away at a new set of weightlifting goals, including a single maximum bench press of 485 pounds. I also stopped fighting my reputation as the "strength guy" and bought into not one but two gyms. The first, Ed Newman's Fitness Center, was managed by Alan Wilhelm and his friend Jim Flake. The second was a union between sports agent/accountant Mel Levine and three teammates, Kim Bokamper, A. J. Duhe, and Bob Baumhower. Dubbed the "Nauti Dolphin," the three-level houseboat, parked on the intercoastal waterway near Fort Lauderdale airport, sounded like a surefire success.

ED NEWMAN'S FITNESS CENTER

706 N.E. 125th STREET
ONE DOOR WEST OF BIG DADDY'S
NORTH MIAMI, FLORIDA

EQUIPPED BY
AMF
WORLD CLASS
A.E.C.
NAUTILUS
AND
YORK

SPECIAL FEATURES
WHIRLPOOL
HEALTH FOODS
CLINICS BY
ED NEWMAN
STUDENT PLANS

MIAMI'S STRONGEST DOLPHIN

Ed Newman's Fitness Center flyer (–1982)

when you're not looking at the inside of your eyelids—or checking out the other sunbathers—you can always raise your eyes over the rail and take in the breathtaking beauty of Marina Bay itself.

★ Nauti Dolphin ★

Your hosts from the Miami Dolphins:

Kim Bokamper, Bob Baumhower, Ed Newman, and A.J. Duhe. During the off season (when not playing or training), these men will serve as staff members of the Nauti-Dolphin. Superb examples of proper conditioning, they will personally work with you to help you achieve whatever degree of physical fitness you desire.

JOIN US

Do something good for your body and nice for your spirits: join

Application for Membership   ☐ INDIVIDUAL   ☐ FAMILY

Nauti Dolphin flyer with Bokamper, Baumhower, Newman, and Duhe (–1982)

With the business of my future reasonably addressed, I directed my energy to the 1982 football season. I returned to Biscayne College and ran into Dwight, who, to my great delight, was social and engaging. He even suggested a double date with Cathy and his girl, Dinah.

A few nights later, the four of us were laughing, sharing stories, and getting on as good friends. Dwight tilted his head toward me and complimented, "I ain't never seen nobody 'doodad' better than Ed."

"Doo-dad what-dad?" interjected Dinah with a playful laugh.

I explained the details of the tandem blocking maneuver and boasted, "Our running backs love us for it!"

"That's right," said Dwight.

"You know, Dinah," I elaborated, "I couldn't do it without Dwight. But man, he made it difficult for me when he first joined the team. Remember that, Dwight?" I toasted our center for the great distance he had come since those "Jus' shut up and play football" days. I caught his eye and praised, "We've got something good here. And if we continue at it, I think we'll emerge as the league's best center/guard combination. Sound good to you?"

Dwight nodded, and our four glasses clinked.

From the silence that followed, Dinah introduced a new subject. "Ed," she said, "Dwight tells me you're very strong—'football strong,' as he puts it."

"Um-hm. He sure is," Dwight piled on.

"He ought to be," piped Cathy. "He spends half his time at the gym."

"It pays off," Dwight encouraged. "Take this…" He looked at the girls and shared, "Last year, Lundy tested our strength with a 225-pound bar. I felt good when I lifted it twenty-two times. But Ed here grabbed that bar and passed twenty-two reps like it was nothing."

"How many times did you lift it, Ed?" Dinah inquired.

Trying to be humble but true, I answered, "Maybe forty-two? I'm not sure. I kind of lost count."

Dinah's jaw dropped, and Dwight affirmed, "Oh yeah, football strong."

***

It was over one hundred degrees when Cathy, our newborn daughter Holly, and I exited the plane in Texas for an invitation-only

185

"Strongest Man in Pro Football" competition. Heat shimmered off the tarmac, and my eyes adjusted to the July daylight when I spotted my weightlifting competitors. All seven were known for their strength, and each had at least thirty pounds on me. I approached the men and noticed that their faces were distorted and puffy, like engorged water balloons. Also disconcerting was how they heaved for air and became drenched in sweat after carrying their luggage a few hundred yards over to the air-conditioned bus.

"Something's not right," I whispered to Cathy.

Assuming they were stressed from the extreme Texas temperature, I declared to the bunch, "This heat is nothing. Come to Miami in this type of shape, and you won't make it one day."

"Nah, man. It's not that," one All-Pro casually admitted. "We're juiced up."

Juiced up? My eyes bulged. "Really? Steroids?" I couldn't believe that someone would inject performance enhancers for any reason, let alone to win the small monetary prize associated with this competition. "Aren't you worried about your health?" I inquired with genuine concern.

"Nah, we'll be okay," the guy responded.

"But what about the NFL's mandatory blood screenings?" I questioned.

"We know what we're doing," said another. He explained how they had used a water-soluble form of the steroid so that it would flush out of their systems before any testing was done. "I'm surprised you don't use," the guy added. "I always assumed you did."

Me? I tried to hide my discomfort. Steroids stained the nobility of competition. They set a terrible example for our fans and unbalanced the playing field because those who abstained had to work that much harder to get ahead.

"No," I righteously responded, "I don't use steroids. I tame the weights in the old-fashioned way—through perspiration and perseverance."

The guy gave me a pained look.

The strongman competition began the following day. In front of over six hundred screaming spectators, the opening actor placed tape on his wrists, powdered his hands, and smashed his palms into his forehead. *Whump! Whump!* Clouds of chalk suffused the air. I cringed while the crowd *ooh*ed and *aah*ed at the showboat spectacle.

After tightening the leather belt around his waist, the contender stomped over to the preloaded bar, bent at a 160-degree angle, and began deadlifting the 700-pound load eighteen inches from the floor. With gritted teeth, the guy used incredible power from his back, hip, and leg muscles to progress through several lifts.

"Six! Seven! Eight!" the crowd counted him along. By his fourteenth lift, the competitor's grunts got so loud that he sounded like a bear roaring. Several reps later, he slammed the weight to the ground, buckled at the knees, and flopped spine down, where he writhed like a dying cockroach on the floor. The fans fawned over the phony fool.

A whimper in the audience stole my attention. I looked around and saw my innocent Holly in tears from the loud noises. Cathy hushed her and mouthed to me, "This is disgusting." I frowned because it was far afield from the ideal of classic competition.

Come my turn, I did my best. Yet it was impossible for me to keep up with the users. I lost all heats except for the bench press, where I still managed to snag second place with fourteen reps at 400 pounds. Years of shock week and strength building came through. The users couldn't believe that a clean athlete could do that.

"Really? No steroids?" one incredulously pressed at the event's conclusion.

"Really. No steroids. Never," I answered because I'd take integrity over chemical cheating any day.

CHAPTER 26

ANOTHER SEASON, ANOTHER OPPORTUNITY

Nineteen eighty-two. Another season, another opportunity, and so much more to achieve. I joined Kuech, Toews, and Stephenson for lunch on our first day back at camp when the conversation turned to a potential strike. I enthusiastically shared the legal nuances underpinning the player/management dispute with my brothers when midbite and mid-thought, the team's first-round pick, offensive guard Roy Foster, strutted over to our table and introduced himself.

"Hey, guys," said the large rookie with a thick torso, a well-groomed goatee, and five giant black-and-white cookies in each hand. "I'm Roy. Roy Foster."

"How you doing, Roy? I'm Ed. This is Bob, Jeff, and Dwight." I motioned toward my compadres, all of whom peeked up from their plates and gave Roy a nod hello.

"Ed?" Roy casually continued. "You wear number 64, right?"

"Yep, that's right. Why?"

"Well," he expanded, "I wore 64 at USC. And I'd like to keep things consistent for the homies. Any chance you'd swap numbers with me?"

WHAT? I nearly choked on my soup. Who did this guy think he was? Did he really think that I'd just give up my number? I mean, I had worked so damn hard to cultivate fan recognition around 64. I wasn't going to walk away from that.

Oblivious to his emotional trespass, Roy took a bite of a cookie and waited for me to respond.

"No way!" I scathed. "Get the fuck out of here, you damn rookie!"

Now, somewhat startled, Roy creased his forehead and sputtered through a mouth full of crumbs, "Bu...I'll pay you for it."

This guy had some gall! I lamely shook my head and sarcastically suggested, "How about you ask Dwight over here and see if he'll trade you his number?"

Dwight chuckled. "Right, he'd have to rip it off my back." Then, in a lowered voice, Dwight mimicked the growly timber of the cookie-loving Sesame Street character Cookie Monster and said, "Me want cookie!"

Roy's face dropped. He scurried off with a grunt.

I looked across the table at Toews, who was amusing himself with a semiprofessional freehand drawing of Cookie Monster. I smiled as he added dialogue bubbles over the character's head that read: "Me love #64. Me love cookies. Give me #64! Give me cookies!"

"Oh, that reminds me." Kuech looked up from the drawing and yelled across the hall, "Rooooookieeee!"

Roy pointed inward.

"Yeah, you, Cookie Monster," Kuech confirmed. "Get up and sing!"

Impressively, Roy did not miss a beat. He hopped up on a chair and beautifully belted the ballad, "You've Lost That Lovin' Feelin'." I grinned as I exited the hall because the rookie had talent.

***

My stomach tightened as I stood alongside young blood like Jeff Toews and Roy Foster before our first preseason scrimmage. I knew the coaches would evaluate all of us among the bunch, and there'd be no immunity—not even for an All-Pro like me. In a quick assessment, I noted that I was stronger by far, older but wiser, less emotional, more mechanical, very experienced, and gifted with explosive power. Of course, there were some minor aches and pains. And that knee was slowing me down. But all in all, I was in my prime and perfectly prepared for another superlative season.

Just then, Kuech tapped me on the shoulder. With his finger pointing toward the darkening heavens, he asked, "Don't you think that cloud over there looks a lot like a whale?" I directed my gaze upward, where cumulonimbus clouds were rapidly redesigning. Almost instantly, the temperature dropped fifteen degrees, the winds increased to nearly twenty miles per hour, and the tropical South Florida skies opened.

Shoes stared at the maelstrom with his jaw jutted as horizontal torrents of rain pelted us. Almost as if he were embodying *Moby Dick*'s Captain Ahab, he rasped, "Enough dawdling. Get to your stations now!" When most hesitated, Coach chided, "Anybody can play when it's sunny."

I shook my head in disbelief and followed the rest onto the turf when—*CRACK!*—a tremendous lightning bolt severed a tree branch a hundred yards off the field. We all froze as it lay smoking on the ground. Then *BOOM!* The clouds roared their thunderous response.

"Let's call it a day!" squeaked our photographer Bob Allen from his perilous perch at the top of the metal tower.

Coach didn't waver. "Get out there!" he ordered through gritted teeth.

When the next bolt touched turf, half a dozen of us hit the deck to seek shelter with the worms. Our poor photographer nearly fell from the ladder. It was crazy. Yet rising paramount above the rest, Shula persisted, "Get your sorry asses into high gear, now! Let's see what you got when it gets this bad on game day."

What else could we do? We all, film guy included, threw caution to the wind and soldiered on. Mud splashed our faces, lightning pierced the sky, and torrential rains soaked our gear.

The following day, I awoke feeling sore. As I thought about it, this had been happening a lot recently. It was almost as if my thirty-one-year-old body needed more time to recover than I had before the next workout. I mentioned this to Lundy, who associated the delay with my aging muscles. My lips turned white because no All-Pro wants to hear they're too old to do their job. In desperation, I asked Lundy what I could do to speed up the healing process.

"Ice," Lundy answered. "If you take an ice bath after practice, the instant freeze will stop any inflammation before it begins and enable your muscles to heal more rapidly."

I shuddered at the thought of how uncomfortable an ice bath would feel after a hot practice but told Lundy I'd do it.

The next day, I was down sixteen pounds of water weight, begging for rehydration, and overheated with body temperature tipping to 103 degrees, when I proceeded to the icy slurry that Lundy had set up. I cautiously dipped a toe in, and—*HOLY SHIT!*—my foot flinched because the seventy-degree differential was too drastic. But the little voice within wouldn't have it. *Don't be a pussy*, it berated. *You can't inch into this tub.* So with a "one, two, three" count off, I plunged my body neck deep into the sludge.

Oh my God! The extreme sensation felt like searing heat exploding beyond the confines of my skull. Blinding white colors flashed in my brain, and every inch of my skin agonized. I wanted out, but I coached myself through it. *Pain is transitory. It will go away.* Eventually, the feeling eased to just uncomfortable, and I stayed in for another twenty minutes. My lips turned blue, my body numbed, and I neared hypothermia. But it wasn't until Roy Foster walked by and gave me a "what the fuck you doin', old man?" look that I decided to call it. I pulled myself out of the tub, stumbled to my locker, and committed to doing it every day in the preseason because I could feel it was already working.

***

The NFLPA and Management Council were locked in a circle of death around the expiring collective bargaining agreement. This time, however, unlike what happened in 1974, the union threatened to strike during the regular season. Management stalled on the assumption that we'd break rank when the paychecks stopped, but the NFLPA had an interesting workaround: a midseason strike. As one of the team's player representatives, it was my responsibility to run the plan by the troops.

I hollered into the locker room one day after practice, "If you pay union dues, get your ass in here for an important meeting!" When all but Kuech filed in, I walked to the front of the room and outlined the union's plan to demonstrate player unity with a "solidarity handshake" before each preseason game, followed by a leaguewide walkout after the second game of the regular season.

I studied my teammates' faces to see how the information landed. Some appeared in agreement. Others looked confused or worried. The heated debate that followed made it clear that most were concerned about lack of pay. I explained how the NFLPA planned it this way so we'd have the cushion of two paychecks before the strike.

"Management is profiting hand over fist on our broken backs," I urged. "We've got to do something about this now."

"Come on," piped wide receiver and fellow player rep Jimmy Cefalo, "let's vote and go for unanimous. Say *yea* if you agree and *nay* if you don't."

I closed my eyes and waited. I hoped most understood that we needed to shift the balance of power to enable future players to earn far more pay through competitive bidding. Though, I feared that some would reject the proposal.

"Yea!" a chorus of players bellowed back. I opened an eye and listened for a dissenting *nay*, but not one came in. The decision was unanimous. The Dolphins were all in.

Fast-forward to August 14, 1982, when the Washington Redskins initiated the solidarity handshake en masse. I tensed as Shula extended his arms wide to block the Dolphins horde and threatened, "Don't you fucking dare fraternize with the opposition." But nothing was going to stop us. With our priorities straight, we plowed ahead like the bulls of Pamplona and met Washington midfield. For the moment, the artificial "hate your opponent" culture faded, and we grasped hands as brothers bonded in this battle.

After that, it was game faces on. In the privacy of the locker room, Shula withdrew his complaint and complimented us for sticking together. "But," he cautioned, "don't allow this dispute to distract you from your main goal of winning." Persuasive as he was, we weren't turning back.

A little over a month later, on the eve of the strike, Shula gathered the team leaders and tried to sway our thinking once more. "We're a championship-caliber team," he stated. "Don't sacrifice your chance for a Super Bowl berth for this bullshit. If you show some leadership and continue with the season, other teams will fall in line."

A true-to-form Kuech distinguished himself by saying, "I'm coming to work tomorrow no matter what, Coach." The others hesitated. I brazenly asked Shula, "Aren't you actively soliciting bids from other teams for when your contract expires?"

"What the fuck does that have to do with anything?" Shula snarled.

If I had any balls, I would have answered, "It has everything to do with everything!" because Shula was tapping into the same bargaining power we were so desperate to secure. But instead, I explained that we also wanted to shop our services around.

This seemed to irritate the Don even more. "God damn it, Newman!" he screamed. "I'm not a player. This strike isn't about me."

Upon seeing that our minds were made up, Shula flipped his hand and scoffed, "Get the hell out of here!" With that, the season came to a halt.

***

193

Remarkably, the striking Dolphins took to the fields of local junior colleges and ran voluntary practices under the substitute coaching of Don Strock, Nat Moore, and Glenn Blackwood. On any given day, 50–60 percent of my teammates showed up for Shula-style practices—just no hitting. Meanwhile, in what seemed like another world, Kuech crossed the picket line and held court with the press while getting ready for a practice of one. We all have our reasons to dissent, and a dearth of pay is a powerful one. Nonetheless, no one, not even the lone wolf, got paid because the league locked all the players out.

It was an uncertain time. No play. No pay. Very little news. Days passed, weeks passed—and we got nothing. Fans begged for ball. The press ginned up their stories. NFL commissioner Pete Rozelle emerged as the solo voice for the league, and Don Strock and I spoke on behalf of the Dolphin players.

With the extra time, I focused on my gyms, both of which were suffering financial distress. With insufficient funds, the Nauti Dolphin CEO Mel Levine asked the Dolphin partners to put up more money. In the context of the strike, we couldn't do that. So instead, Kim Bokamper and I hit the high school circuit to promote the gym.

As for Ed Newman's Fitness Center, a disconcerting visit revealed that my equal, one-third partner Jim Flake was stealing cash from the register, selling cocaine, and making things so untenable for our other partner Alan that he wanted out. Even worse was when I found a pile of unpaid bills, a checkbook with insufficient funds, and—*fuck*—a stash of anabolic steroids in the gym's front desk drawer. *No!* This was the antithesis of my brand. Immediately, I put a plan in motion to exit the venture.

***

After eight long weeks, the NFLPA and management council came to a consensus on free agency, league revenue, and severance-pay packages. All voted to end the fifty-seven-day strike. Immediately, the Dolphins hearkened to Shula, who tightened the sails, ran sharp practices, and expertly played the talent he had. We surged through the season, and sure enough, the sponsors jumped on the bandwagon.

Adidas paid big money for some of us to wear their shoes. Fortunately, they made them in a size 13 doublewide. Häagen-Dazs offered unlimited tubs of ice cream for endorsing their product. Three pints of rocky road, please. Gas stations distributed isolated action shots of six Dolphin superstars at the pump. I collected the novelty giveaway each time I filled up. And a local Jewish millionaire offered me $10,000 to show up at his son's bar mitzvah. That one I turned down because I didn't want to cheapen my faith. The popularity even bled into the Ed Newman Challenge, where blood donations surged. All was right in the world, especially when I made All-Pro and Pro Bowl again, and the Dolphins clinched yet another playoff berth.

But remember, Chaos likes to keep you in check. On one clear-skied, brisk-aired December evening, it tapped Buffalo Bills' defensive end Ben Williams to do its bidding. It all went down during a pass play when Williams leaped high into the air to block one of Woodley's passes, and Laakso countered with a punch to his chest. Rather than try to regain his footing, as most free-falling guys do, Williams allowed his body to go limp. In doing so, he put a bullet in the chamber. Less than a second later, the weight of his 251-pound body crashed into the back of my right calf.

Pop! All my pores opened, and perspiration flowed out of me at a freakish rate. In a dreamlike state, I limped to the sideline, trailing a stream of sweat behind me. After a quick examination, Dr. Charles Virgin confirmed I had suffered another medial collateral ligament rupture—this time in my right knee.

Shit. This was a bad injury. It would require surgical repair and a long, difficult recovery. I was so disappointed that I'd be out for the remainder of the '82 season. I mean…we… *I*… was doing so well. God damn it! We were on the trek toward the Promised Land, and like Moses, I'd be denied entry. Meanwhile, my good friend Jeff Toews would continue with the cohort toward the Holy Land.

Nineteen eighty-two. Another season, another opportunity, but unable to achieve. I was relegated to cheerlead from the stands in that darn oversized cast as my teammates marched through the post-season and straight into Super Bowl XVII. My melancholy increased when we arrived in Pasadena, and they bounded off the plane while

195

I hobbled about. In meetings, Shula shined his light on the active troops. I faded into the shadows. When we met with the press, the reporters lined up to speak with Kuech, Toews, and others while they simply passed me by.

Before long, it was gameday: Super Bowl XVII. Can someone pass the pom-poms, please? I cheered my team along as we maintained a four-point lead late into the fourth quarter. But when Washington was in a fourth-and-1 situation on the 43-yard line, quarterback Joe Theismann flipped the ball over to his fullback John Riggins, who captured the momentum and bulled through the Dolphins' defense, spoiling the show with a touchdown. My heart sank. I felt powerless because there was nothing I could do. Those feelings worsened when Theismann put another six points on the board and secured the win: 27–17. Super Bowl XVII was over. It felt like my being was vibrating, yet I was stuck in place.

Ed Newman post-knee surgery (–1982)
Photo credit: The Miami Dolphins

CHAPTER 27

THE PLAN B PACT

"There are only so many knocks in the can," Jim Langer used to say. "Knock it once, it's a can with a dent in it. Knock it twice, same thing. But knock it a thousand times, and it's a useless lump of crap." Why would my can be any different? I saw the progression. All of yesteryear's greats had their moments in the sun. But the sun always sets—sometimes tragically. If it wasn't Chaos, then Father Time got them. I thought through the long list of retired vets. There was Buoniconti, Csonka, Den Herder, Fernandez, Griese, Little, Langer, Wayne Moore, Morrall, Stanfill, Yepremian, and now, Newman?

No! No! I shook away the gut-wrenching thought. Not Newman! I wasn't over the hill. I was an All-Pro in the prime of my career. I could rebound from injury. I could come back better than ever. But just because I could, didn't mean I should. I wondered, Was an NFL reascension really worth the effort? Was it worth the risk of further injury? Yes. I resolved, definitely yes, because I still had more to show.

Nonetheless, I needed to figure out that nagging question of my plan B. I needed to engage in something viable and concrete. Restless nights followed depressed days, and I neared rock bottom when the

Nauti Dolphin went belly up. In the recess of my mind, I could hear my Nana Anna ask a toddler version of myself, "What do you want to do when you grow up?" Twenty-five years later, and I still had no answer to give.

Then one evening over dinner at Miami's treasured Joe's Stone Crab, Andy and our mutual lawyer friend Michael Genden gave me counsel. "You've got a good brain," Genden said while cracking open a jumbo stone crab. "You could use that brain in law."

This again? I resisted, but Andy wouldn't allow it. "Genden is right," he chimed in. "Look at the facts, Ed." Andy recounted several examples where I had acted a lot like a lawyer in the context of the NFL.

Despite their persuasive arguments, the idea still did not resonate, and even if I humored them, the logistics alone would make it impossible. I explained, "It's one thing for me to attend classes in the offseason when there's no practice, but another in the regular season when Shula has every minute of my day scheduled."

"Alan Page," interjected Andy. "Didn't he go to law school while playing for the Vikings? There are probably others too. Those guys found a way. I'm sure you could as well."

I took a big breath, itched at the skin held hostage under my leg cast, and shook my head. "I don't know. Law school and football are like jealous mistresses. Neither wants to share with the other, and both require total dedication." I looked from Andy to Genden and added, "You know I'm fully faithful to football."

This prompted an enthusiastic Genden to spurt out, "Night school!"

Hmm. Night school? I had never considered it before. It was a simple solution that could actually work. And to be fair, a law degree was a stunning prize. But before I got all swept up in the possibility, the fear of rejection took over. There was the application process, the entrance exams, the evaluations. *No.* I resolved that it would be too hard.

"Get your Duke transcripts ready, Ed," Andy persisted. "I'm going to make an appointment for us to meet with Jeannette Hausler, the dean of admissions at the University of Miami School of Law. She's a straight shooter, and she'll tell you if this is possible."

"You're kidding, right?" My light laugh ceased when I realized that Andy was being serious.

The sight of the short and stocky woman in her midfifties, with extremely curly gray hair, standing outside the dean's office took my breath away because she had a striking resemblance to my Nana Anna.

"Hi, Dean," Andy piped in a familiar voice and started to introduce me. But as fortune would have it, a student passing by cut him off and asked for my autograph. The fan gushed about what I had done for the South Florida Blood Service with the Ed Newman Challenge. I beamed because an introduction was no longer necessary.

Once settled in the dean's office, Andy inquired about my law school prospects. The dean scanned my transcripts, interlaced her fingers, and advised that with my academic credentials and community involvement, she'd support my admission into the university's night division if I scored a 140 or higher on my Law School Admission Test (LSAT).

Cha-ching! My vision sharpened. Every fiber inside of me buzzed. The dean was talking about plan B—my plan B! I didn't expect this. If I could pull it off and earn my juris doctor, I'd have the qualifications for a long and rewarding career. My mind raced. I got very excited.

Yet as Andy drove me home, reality crept in. There were some big trials ahead. Just to rebound from my knee injury and get back to All-Pro levels for the '83 season would require mind- and body-bending efforts. I'm talking major time at the gym and major rehab. *Ugh.* I wasn't sure there'd be enough hours in the day. I'd have to become some type of superman—super-brainy, super-brawny, and super-efficient to pull it off. I'd need to train like a maniac, study like a maniac, squeeze the grape to get every drop of juice out while still being a husband and a father.

But then I told myself to slow down. This was a first-and-ten situation. There was a yearlong journey ahead. I still had to take my

LSAT, apply to UM, and get accepted into the 1984 program. Then I could advance the ball from there.

***

By the time the '83 preseason opened, my knee was fully functional. I reported to camp stronger than ever with a 500-pound bench press and was ready to dominate as Miami's starting right guard. I noted that this team was something special. We had acquired superstar quarterback Dan Marino in the first round and struck gold in the eighth round with wide receiver Mark Clayton. The O-line also looked powerful, with Kuech at left guard, Jon Geisler at left tackle, Dwight at center, and Laakso at right tackle. As for the D-line, the Killer Bees were primed to sting.

Despite the team's brilliance, I found that my energy for football was becoming more focused and serious because, well, I had other things on my mind, like that imminent LSAT. It was strange. Where I used to get psyched up for a pregame cheer, I now grew impatient with that *"rah-rah"* stuff. And when Coach called us together for an all-hands-in ceremony, I'd lean back and remain around the periphery because all I cared about was assignment, technique, and results. Did I get my man or not? Even when we suffered a defeat in that tremendous 12–4 season, I moved on quickly because there was little to gain from prolonged lament.

My increasing emotional numbness became most apparent after our sudden-death loss in the postseason against Seattle. We were out, and another one of my All-Pro seasons was over. Yet I had no regrets, only dashed expectations. With '83 behind us, all I wanted to do was look ahead to '84.

***

Barely days into the offseason, I enrolled in an LSAT prep course, took several practice exams, and visited UM's campus to procure all the first-year legal texts. I did this because I knew that if accepted, I'd experience a tsunami of reading material just as a wave of Miami Dolphins practices and games crashed in on me. I took my LSAT and hit my mark—actually, three points above it, with a score of 143. I then wrote my essays, completed the paperwork, and submitted my law school application. All the while, I said nary a word about it to anyone because it wasn't worth the distraction until it was a real thing.

Then, on one fine spring day, when all the flowers were beginning to bloom, the highly anticipated letter from the admissions office arrived. My heart fluttered as I walked from our mailbox to the front door and opened the envelope. With bated breath, I carefully unfolded the university's response to my application: "Waitlisted."

Shit. I sighed. At least there was still hope. After all, being waitlisted was far better than being rejected.

May and June passed. Each day felt like an eternity. I worked out like a demon, got ready for the '84 season, and continued studying the law school 1L materials, just in case. I even prayed a little in those rare moments when I had time to myself.

And then, on one fine summer day, when the flowers in my front yard were in full bloom, the second letter from the admissions office arrived. I asked Cathy to open it to ease the potential pain of rejection. If I didn't get in, I'd have to make a whole new plan B.

My confident Cathy tore open the envelope, skimmed the first paragraph, and announced with a beaming smile: "Accepted!" She confirmed that I processed the news by reiterating, "Eddy, you got in! You're going to be a lawyer!"

Shit. This was a horse of a different color. I was going to law school. Immediately, my mind shifted. I had to tell Coach. He deserved to know. So the moment I cleared my NFL preseason evaluations, I took a rare right from the locker room toward Coach's open office and waited for him to address me.

"Newman?" A startled Shula looked up from his mahogany desk and probed, "What's the bad news?"

"There's no bad news here, Coach. It's good news," I explained. I sat before him and shared my plans of going to law school at night while playing football by day.

Coach closed his black book. With an unusually soft face, he informed, "You know, Ed, one of my kids went through law school. It's a big undertaking." Shoes gently crossed his arms and asked, "You sure you can carry the extra load?"

I assured Coach that my first loyalty remained with the team— always. That said, I explained how becoming a lawyer was also important to me.

Shula jutted his chin and took a more serious tone. "You are one of our key players. All of us depend on you." He explained, "While I believe that law school is a worthwhile undertaking, I cannot accept any letdowns. Especially not when Kuechenberg is out on IR for the full season with his eye injury."

I nodded. I wouldn't let him down.

Shula scratched his nose and finished his thought, "I give you my blessing, but know this: if you fall short in any way, if you falter or let the team down, then I will ask you to leave law school immediately."

I interpreted the Don's words as a contract and promised that there would not be a conflict. "If night school gets in the way," I assured Shula, "I'll take a leave of absence from law school. I swear on it."

With that, I extended my arm, and we shook on the plan-B pact.

CHAPTER 28

OIL AND WATER

"BRRIIING!" The alarm blared ninety minutes before the sun rose on my first day of straddling the two worlds of school and football. There'd be a morning and an afternoon practice, a team meeting, a pair of evening classes, and a lot of studying and driving in between. Even though I had considered the tremendous amount of effort required to pull this off, now that it was real, it felt like I was on a roller-coaster ride, at that point where the cart is perched at the pinnacle, poised for the plunge. Your heart pounds. You close your eyes. All ten fingers extend to the heavens, and you scream at the top of your lungs, "YAAAAHHHHH!"

"Morning, Daddy." Stephani broke my emotional freefall with a peck on my cheek. She turned toward her little sister and encouraged, "Come on, Holly. I'll help you up." With her hand extended, Stephani hoisted Holly onto the mattress for a game of "hop on Pop."

My heart fluttered at the sight of my vivacious girls. I jumped out of bed, swooped each under an arm, and took them to the kitchen to enjoy breakfast together. We ate, and we laughed. After fifteen perfect minutes, it was kisses and out the door because three hours of homework needed to get done in less than ninety minutes at Biscayne College's law library. Coach's 9:30 a.m. meeting would kick off with or without me, and I didn't want to think of the consequences of being late. With one foot out the front door, I called to Cathy, "I love you!"

"Da-da. Wai…" Holly tottered over with her golden blonde ringlets and bright blue eyes. She raised her hands to the sky and pled, "Uppa!"

I knelt down to kiss my little girl and begged Cathy for a hand because I really had to go. Ugh. Things were already starting to feel hectic, and this was just the beginning.

After Coach's meeting, it was helmet on, practice, break for lunch, and to the weights. Next, film analysis. *Tick…tick…tick.* My eyes tracked the clock. At 4:00 p.m., I shut my playbook and hurried out the door to meet my girls for dinner at some dive near the university. *Oh, heavenly gifts.* The embraces of my wife and daughters revived me. But I couldn't linger because the professors would take the field at 6:30 p.m. On campus, it was thinking cap on, class, break for coffee, and to the stacks to digest hundreds of pages of legalese. *Faster. Go faster!* I tore into the material. But man, I was so tired that I laid my head down to rest just for a second, and before I knew it, I was sound asleep.

"THE LIBRARY IS CLOSED! THE LIBRARY IS CLOSED!"

The librarian's high-decibel screeches startled me awake. It was midnight. The final whistle had been blown, and I needed to retire for the evening. I wiped some drool from my face and stumbled to the parking lot. With my car's AC going full blast, I grabbed a short-bristled brush and rhythmically stroked my hair to stay alert through the thirty-minute journey south on US-1. Once home, I crawled into bed and logged six hours of precious sleep.

Wednesday, it was the same thing. Thursday and Friday too. Even though I was determined to achieve the mark, it became clear that football and law school mixed about as well as oil and water. Nonetheless, I told myself I'd get it done with constant stirring.

September. Stir. Stir. Stir.

We faced Washington, New England, Buffalo, Indianapolis, and St. Louis. Dan Marino instantly proved himself as a super-genius. Large, strong, fast, and blessed with perfect ball control, the second-year quarterback merely required a three-step setup to deliver passes that fell from the heavens into the arms of any eligible receiver. Duper and Clayton were happy to oblige. They put on a spectacle week after week as they engaged in a friendly competition to outdo each other. This, combined with Green's extended reach, Dwight's supernatural balance, Giesler's grit, Foster's hustle, and my strength, made the '84 Dolphins a notch above the rest. We produced 164 points compared to our opponents' 76 in those first five games and never gave up the lead!

In my parallel academic universe, I was a good student. But it was hard to show strong with all those Dolphin demands on my time.

October. Stir. Stir. Stir.

I started to get worn down by the triple whammy of sleep deprivation, endless study periods spent idly at a desk, and the physical beatings of football. Subtle and not-so-subtle anti-jock remarks also took a toll. One classmate sniped, "You don't deserve to be here." Others treated me like a dumb jock. Even Coach Sandusky reproved, "It's ridiculous you're going to law school. I would never let you defend me."

"Well, no," I countered. "But you better watch out, or I'll prosecute you."

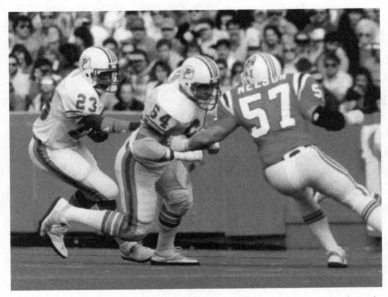

Ed Newman kicks out Patriots linebacker to create an inside lane (1984)

Photo credit: Miami Dolphins

November. Stir. Stir. Stir.

Our win-loss record remained flawless through November 11. But there was no time to celebrate. There was no time for anything! I missed my girls. My body yearned for longer sessions in the ice bath. As for my brain, it grumbled as if it was being hammered from the inside out at the never-ending acquisition of specialized knowledge. Yet my commitment to succeed remained because I owed it to my family. I owed it to my fans. Heck, I owed it to myself.

Then, on November 26, I suffered a disruption that threatened everything. We were squaring off against the Jets when my tremendously powerful opponent, Joe Klecko, shook me as all my strength was concentrated on pushing his breastplates upward. Within a few plays, Klecko dislocated my left and right shoulders. I mentally struggled to quantify the searing pain coursing through my arms. Wasn't I invincible? I secretly wondered if the injury resulted from all those hours hunched over legal texts. I debated if I should tell the

Dolphins hierarchy, but after a measure of soul-searching, I decided it was better to treat the discomfort privately than admit to the team that I was vulnerable.

December. Stir. Stir. Stir.

Ed Newman picks up Raiders' defensive back to protect Dan Marino (1984)
Photo credit: Miami Dolphins

I was fatigued, dragging, and grabbing for the will, but I knew this was not the time to let up. We still had games to win. Coach's late-season announcement that I was voted First-Team All-Pro and invited to the Pro Bowl again gave me an instant lift. Oh, how I yearned to relax in the peaceful accommodations associated with the Pro Bowl prize.

When we advanced into the postseason with a remarkable 14–2 record, it dawned on me that with this crew, we might just soar through the playoffs and into the Super Bowl. This triggered a new set of thoughts. If we made it to the big game, it might overlap with a law school final. This was an unusual conflict for a professional football player that needed to be addressed immediately, so I met with Dean Hausler, who told me she'd take care of the details if it came to that.

January. Stir. Stir. Stir.

On January 6, 1985, we beat Pittsburgh in the AFC Conference Championship and fulfilled my happy prophecy. The Miami Dolphins were Super Bowl–bound at the same time as a law school final. Now this was oil and water at its finest blend.

Dean Hausler arranged for me to take the exam early, and I nearly did backflips through the parking lot once that test was behind me. School was out for winter break, and I could fully align my efforts with the troops. A Super Bowl appearance is the stuff of heroes. It deserves to be front and center.

***

GAME DAY

Super Bowl XIX
January 20, 1985
53 °F, clearing fog
Stanford Stadium (Stanford, California)
Miami Dolphins vs. San Francisco 49ers

This was my third Super Bowl, the second one I'd compete in, and the first where I'd start. Over eighty-four thousand football fans screamed, and nearly one hundred million worldwide viewers fixated on me as the announcer called my name and I ran through the tunnel. It was amazing. Fireworks kicked off the show along with the national anthem and a satellite presentation of President Reagan doing the coin toss from the White House. After San Fran won the toss, it was go time.

I showed strong right from the start, and Miami jumped to an early 10–7 first-quarter lead. However, in the second quarter, San Francisco's superstar quarterback Joe Montana and his 49ers just started grinding it out. Featuring a run game, the 49ers' time of possession forced us to play catch-up ball, where Marino passed a lot. Tony Nathan was our go-to guy. He was like silk the way he slipped into the secondary on a run/pass fake and snagged an easy ten-yard reception. Even so, San Francisco scored twenty-one points compared to our six, and our lead was lost. It slipped even further in the second half when San Fran put another ten points on the board.

During this time, I was positioned on the bubble, dancing with three formidable men—most notably, left defensive end Lawrence Pillers. After having battled nearly one thousand warriors in my previous 166 Dolphins games, I knew how to stave off Chaos. I kept my head on a swivel, churned my metal-braced legs with forward momentum, planned for worst-case scenarios, and protected myself behind a marvelous shield of muscle. However, it wasn't enough. When Green slammed Pillers to the ground at the end of the fourth quarter, Pillers directed his crash into my planted right leg and—*pop*—adrenaline obscured the pain. I assumed it was merely a hyperextension. But a bad limp accompanied my heartache ten minutes after our 16–38 defeat. *God damn it.* Nobody remembers Super Bowl losers, and I was sure Pillers had stretched some knee ligament to the threshold.

Deep in denial, I told myself I wouldn't accept a limit like this. I had worked too hard to let anything stop me when the Pro Bowl in Hawaii was just one week away. I desperately needed that rest and relaxation. So I set off for paradise and insisted that I play even when the head coach inquired if I was injured.

Come game day, I ignored the dull and highly focused pain running down the medial side of my right knee. While in '81, Randy White told me to "make fun, not hurt," now it was me pleading with the Manster to take it easy.

Four quarters and a win later, I returned to the sideline, removed my helmet, and sat there for a while. When the last of the fans trickled out, and the cleaning crew appeared, I assumed that Cathy was probably growing very impatient. But I remained on the bench. I needed to sit alone for a little while longer.

In the quiet stadium, the throbbing pain in my knee faded, and an overwhelming sense of euphoria flooded in. I realized that I had just accomplished the near impossible. I had mixed oil and water—football and law school. Few, if any, could boast such a feat. With a glow on my face, I reveled in the fact that this was the happiest moment of my life.

Ed Newman celebrates a tremendous season (−1984)

Photo credit: Miami Dolphins

CHAPTER 29

A SEPARATION

The palm trees lining US-1 gently swayed in the breeze, and little rays of sunlight fought through the clouds as I drove toward the University of Miami for the first day of the 1985 spring semester. As I wove between slow-moving cars, I silently rejoiced that this term would be a piece of cake because it was the offseason and there'd be fewer demands on my time.

I decelerated at the yellow light just off campus, and while I waited for the signal to turn, I fantasized about my law school graduation. It was three and a half years in the future, in May 1988. I imagined I was dressed in game-day attire amongst a sea of traditionally black-gowned students. As I advanced to collect my diploma, my uniform magically morphed from that of a Miami Dolphin to that of a professional lawyer. My eyes glistened at the dream of retiring from football as a juris doctor. It was doable. Only three more semesters of double duty, and—

"Honk! Honk!"

The horn of an impatient driver snapped me back and sobered me to the likelihood that so much could go wrong. There was injury.

Father Time. Cuts and Chaos. I might falter. I might let Shula down and, per our agreement, be forced to leave law school. But I didn't want to entertain those thoughts, especially when there was so much that could go right. I mean, I could thrive. I could make All-Pro and Pro Bowl again. I could improve my odds of getting selected into the NFL's Hall of Fame. With persistent hard work, I trusted there was nothing I couldn't do. And besides, that knee thing was already out of my mind.

This positive thinking fueled me to forge ahead with the same intensity as ever before. I pushed the physical limits and trained alongside UM's football team, where I transitioned into a Herculean creature and closed in on a bench press of 535 pounds. I pushed a different set of mental limits in my studies, boosted my GPA, developed my power to think and communicate critically, and took a summer internship with personal injury attorneys Michael Genden and Gabe Bach.

***

I returned to camp for the '85 season feeling confident because I was stronger than ever and fully prepared to stir oil and water all over again. I treated our August 10 preseason debut against the Vikings as child's play. At the snap, I jumped back into pass protection and looked to the right, where I saw Vikings' second-string defensive end Doug Martin slice to the inside in an effort to gain clear passage at Marino. When Green knocked Martin to the ground, I rotated my focus to the Vikings' inside linebacker. However, below my vision, a determined Martin scrambled on his belly toward Marino, and one of his shoulder pads bumped my right shin. It was nothing. But the next thing I knew, I couldn't support my weight, and gravity pulled me down.

"Help." I waved for Lundy. As the team trainer escorted me to the sideline, the roar of the fans faded from my consciousness. I couldn't believe what was going on. I was a first-team All-Pro—a master of Chaos, not a victim of it. I blinked my eyes rapidly and told the team's orthopedic surgeon that Martin barely grazed me.

"Be that as it may," the doctor responded, "it looks like you've ruptured both your medial collateral and anterior cruciate ligaments." With a sad look, he opined that the ligaments were already damaged from an earlier injury.

An earlier injury? Oh, I could pinpoint it. It was that mishap in Super Bowl XIX when Pillers hyperextended my knee. *Damn it.* I cupped my eyes at the recurring nightmare. My injury would require surgery again. Rehab again. All this would be coupled with unimaginable pain. *God damn it.* Even worse, I'd be out on IR for the entire '85 football season. I had worked so hard and gotten so strong for nothing.

***

"I can break down film. I can assist Coach Sandusky. I can help in any way," I told Shula shortly after my surgery. Shoes sympathetically stared at me. "Coach, really," I said, "I can do anything…" and then my voice trailed off because I was too tired to fight.

Coach must have felt my pain. His face relaxed, and in a soft tone, he encouraged, "Make the most of law school while you're out, Ed. Get a jump on your course credits." With a rub of his nose, he continued, "Do what you can to stay on track. Just make sure you show up here from time to time so we know you're still interested."

It was another player/coach pact, and my heart swelled because Coach's treatment was totally decent. He could have demanded more. But like a father, Shula respected my bigger picture. He gave me the space I needed to pursue it, and I vowed not to let him down.

I next met with Dean Hausler, who was also compassionate. She suggested I become a day student and accelerate my graduation to spring 1987. Arrangements were made, and I was back on campus as a full-time student.

Between my studies, I lifted weights, pedaled with one foot, and did whatever else I could to recoup quickly. When that cast came off, I returned to Biscayne College and launched into wind sprints. At first, I was clunky. But by mid-November, I was moving well.

213

Coach noticed and appeared at my locker one afternoon, donning a strange look. "Newman," he said, "I've been watching you from my office. It looks like you're recovering nicely." He adjusted himself and asked, "What's it been...two months since you've been out of the cast?"

"That's right," I answered. "I'm training for next season."

"I see," said Shula as he jutted his chin and drilled his gaze into mine. "With how things are shaping up, I need you this season. Are you ready to be elevated to active status?"

I stumbled back in surprise. Did Coach really need me now? Roy Foster was solid at left guard, and we had capable understudies in Ronnie Lee, Jeff Toews, and Steve Clark. I doubted the doctors would even clear me. And if they did, how would I manage football alongside my classes? Then I realized this was a test—another one of Shula's tests. He wanted to see if I still had the fire in my belly, which I did, so I responded, "Sure, Coach. I'll suit up whenever you need."

"Oh, okay." The Don was caught short by this. He sputtered that he'd speak with the team doctor and scurried off.

***

The Dolphins ended their '85 season with a 12–4 record and a sudden-death loss against New England in the postseason. While New England went on to face the Bears in Super Bowl XX, my teammates went on their way. As for me, it was back to the negotiating table because my contract had expired, and I needed to reopen discussions for the 1986 season.

I knew to approach this round of negotiations differently. As an older and recently injured player with law school in the mix, I couldn't put in an epic commitment to conditioning if the team wasn't all that invested in me. So I proposed to Andy that we demand a signed contract before the end of April to gauge the Dolphins' interest.

"It's a nice idea," said my brother-in-law/agent. "But won't the Dolphins delay?"

"Well, that's the point. They probably will, but I don't have to accept it." As frenetic anxiety charged through my core, I threatened, "If they can't lock me into a solid contract early on, then…" I couldn't say the words.

"Then what?" probed Andy.

"Well," I explained, "the last thing I want to do is quit. But"—I stared off in the distance—"if they don't give me a satisfactory contract by the end of April, then I'll stop training like a crazed warrior because I can't continue at this rate on a hope and a prayer."

"It's risky," advised Andy, "but I'll call Stonewall to start the conversation."

The three of us met on neutral turf to discuss terms. Stonewall appeared tired from a long season, so I got straight to the point. Outside of asking for comparable All-Pro guard compensation and a "no-cut guarantee," I explained that we needed to conclude negotiations by April 30.

Stonewall's little body stiffened. His jet-black eyebrows raised, and his hawkish nose slanted downward. "What's so magical about the end of April?" he inquired.

I explained how I had done this dance several times before and was no longer interested in the team's posturing. I stated, "If the Dolphins love me, they'll get off their ass and show it."

When Stonewall didn't bat an eye, I elaborated that I refused to put in a thousand more hours in the gym only to be held hostage in the holdout game. "There's a limit to how far I will go," I explained. "But if we're in the ballpark by the end of April, I'll report to camp in All-Pro shape."

With a smug smirk, Stonewall probed for an opening offer. Andy laid out my terms. Stonewall scratched his head and retorted, "I've seen guys get fat and slow once they've tasted guaranteed money. How can the Dolphins be sure you'll deliver as you say you will?"

I tensed in umbrage. "My word is my bond, William. If I say I'll be All-Pro, then I'll be All-Pro."

An uncomfortable Stonewall confirmed, "You mean that not reaching an agreement by April 30 is a deal-breaker?"

"Well," I answered, "if I don't have a signed contract by then, I'll stop working out."

Stonewall shrugged. With a passive face and a monotone voice, he said, "You're not going to dictate the terms. If you stop working out, that's on you. And if you don't come to contract, then you'll at least be considered 'one of the family.'"

One of the family? Stonewall's insensitive words cut deep. They implied that I was old, injured, worn out, overvalued, and overdue to be replaced. *No!* I didn't like it.

I told Stonewall, "This is not a bluff. You better take this to Shula and Robbie because April 30 is an important date for me. I'll be expecting your call."

The meeting ended with a noncommittal handshake followed by deafening silence.

***

The months passed. I trained every day and entered into a new realm of near-demigod strength. I occasionally crossed paths with Shula at Biscayne College. He could see I was strong, healthy, and committed. But it was awkward when not a word was spoken about my deadline.

And then it was April 30, and I got nothing but the void. May 1, same thing. It broke my heart that a little part of the All-Pro in me was vanishing with each passing day. I consoled myself that getting nothing in April or May was far better than getting subpar pay in July or August.

As promised, I stopped showing up at Biscayne College. I secretly hoped my absence would be noticed. I prayed Stonewall would reach out. But soon the team's silence filled my soul with resentment. *God damn that pencil-necked Stonewall.* And then, I kind of just accepted it.

Like two ships passing in the night, I steered toward the law while the Dolphins steered toward the '86 season. For the first time in over a decade, I didn't stress myself in the weight room. Of course, I lifted out of habit, but not strenuously. Then it was June and early July.

I needed to tell my fans what was going on. They deserved to know. Andy and I asked all the local sports reporters to gather at his office for a televised press conference. On July 18, 1986, I held back tears as I told the media I was healthy and eager to play, yet I couldn't don the pads without a signed contract. Near quivering, I clarified that the Dolphins and I had entered good-faith negotiations, but I wanted more than they were willing to give. As a result, we were at an impasse. I emphasized, "I have not quit. This is not an announcement of retirement, but the Dolphins are freezing me out, and unfortunately, that might be the end of it."[4]

Camp opened the following week. A bunch of inexperienced players tried to fill the shoes of Kuech, Laakso, Toews, and now Newman. Marino wasn't getting the protection he needed, and when Steve Clark got knocked out in a preseason game, the press clamored, "What about Newman? He said he was 'ready to play.'"

Next thing, Shula's office tracked me down while I was preparing interrogatories at my legal internship with Dick Lapidus. Mr. Lapidus gave me a nod to take the call and stayed nearby, listening on. My heart thumped wildly as I took an even tone and spoke into the receiver, "Ed Newman here. How can I help you?"

"You need to get into camp immediately, Newman," blurted Shula.

What? I listened closely as Coach explained how he had gotten me the contract terms I wanted, including a no-cut guarantee of $250,000. My eyes widened. My heart would have soared in other circumstances because this meant that Coach believed in me. But reality had a sobering effect. I hadn't trained in over three months. I was no longer in All-Pro shape. It wouldn't be fair to the team, my fans, my family, myself, or my legacy if I played. The last thing I wanted was for folks to natter about how "Newman played one season too many." And then there was Chaos. Without the proper

---

[4] "Dolphins' Newman Quits to Pursue Law," *South Florida SunSentinel*, July 19, 1986, https://www.sun-sentinel.com/news/fl-xpm-1986-07-19-8602120444-story.html.

measure of training, I no longer had the foundation to protect myself from my great nemesis. Too much was at risk.

I took a deep breath and sorrowfully explained, "Coach, I'm not in shape. It's not safe for me to return to the field. You and the team deserve better."

Shula assured, "Don't worry, Ed. Coach Sandusky and I will give you the time you need to prepare. You won't play until you're ready." Oh, how I wanted to believe him. And while Shula probably meant every word he said, I knew that when the rubber met the road, he'd have no qualms in prematurely playing me if it helped ensure the team's success.

I moved the phone from one ear to the other. I opened my mouth and closed it. Lapidus offered me his support without saying a word. I wanted to say yes to Shula because I missed being a Dolphin. I even convinced myself I could rebound if I trained like three men. But somehow my head trumped my heart. In nearly a whisper, I responded, "Coach, it means everything to me…but…I just can't. Nobody wins if I return." On those last words, it felt like my soul was being vacuumed out of my body. I limited further pain by begging off.

Lapidus left the room. I stood there for a while, processing everything. I couldn't believe I said no to Shula. He wanted me back. He offered me everything I had asked for, and I still turned him down. As I lingered, reality crashed in. This was it. Over. No more football. *No more football!* It felt like I was in free fall—leaping from the heights of a well-paid, high-profile professional ballplayer, hoping to land on my feet as a competent lawyer.

For an irrational second, I thought about calling Coach to tell him I had reconsidered. But I reminded myself that my NFL bonds were compromised the moment the team missed my deadline. I took in one more big breath, cleared my head, and affirmed that I could no longer worship the gods of strength when the gods of justice were considering my petition. But football was core to my being. The thought plagued me for hours: Who would I be if not a Miami Dolphin?

CHAPTER 30

A BETTER NARRATIVE

The question of who I was, if not a Miami Dolphin, plagued me late into a sleepless evening. I tossed and turned, feeling lost and confused. Finally, my dreams rescued me and brought me to a more comfortable place: the locker room. It was game day, and I was gearing up for battle. In full uniform, I descended the tunnel, sprinted past spirited cheerleaders, and charged onto the field. Fireworks blasted in the background, and the announcer boomed over the PA, "Right offensive guard, Ed Newman, number 64." It was surreal. Goose bumps, adrenaline, a deep sense of well-being, and a supreme confidence took over. I could feel the crowd's energy. It was exactly as I remembered. But then my aching shoulders pulled me awake: 5:00 a.m. Reality. Life as a civilian.

Rather than lying there, I got out of bed and sought distraction in the sports pages of the Miami Herald. I wanted to see what was going on with my team. *Ugh.* It dawned on me that the Dolphins were no longer "my team." Just as Stonewall had so callously put it, I was merely "one of the family." I flared my nostrils in anger at his insensitive words and opened the paper to an article detailing how my brothers were competing for a spot on the '86 roster. It felt otherworldly to be outside of that cohort. With a tiny smile, I realized that at least I didn't have to prove myself. I mean, for the first time in fourteen years, I didn't have to fool the Turk, finish the twelve-minute run, or suffer the headaches associated with the Oklahoma drill.

I flipped to another article, this one analyzing an upcoming preseason match. I envisioned Coach Sandusky psyching up the O-line. I could hear him saying in his gravelly tone, "You guys are the foundation of the team's offense. If ever there was a day to give it your all, this is it." Even though his words were imagined, my heart beat as if it were preparing for battle.

Cathy picked up on my restlessness. "Come on, Eddy," she tried to comfort me. "Let's take the girls to Wagon's West for breakfast." She lovingly ran her fingers through my wild hair and continued, "After that, we'll go for a bike ride. It's going to be a beautiful day."

My wife's antidote worked miraculously, and my melancholy melted to pleasure as I showed off my flock on a bike ride around our neighborhood. When we arrived at an unpaved road lined with oversized boulders, I hopped off my bike, pointed toward the street, and engaged the imaginations of my daughters.

"Look, girls," I said, "there are the rocks. Where are the monsters?"

"Monsters?" Holly nervously asked.

"Daddy is being silly," Stephani clarified.

"Are you so sure about that?" I joked. "Haven't you ever heard of 'rock monsters'?" And so began a hunt to find make-pretend rock monsters. Stephani squealed, Holly giggled in delight, and I occasionally popped up from behind a rock and roared.

The extra family time was exactly what I needed to stay grounded during this painful period. Still I wrestled with my sense of self when I was alone at night. Everyone tagged me as a ball player. They'd say things like, "Ed Newman. Oh yeah, isn't he that Dolphins guy?" But that wasn't exactly true anymore. Now I was more out than in. Trying to reconcile the disparity, I realized that even though I was retired from the team, I didn't have to totally abandon the ballplayer within. I still had Dolphins celebrity value. I could keep a toe in Miami's waters and participate in the team's active alumni association. I could volunteer at golf tournaments, engage in fan clubs, and hang with the likes of Kuech, Little, and Laakso at Robbie's lavish programs. I could even restart the Ed Newman Challenge.

On that last thought, I called Pam Gadinsky of the South Florida Blood Service to see if we could launch another campaign. Pam regretfully stated that the run was over, but she introduced a related topic before hanging up.

"Ed," she excitedly shared, "we've petitioned the City of Miami to change the name of the street bordering our office from 'NW 17 Street' to 'Ed Newman Street.' We've done this to recognize your contributions."

I gasped. A street named after me? This was too much of a prize. I humbly protested, "Pam, it's an incredible honor, but I didn't do that much."

"Yes, you did!" Pam insisted. She explained how, through my efforts, the South Florida Blood Service collected tens of thousands of new whole blood donations, with a significant increase among first-time donors. "Don't you see?" she expanded. "You essentially changed the blood donation culture of South Florida forever."

My chest swelled. I much preferred this narrative. "Ed Newman. Oh yeah, isn't he that Dolphins guy who helped a lot of people?" I smiled. All who drove by NW 17th Street would see my name.

Miami names street for Newman

Football star honored as blood service spokesman

"Wow, this is better than going to the Super Bowl!"

That was Ed Newman's reaction as the veil was lifted on the sign dedicating a portion of Northwest 17th Street in Miami to him. It was the first time a city street in Dade County was dedicated to a sports figure.

The Miami city commission voted the dedication because of Newman's extraordinary service to the community as a spokesman for the cause of blood donation during the past four years. The street bearing Newman's name runs alongside the main facilities

THE SIGN UNVEILED, ED NEWMAN BEAMS TO AN ADMIRING CROWD Walter Pierce (Left) and Dr. Peter Tomasulo (Center) Express Thanks to Newman

Lifeline article regarding Ed Newman Street (–1986)

Photo credit: South Florida Blood Service

***

My identity became more rooted in the law with each passing day. School and a legal internship more than filled my time. Before I knew it, graduation day arrived. As I sat on a metal folding chair at the front of the Hyatt Regency auditorium, I listened to Dean Hausler challenge the graduating class to rise to the occasion. Her words made me think about what I could do. I then marveled at what I had done. The hurdles I had cleared. The twists and turns that led me to this point. While I had dreamed of graduating from law school as a ballplayer, achieving even a fraction of that was more than significant.

When the Dean invited me to collect my diploma, it registered high on my emotional Richter scale. I danced across the stage in my black graduation robe that coincidentally had a velour purple patch covering the breastplate lapels. *Ed Newman, juris doctor, ALL RIGHT!* The whole thing felt a lot like that time when Shula called me up to collect my winning Super Bowl ring. This diploma was a new trophy I'd cherish forever.

When the proceedings concluded, Mom encouraged me to mark the moment. Cathy took us out to celebrate. Andy and his wife, Ellen, toasted me with an expensive bottle of wine. Stephani and Holly took turns wearing my graduation cap, and Marvin pulled me aside to offer some words of wisdom.

"Son," he said, "you know, I try to avoid lawyers like the plague, but I've come to realize there are times when you need them. Be a good lawyer," he advised. "Let the judges, attorneys, and clients know you have a solid moral compass."

"I will, Dad," I promised. "That's who I am."

However, I quickly learned this was easier said than done because unsavory practices had permeated the legal ecosystem. For example, when I joined Floyd, Pearson, et al. as a sports agent, my competition regularly paid college athletes before their amateur status had run out. This scandalous practice violated Florida law and the NFLPA licensing agreement. Not interested in drawing a penalty flag, I shifted away from sports agency.

I found similar unethical scenarios when I opened my own law practice in 1992. Some tried to hire me to launder money or unlawfully hide assets. One joker asked me to suborn his perjury. Another wanted representation in a personal injury suit for a shotgun wound he took to the ass while robbing a house.

Through the ups and downs, I realized that this plan B wasn't a perfect fit. While I loved the law, I didn't love how the task of acting in the best interest of my clients occasionally threatened my moral code. I resolved that I wanted to be truer to myself and have more agency to better the world.

***

It has been said that angels are the messengers of God. Sometimes angels walk among us. Enter my friend and former boss, Michael Genden, who listened patiently while I groused about the realities of lawyering. Genden shared his plans to run for judge and suggested I run alongside him.

Me? A judge? My mouth watered the moment he said it. *Yes.* It certainly was a purer path—idealistic, moral, and good. *Whoa.* In my heart, it felt right. I was a do-gooder, a leader who steered toward the light and away from the dark. I could help others do the same. And then the parallel occurred to me—Samson, my childhood hero. He was a warrior and a judge. My father once said I was a little like him. As a young man, I could only aspire to walk the path of Samson. Yet here I was, discussing a way to do it. I loved how this story would provide an even better narrative. "Ed Newman. Oh yeah, isn't he that Dolphins guy turned judge?" I knew it then. I wanted to be the "Honorable Ed Newman."

Though, I wasn't naive. I knew that like entry into the NFL, the passage to judgeship would be long and difficult. It would require substantial personal investment, fundraising, campaigning, and a major remarketing of my name. I'd have to put myself out there and be vulnerable to the voting public. They'd scrutinize me and consider: Is Ed Newman worthy or not? No matter. I resolved that just like I proved my merit to Coach Shula, I could do the same in this arena. With enough gumption, I'd get it done. After all, it was just another challenge—and I loved a good challenge.

CHAPTER 31

TOUGH ON THE FIELD... TOUGH ON THE BENCH!

"You ready to win this thing?" probed political consultant Phillip Hammersmith in the spring of 1994 as he invited Cathy and me into his office. The middle-aged advisor fiddled with his blinds. As sunlight flooded the room, he fixed his eyes on my hands and abruptly blurted, "Where's your ring?"

"What ring?" I asked.

Hammersmith raised his voice and clarified, "Your winning Super Bowl ring!"

"Oh," I answered, "it's at the bank. Locked up. I barely wear it."

"No!" Hammersmith retorted. "That won't do." He shook his head and insisted I keep my championship ring on all the time. "It will get you votes," he passionately proclaimed.

I considered Hammersmith's suggestion. It had been nearly ten years since I hung up my cleats, and leaning on my NFL appeal to win this campaign didn't feel right. I shared this perspective with Hammersmith, but he wouldn't hear it. With some gestures that looked a lot like he was tossing a football from one hand to the next, he urged, "All people in South Florida—no matter their ethnicity, faith, gender, or ideology—root for the Dolphins." With a serious look, he insisted, "You can't miss out on all that goodwill. Let them root for you."

I objected, "I'd hate for my critics to say I'm shamelessly running for judge on my football credentials alone. They'll harp that playing ball doesn't qualify me for the bench, not by a stretch. And I think they're right."

"I don't agree," Hammersmith interrupted. "The qualities you exhibited in the NFL, like hard work, determination, goal setting, and achievement, transcend both arenas. Don't fight it, Ed." Upon reflection, I realized that Hammersmith was right. With that, my two worlds merged.

***

Preparing for a judicial campaign was much like preparing for a football game. There was strategy, assignment, knowing your competition, and studying their weaknesses. There was also leaning into your strengths to get your man (or woman) and keeping your feet moving to gain an edge. With the guidance of Hammersmith, we mapped out a plan for me to win out over prominent Miami lawyer Phillip Brutus in the autumn election.

Soon the slogan "Tough on the Field…Tough on the Bench!" displayed prominently in Dolphins' orange and aqua-green lettering alongside my name on billboards across Miami's highways. "Vote for Ed Newman" swag was printed, and I was off to numerous political proceedings.

Let it be known that campaigning was far more challenging for me than any football practice I had ever endured. Inherently introverted, reserved, and awkward in crowds, I was not a natural. However, as Hammersmith predicted, potential voters gravitated toward me, if for nothing else than to see my Super Bowl ring. It was easy, dare I say even enjoyable, to talk sports with these longtime Dol-Fans.

Good got even better when several teammates stepped up to assist me on the battle to the bench. Dolphins tight end turned radio/TV showman Joe Rose invited me on his live WTVJ-TV broadcast. After bantering about our time on the gridiron, the conversation turned to my campaign. Rose joked with the audience, "Ladies and gentlemen of Miami-Dade, I've never seen anybody work as hard as this Ed Newman here. He's as honest as the day is long and cannot be corrupted. Trust me, I've tried." Now taking a more serious tone, Rose added, "Whether you're rooting for Ed or somebody else, just remember to vote on September 8."

My teammates' support continued to pour in with Larry Little and Ralph Ortega, both heroes in their respective Black and Hispanic communities. They vouched for me on political ads that were broadcast hundreds of times on local, targeted radio. Others, including Bob Kuechenberg, Eric Laakso, Jon Giesler, Roy Foster, Dwight Stephenson, Mark Clayton, Mark Duper, Nat Moore, Dan Marino, Dick Anderson, Nick Buoniconti, Manny Fernandez, Kim Bokamper, and Jim Mandich, participated in my fundraisers. They talked me up, endorsed my qualifications, and impressed the generally much smaller voters. Even Coach Sandusky marched on my campaign trail. I wondered, Would Shula?

"Coach?" I raised my eyebrows and asked for his endorsement at one of Robbie's events.

With a grab of his chin and a fold of his arms, the seasoned sailor explained, "I'm sorry, Ed. If I were to endorse you, hundreds of others would be lining up at my door asking for similar favors."

I persisted, "Couldn't you give me a factual quote? Something you could stand by?"

Coach squinted his eyes, and with a swipe to his nose, he agreed. In short order, the following words appeared on my campaign flyers, which were distributed to tens of thousands of voters and Dolphins fans across Miami-Dade, just as the NFL's 1994 preseason was kicking off.

> "I remember in 1984, Ed Newman starred as an All-Pro offensive guard. The Dolphins went on to the Super Bowl. Simultaneously, Ed commenced night classes in law at the University of Miami. There never was a conflict. Ed is a hard worker and practices discipline in whatever he does."
>
> **Don Shula**
> Head Coach
> Miami Dolphins

Excerpt from Ed Newman's judicial campaign flyer (1994)

As with the twelve-minute run, my initial burst of campaign energy teetered as the clock wound down. While I loved meeting the civic-minded people across Miami's large and diverse communities, I found the endless networking exhausting, especially when I was also running my private practice. With full days, it felt a lot like I was stirring oil and water all over again.

Cathy emerged as my winning edge. She helped me stay the course. With her warm and friendly smile, Cathy stood by my side and initiated thousands of conversations. I could not have done it without her. Nor could I have done it without the selfless support, positive validation, or monetary contributions from many others. There were lawyers, clients, union reps, members of bar associations, colleagues, UM law professors and alums, South Florida Blood Service personnel, Andy, and other family and friends who helped. And then it was go time.

***

ELECTION DAY

Miami-Dade County Court Judge
September 8, 1994
84°F, mostly cloudy
The Newman Residence (Miami, Florida)
Ed Newman vs. Phillip Brutus

I wanted to pace back and forth as I watched the division tallies scrawl across the screen alongside friends and family. When only 1 percent of the vote was in, Judge Michael Genden prophesied, "You're going to win strong, Ed."

"It's too early to know," I responded. But deep inside, I trusted that my patented formula of relentless hard work would pay off. Feeling anxious, I distracted myself with some food at the appetizer table. When the first quarter turned into the second, third, and fourth, my lead broadened into a landslide, and the massive knot in my back loosened. Miami had spoken. They wanted Newman. Glasses were raised, and all in attendance toasted the victory that felt a lot like winning a Super Bowl.

In the following months, I unwound Ed Newman, PA and met with the administrative judges for placement. I found my conversation with Judge Dakis of the Domestic Violence Division most intriguing because the intelligent magistrate skillfully connected my past with my present.

"O. J. Simpson," she opened, "do you know him?" Judge Dakis was referring to the former Buffalo Bills/49ers' NFL Hall of Fame running back, who was currently in the news with his approaching double-murder trial of ex-wife Nicole Brown Simpson and her friend Ronald Goldman.

When I explained that I had crossed paths with O. J., Judge Dakis probed for detail about his character. I disappointedly shook my head and shared, "He's an embarrassment. Ever since the early '70s, I've heard stories about his domestic violence problem. And now with these accusations," I expanded with a frown, "O. J. is continuing to drag the NFL and the reputation of the players through the mud."

Judge Dakis waved her hand, encouraging me to go on. I elaborated, "It's natural for people to generalize, so when they hear about guys like O. J., they assume most ballplayers are woman abusers. But I believe that the rate of domestic violence among football players is no worse than that of the general population." I stated, "Ballplayers just get more ink when it comes to such transgressions."

Judge Dakis rested her thin chin on her tightly clasped hands and inquired, "Does the NFL get involved in matters of domestic violence?"

"Yes," I answered. "The league wants a wholesome product. I've even seen Shula fine players before for domestic violence."

Judge Dakis thanked me for sharing my perspective. She explained how historically the clergy and family had taken responsibility for mediating such matters but that she wanted the courts to take a more active role. She gathered some papers on her desk, aligned the edges, and concluded, "I think we have an opportunity here. If you, a former ballplayer, were to stand firm as a judge against any form of domestic violence, it would send a strong message to the people of South Florida that such behavior is not okay. What do you think?" Judge Dakis's eyes met mine, and she asked, "Would you like to join our team?"

Her mission resonated deeply, so I affirmed that I was all in.

***

A rookie again. I placed my long, XXL black robe over my shoulders, fastened the top button, and glided past the room reserved for jury deliberation on my first day presiding as Judge Newman. Hyper, intense, ready to impress, a little clunky, but well-versed in the playbook of Florida statutes, case law, and rules, I was prepared to make my mark in this arena.

The mahogany door sealing off the courtroom opened. I peeked in as my bailiff boomed: "All rise for the Honorable Ed Newman." I watched as approximately forty people stood at his command. It was surreal but not a dream. Goose bumps, adrenaline, a deep sense of well-being, and a supreme purpose took over. I could feel the crowd's energy. It was unlike anything I could have ever imagined. I ascended the ramp, surveyed the courtroom, offered my sincerest thanks, and invited everyone to take a seat. 9:00 a.m. Reality. Time to do some justice.

ON THE HOP

Nineteen Years Later—Summer of 2014

"Order in the court!" boomed my friend, former teammate, and now bailiff Tony Nathan from the front of my courtroom as he smoothed out some ruckus being caused by an angry defendant. The din settled, and I thanked my man for taking control. With a swivel of my head and a playful grin, I asked how he thought Shula would react to such a disturbance. Tony looked at the floor and said softly, "Wouldn't stand for it, Judge."

"That's right," I affirmed. "Shula wouldn't be kindly disposed to someone acting out like this. Nor am I." With my chin jutted, I returned my gaze to the defendant and explained, "We've got to keep some order around here. Otherwise"—I paused—"we'll be left only with Chaos. Now, please wait your turn."

After several cases were closed and bench warrants administered, Tony and I meandered to the antechamber of my office to decompress over lunch. Between bites of an overflowing Cuban medianoche sandwich, Tony rubbed at his salt-and-pepper beard and asked if the Dolphins had called me.

"They sure did," I cheerfully answered. "We're getting inducted into the Dolphins Walk of Fame during the Kansas City game, right?"

Tony nodded.

With a proud jostle of my shoulders, I added, "It's a big honor. Even my Holly is going to fly in for the ceremony. Oh, did I tell you?" My face lit up. "She's pregnant! My youngest is pregnant."

"Now that's some good news," congratulated Tony. "Another grandchild." He extended his hand toward mine for a fist bump.

Judge Ed Newman and Bailiff Tony Nathan (2021)
Photo credit: Mary Beth Koeth

***

Cathy laid out my clothes the morning of the celebration. As I carefully pulled on my ironed khaki pants and pressed white-collar shirt, I caught a glimpse of my reflection. I was 6-foot-2, 270 pounds, and overweight with over 25 percent body fat. No longer lean and buff with solid muscle, everything about me seemed soft. By degrees, my once wild and curly hair was short, thin, and gray. Crow's-feet wrinkles radiated from the corners of my eyes making my sixty-three-year-old face reflect age, wisdom, a life well-lived, and some trials and tribulations. There were three challenging judicial reelections, two horrendous bouts of cancer, and a lot of painful arthritis. Though today, I wasn't thinking about any of that. And even though the man in the mirror no longer radiated youth and physical strength, a deeper look into my dark blue eyes revealed the football player within. *Twelve wonderful years with the Dolphins.* I stood a little taller. *Seven years as a practicing attorney.* I leaned in. *And nearly twenty years on the bench.* I audibly celebrated, "Nice job there, old fella." My heart beat strong at the contented narrative.

The parking lot at Sun Life Stadium was swelling with tailgaters and savory barbecue aromas when Cathy, Holly, and I arrived. Alcohol flowed, kids tossed around a football, and loud rock music resounded through the air. I draped my Dolphins-branded jacket over my left shoulder and wrapped my right arm around Holly's back so we could stroll behind Cathy toward the honoree's meeting place. Despite the chronic pain in my back, I tried to walk tall.

"Cathy!" I called ahead. "Let's take the perimeter path. I want to show Holly the *Perfect Moment in Time* statue."

A few minutes later, we arrived at the approximately fifteen-foot bronze statue featuring Shula on the shoulders of Al Jenkins and Nick Buoniconti.

"You see this, Holly?" I pointed toward the weathered sculpture and told my little girl, "This represents the '72 season. It recreates the moment right after Miami beat Washington in Super Bowl VII and capped off the perfect 17–0 season." I gushed. "This is the stuff of greatness."

The *Perfect Moment in Time* statue (2023)

"Dad," Holly turned to me and asked, "did you get to play with any of those '72-season guys?"

"Yes," I answered. "I was privileged to play with many of them for many years. I was also fortunate to play my full career with Don Shula." I expounded, "He was the best, and under Shula, we won two out of every three games we competed in." I tapped my knuckles and expanded, "This means that with my longevity, I participated in far more wins than most NFL athletes can boast."

"Dad," Holly grabbed my hand and revealed, "I wish I knew more about your time in the NFL. I was so young when you retired, and you don't usually talk about it." My littlest placed a hand on her pregnant belly and earnestly stated, "I think we should capture your story. You know, write it all down."

"Hey, Judge," a fan passing by interjected, "I see you've got your team jacket. You going to be on the field today?"

"Yeah," I humbly responded, "they're honoring a few of us."

"That's great," he said. "Mind giving me an autograph?"

My chest swelled. After nearly thirty years, I still had fans.

A short while later, we approached a substantial gathering of large men, also wearing Dolphins-branded sports jackets, standing around a supersized bronze statue of Joe Robbie. *My teammates.* My face lit up at the sight of these men. A little older, a lot wiser, and at least three inches taller than I remembered, these guys were here on this day to honor us inductees.

"It's so good to see you, brothers." I shook their hands and patted their shoulders.

"Holly, come here." I waved her over and pointed toward the names on the plaques of prior Walk of Fame inductees. There was Nick Buoniconti, Larry Csonka, Bob Griese, Jim Langer, Larry Little, Dan Marino, Dwight Stephenson, and Paul Warfield, to name just a few. I explained to my little girl, "I had the pleasure of playing with all but three of the men listed below."

Despite my elation that so many teammates and former honorees were here on this special day, I was saddened that many others wouldn't be in attendance because they had departed this earth too soon. *Wayne Moore, Bob Matheson, Eric Laakso, John Sandusky and Monte Clark, your memory will live on forever. Rest in peace, my brothers.* Knowing that others couldn't make it because they were too riddled with cognitive impairment or other ailments made me shudder at life's fragility. And then, there were the ghosts of years past. Guys like Jeff Toews, Mark Dennard and Dirty Wally had simply disappeared from player society and never come back.

Just then, Hall of Fame quarterback Bob Griese approached. I pointed toward the names on the sidewalk and said, "You know, Bob, I was such a dopey rookie when I first joined the team. Would you have ever thought I'd get a plaque just a few yards away from yours?"

Sharp as a tack, Griese replied, "Yeah, Ed, you've definitely brought down the value of real estate in this neighborhood."

Griese's stinger caught me off guard. I laughed. But then, always the general, our quarterback called the signal. "All right, Judge. Enough talk. There's a ceremony honoring you." With a wink through his dark-rimmed glasses, Griese added, "Shula will fine you if you're late."

I escorted Cathy and Holly to their seats and hustled as much as I could to my designated spot in the center of the plaza, where a pretty Miami Dolphins cheerleader offered me her arm. Next thing, the voice of former teammate turned broadcaster Jimmy Cefalo opened, "One of the great things the Miami Dolphins ownership has always done is to keep our alumni together." The silver-haired announcer continued, "During the game, we sit together…we're able to renew our friendships. And we make up stories about the past. Some of them are even true." With his arms waving, Cefalo transitioned to the first inductee, the oldest of the bunch—me.

Cefalo touted my accomplishments and thundered, "Ladies and gentlemen, number 64, Ed Newman!"

I stepped forward and waved to the crowd. Cheers abounded, and I took a knee to unveil my plaque. Immediately, fond thoughts of my father and all he had done to contribute to my success flooded in. While it was too difficult for my folks to attend the day's ceremony, I felt their presence. I looked over at Cathy and Holly and noted how happy they were to share in this moment with me. That's when the gravity of the honor sunk in. Just as Dad had encouraged, I used my reputation as a great athlete to do meaningful work, and this Walk of Fame was like a gold medallion for winning at life.

After the presentation, my little girl, with her bulging belly, sat beside my plaque and posed with her arms splayed out, bracketing my name. Cathy snapped a few photos so that one day Holly could show her yet-to-be-born son Jordan that he was also there.

Holly Newman Greenberg at Walk of Fame (2014)

***

Later that day, I gathered with my teammates in the alumni box and watched the 2014 Dolphins compete against the Kansas City Chiefs. Just as Cefalo had mentioned, we told stories from back in the day.

"Hey, D." I turned to Dwight Stephenson and asked, "Do you remember when I put up a newspaper wall between our lockers? How ridiculous was that? And, Chicken"—I looked at Larry Little—"what do you think was going through Al Jenkins's head when Shula made us run Flow 38 and Flow 39 until we nearly dropped?" I shifted to Manny Fernandez and said, "Taco, did you and Stretch really distract the Turk so I wouldn't get busted for missing curfew on that beer run my rookie year?"

Recollections of the good old times flooded in.

When the current-day Dolphins trailed behind the Chiefs at the end of a lackluster second quarter, I turned to Dick Anderson and asked, "How do you think the 17–0 team would stack up against this team?"

After thinking about it, my former teammate turned business-man/senator replied, "Perfectly, of course."

A little while later, a representative from the Dolphins administrative office guided us to an elevator for descent to the stadium's ground level for an on-the-field halftime presentation. I straightened my jacket and blotted the sweat from my face as the elevator doors began to close. Just then, former wide receiver Jim "Crash" Jenson extended his hand from the outside, slipped into the elevator, and announced to the jam-packed car, "No farting!"

"Jus' shut up and get in," huffed an impatient Dwight over the laughter of others. I think Kuech let one slip anyway.

Down the tunnel and to the turf, to the gridiron we will go...

The smell of freshly mowed grass triggered my most profound memories. My body tingled as cheerleaders escorted us to our designated spots. The energy in the stadium built. I waved to the spectators, and while some cheered, it wasn't until the images of the four Walk of Fame inductees flashed across the jumbotron that the fans came to see the significance. The volume steadily increased, and the intense roar of appreciation brought tears to my eyes. *Amazing—an ovation by seventy thousand people.*

Click! The photographers captured the epic moment.

"To the barn!" former teammate and now vice president of the Miami Dolphins organization Nat Moore directed us to exit stage left.

For the moment, #64, almost at the age of sixty-four, with crippled knees and an arthritic back, felt no pain. Instead, with epinephrine pumping through my brain, I was consumed by a single desire: to run on the field. I looked ahead to Little and Dwight and barked, "Come on, brothers. You heard the man. Let's get off the field. On the hop!"

Reflexively, the three of us pushed off. Our feet softly thudded the turf. The wind whipped past our ears. The fans hollered. But then Dwight slowed. He looked at me like I was crazy. Little outright stopped. In his deepest baritone, he boomed, "Yeah, right, Ed. That's a good dream."

But it wasn't a dream. I welcomed the feelings that overcame me: the first time I fell in love with competition, touched turf, played for Coach Miller, wrestled for Coach Blossfield, became an Iron Duke for Coach McGee, and played for Don Shula and his extraordinary Miami Dolphins. Oh, this was quite the journey—addictive, powerful, intoxicating. *God, I did it.* I shuffled my feet forward as fast as I could. Perhaps to the crowd, I looked pathetic, moving that way in my older age. But it didn't matter. This was my moment, and I took it and ran off into the tunnel.

POSTSCRIPTS

I gathered with a few dozen Dolphin vets to celebrate the ninetieth birthday of Don Shula in January 2020. Even though the old man was anchored to a fire-engine-red mobility scooter, I noted that he remained proud and as feisty as a rooster. This was most apparent when, after some alumni publicly roasted the Don, Coach jutted his chin and mounted an entertaining counterattack.

"Shut up, you lazy bastards," he spat. "You wouldn't have gotten anywhere if I hadn't pushed you through it."

When my turn approached, I pondered what to say. I respected the man way too much to take a heavy hand. So instead, I told the "Two Thumbs Up" story featured in chapter 17. I kept my eye on Shula to see how the tale landed and noticed that his face softened and filled with the expressions of an approving father. It made me believe that Coach shared the same gratitude I did that our paths had crossed nearly fifty years earlier. I loved him, and I think he loved me too.

Don Shula and Ed Newman at Hardrock Stadium (2015)
Photo credit: Francis Duhe

Sadly, Don Shula passed away a few months later. My heart hurt just as it did when I said goodbye to my father because Shula also played a formative role in my life. There will never be another like him. Due to COVID-19, few were allowed to attend Coach's funeral, and his celebration of life was delayed by a year and a half. Of course, I attended the tribute. Nothing would keep me from honoring the exceptional man he was.

***

Several others have also shuffled off this mortal coil. Garo Yepremian slipped into the night less than a month before his seventy-first birthday. Bill Stanfill died at the young age of sixty-nine. Best buddies Bob Kuechenberg and Jim Langer passed within months of each other when they were seventy-one years old. While the number of remaining 1972 Miami Dolphins continues to dwindle, I dream that their perfect legacy lives on forever, or at least endures for as long as they walk this earth.

I am seventy-one years old as I write these final words in the spring of 2023. Although it concerns me that I'm passing the age of many of my deceased contemporaries, I'm taking reasonable care to stay in good health with exercise, a proper diet, and a knee replacement. I hope that with some kindness from the fates, I'll be able to take all five of my grandchildren to see my Dolphins Walk of Fame plaque many years in the future.

Ed Newman with grandson Jordan Greenberg (2019)

***

While this story focuses primarily on my football days, another volume could be written on my very fulfilling legal career and all the incredible people within the professional community who have touched my life.

ACKNOWLEDGMENTS

This book would never have happened without Holly's grit and determination. She stayed the course through several ups and downs. The sacrifice was great, and the impact on her husband, Blair, and their two sons, Jordan and Henry, was significant. From the bottom of my heart, I thank you for enabling her to make my story and its lessons eternal.

A hearty thanks goes to Trudy Newman, Eugene Russo, Tony Nathan, Andrew Leinoff, Dwight Stephenson, Larry Little, Andy Cohen, and Jim Steeg for providing content that rounded out the narrative. The *New York Times* bestselling author Michael Ennis contributed significant feedback on the flow and structure that substantially improved the manuscript—no doubt he was our MVP. Friends, including Mindy Pava, Terry Hauser, and Michael Ranieri, enhanced the story with detailed feedback. Others, including Brooke Vitale, Chip Namias, Daniel and Nicole Shemesh, Clint Greenleaf, Juan Tamayo, Nate Rubin and Meital Gueta-Rubin, Melinda Martin, Chris Rutherford, Kenneth Roy Monterroyo, Syosset classmates, and many, many Phi Delta Theta brothers helped in the publishing process. Finally, our family, most notably Cathy Newman, Blair, Jordan and Henry Greenberg, Stephani and Jared Zuckman, Donna and Jim Fredkove, Barry Greenberg and Barbara Rubin-Greenberg, and Gaby Tuci all listened closely and cheered us along throughout the four-year journey. Now, all hands in and repeat after me, "Go, team, go!" Together, we did it!

ABOUT THE AUTHORS

EDWARD NEWMAN

The "Perfect Season" Miami Dolphins selected Ed out of Duke University in the sixth round of the 1973 NFL draft. Ed played twelve seasons for Coach Don Shula and participated in one winning Super Bowl and two American Conference championships. The four-time All-Pro reluctantly broke from the Dolphins after a knee injury. The team honored him as one of the "Top 50" players within the first fifty years of the franchise.

Ed served as a civil litigator from 1987 to 1994. After a successful election campaign, he was commissioned as a County Court Judge in and for Miami-Dade, where he presided for twenty-eight years.

Ed has been happily married to his wife, Cathy, for over four decades. They reside in Miami, Florida, but often travel to Connecticut to visit their daughters, Stephani and Holly, sons-in-law, Jared Zuckman and Blair Greenberg, and five grandsons—Benjamin (nine), Jordan (eight), Andrew (seven), Charlie (seven), and Henry (five). Ed boasts that his best friends call him "Papa."

Ed Newman with his grandsons at his seventieth birthday celebration (2021)
From left to right: Charlie, Andrew, and Benjamin
Zuckman; Jordan and Henry Greenberg

HOLLY NEWMAN GREENBERG

Holly was born and raised in Miami, Florida, where at a young age, she became a Miami Dolphins fan simply because it was "her father's team." After graduating from Miami Killian Senior High School, Holly followed in her father and grandfather's footsteps by attending Duke University. She graduated in 2004 with a bachelor of arts in psychology, along with summa cum laude and Phi Beta Kappa honors. Holly earned a master's degree in organizational psychology from Teachers College of Columbia University and used her credentials to shape the culture of numerous Fortune 500 companies.

Following the birth of her children, Jordan Louis and Henry Theodore, Holly shifted her focus from corporate America to her family, where she fulfilled her dream of memorializing her father's story. Holly lives in Connecticut with her sons and loving husband, Blair Greenberg.

The authors, Holly and Ed Newman, then and now (1982, 2012)
Photo credits: Carousel Designs (left) and Newman Archives (right)

Printed in the USA
CPSIA information can be obtained
at www.ICGtesting.com
LVHW090836250124
769463LV00002BA/194